THE SPIRIT WHO HEALS

"A wonderfully inspiring blend of Bible teaching and powerful testimony. This book will become required reading for all who want to get involved in divine healing.'

Revd Dr Mark Stibbe, St Andrews Chorleywood

'An excellent, well-researched personal and practical encouragement and a reminder that healing is still an important part of the church's life in the twenty-first century as in the first century. An important and enjoyable book for the whole church.'

Sandy Millar, Holy Trinity Brompton

'Is healing in the atonement, and therefore do we have a right to our healing or is it a grace of God and a sign of the kingdom? Peter undertakes this vital theological truth with such clarity of teaching, humour and depth of insight that the fog is cleared rapidly away. The testimonies are very exciting too! It should be read by all involved in the healing ministry.'

Revd Paul Springate, Harnhill Centre of Christian Healing

'This is the book Peter Lawrence has always wanted to write. And it shows! Amidst the welter of conflicting views about healing, Peter is at pains to avoid proof texts but to collect the whole teaching of Scripture on the topic. Thus he shows the shallowness of some current ideas like "Healing is in the atonement" or "Name it and claim it". Healing springs from the activity of the Holy Spirit. Jesus healed that way. So did the first Christians. It is no different today – there are no techniques. The book is warm-hearted, cool-headed, well written, illustrated with 40 personal examples, and hilariously funny. Buy it, learn from it and lend it!'

Dr Michael Green, Senior Research Fellow, Wycliffe Hall, Oxford University

'With his welcome mix of teaching and testimony Peter has given us a treasure – a book to clear the head and fire the heart.'

John Mumford, National Director, Vineyard Churches UK

The Spirit Who Heals

PETER LAWRENCE

KINGSWAY PUBLICATIONS
EASTBOURNE

Unless otherwise indicated, biblical quotations are from
the New International Version © 1973, 1978, 1984
by the International Bible Society.
RSV = Revised Standard Version
KJV = King James Version
GNB = Good News Bible

ISBN–10:1 84291 229 1
ISBN–13: 978–1–842912–29–4

06 07 08 09 Printing/Year 10 09 08 07 06 05 04 03 02 01

KINGSWAY COMMUNICATIONS LTD
Lottbridge Drove, Eastbourne BN23 6NT, England.
Email: books@kingsway.co.uk
Printed in the USA

To my friends in the Parish of Canford Magna

Canford Magna Parish Church

The Lantern Church, Merley   *St Barnabas Church, Bearwood*

Contents

List of Healing Stories

Acknowledgements

Thank you to:

Melanie, who prepared the manuscript for me with great skill and alacrity, and to St Barnabas Church, Bearwood, who allowed her to do it during office hours.

So many of you who allowed me to use your stories for God's glory.

Bishop David Stancliffe, Bishop of Salisbury, who gave me a sabbatical in which to do my research.

The Revd Peter Byron-Davies at Terra Nova Publications, for granting me permission to use one or two stories from my earlier books, *The Hot Line* and *Doing What Comes Supernaturally*.

Those who so kindly provided endorsements.

Kingsway, who risked publishing me for the third time.

My wife Carol, who moved house for both of us while I was writing this book, and encouraged me in the good times and the bad.

My three beautiful daughters, Amanda, Heather and Hazel, who allowed me to write another book. So I put them in it. See if you can find them.

God, who is a bit special. May he bless you as he has blessed our family.

1

My Search for Biblical Healing

As the chattering of the gathered throng faded and the lights dimmed, an old 16 mm projector whirred into action like a helicopter taking off. At once I found myself in India, at the back of a large but flimsy stage, looking out on thousands upon thousands of attentive, eager faces. Between them and me, at the front of the platform, making good use of a portable generator-powered loudspeaker system, an American called T. L. Osborn was expounding the gospel of Jesus Christ, as he saw it.[1]

'Jesus died for our sicknesses as well as our sins,' he claimed. 'If we believe in him with all our hearts, we will not only be saved and go to heaven when we die, but we will also be healed here and now of every kind of disease.'

I had never heard anything like this before in all my 19 years, and I was grateful for the darkness that hid my reaction from my strictly orthodox friends at this somewhat

---

[1] The film was entitled *Athens of India*, which was produced by the T. L. Osborn Foundation, Box 10, Tulsa, Oklahoma, USA 74102. The healings took place in Madurai.

unorthodox Christian Union meeting. I knew I wasn't supposed to believe all this stuff, but I loved it from the moment I first heard it.

I was brought up spiritually in an evangelical, definitely not charismatic, Anglican church, where I was born again by the Spirit, delivered of demonic fear and learned to speak in tongues by reading books our church didn't recommend. The Holy Spirit and spiritual gifts didn't feature much in the *Book of Common Prayer* that we used every week, and not at all in our pulpit. But I was now at King Alfred's College, Winchester, training to be a teacher, and my home church leaders could only get at me during the vacations.[2] A very Pentecostal student brought these films of healing evangelist T. L. Osborn to our CU meetings, and I simply could not get enough of them.

After he'd finished preaching, T. L. Osborn invited people who needed healing to come forward onto the stage, where he laid hands on them in the name of Jesus. Almost instantaneously, power came upon the sick, with the result that blind eyes were opened, deaf ears unstopped and crutches thrown away, followed by dancing and jigging around with great merriment. People may have difficulty believing that a death on the cross 2,000 years ago can guarantee believers a place in heaven when they die, but when the same cross heals the blind and lame before our very eyes, it is a shade more convincing. I returned a few weeks later to

---

[2] I was at KAC from 1966 to 1969, where I was very fortunate to study English under Harry Blamires, who himself had studied English under C. S. Lewis. Harry has written a number of literary books, including *The Christian Mind*, which has become something of a Christian classic (London: SPCK 1963).

watch another film, this time from Indonesia, with very similar results.[3] I was hooked instantly; I bought and read all Osborn's books and believed his message completely. I will always be grateful for these presentations because they switched on in me a light that has never gone out.

In those days, I was studying English and knew very little theology – other than what I'd picked up in my daily Bible notes. What I saw and heard in the films, with the quoting of much Scripture, seemed to me to match what Jesus did.

'Which is easier: to say, "Your sins are forgiven," or to say, "Get up and walk"? But so that you may know that the Son of Man has authority on earth to forgive sins...' Then he said to the paralytic, 'Get up, take your mat and go home.' And the man got up and went home. When the crowd saw this, they were filled with awe; and they praised God, who had given such authority to men. (Matthew 9:5–8)

I was not surprised to read they were filled with awe, praised God, or ended up believing in a Jesus who can forgive sins. I found myself in the same position after I'd seen a couple of T. L. Osborn films.

I tried believing in what Jesus had done on the cross, really believing, for four or five years, praying and laying on hands, quoting verses of Scripture, addressing sicknesses whenever and wherever I met them, but no one testified to feeling even a little bit better. Not enough faith, I supposed. Undaunted, my belief in Jesus' love for us still led me to offer myself for ordination in the Church of England. They

---

[3] The film was entitled *Java Harvest*, also produced by the T. L. Osborn Foundation. I did not know at the time that the events took place during the Indonesian revival of the sixties.

seemed to approve of people who had questions to ask and were still working things through rather than believing they had all the answers, and I was joyfully accepted amongst the fraternity. My bishop rang me up after the interviews, positively rejoicing he had a candidate with doubts, who seemed to him to be just what the Church of England needed at the time.

I went for further interviews at the theological college in Nottingham, hoping to get a place there as my girlfriend was about to start at Nottingham University. This seemed to be a good idea, but telling my interviewers was probably not such a good idea as I found myself being made to jump a few hurdles. They invited me to attend a lecture while I was there, which went something like this:

> Signs and wonders, healings and miracles were commonest in the Bible during two major events:
>
> a) The Exodus event.
> b) The Jesus event.

The Exodus from Egypt was the special time when miracles helped the Jews to believe in God, to become a nation and to enter into a covenant relationship with God as his chosen people – the Old Testament (Covenant). The coming of Jesus into the world was similarly a special event when signs and wonders helped people to believe in Jesus and to enter into a new covenant relationship with God – the New Testament (Covenant). Once these had happened, and the Bible was written, there was no more need for supernatural events such as healing, which is why we don't get miracles today.

The lecturer's experience of non-healing appeared to

confirm his theology, though I suspect he'd never been to India or Indonesia, nor heard of T. L. Osborn. And I couldn't help thinking there were a few billion people around today who would benefit from some supernatural help to believe in Jesus, rather than just being told he had a book out.

When I returned to my interviewers, I expressed some doubts to them about the lecture I'd just heard, but even so I was given a place to study theology at St John's College, Nottingham.[4] What I had just heard, however, gave me an interesting dilemma to ponder. Starting from the same Bible, one person concluded that God now wants to heal everyone while the same pages convinced a second person, a more academic and theologically trained person, that God now wants to heal no one. They did, of course, quote different verses.

While I was in Nottingham, the charismatic Fountain Trust went from strength to strength. At one of their meetings, Tom Smale gave me a book on healing which he'd just brought back from America, written by Francis MacNutt.[5] It was the best and easiest book to read on healing that I had ever encountered, and one idea in particular really appealed to me:

> The gift of healing is . . . where the person praying already knows in some mysterious way the mind of God, and can speak in His person.[6]

---

[4] I trained for the ordained ministry at St John's College, Nottingham, 1972–76.

[5] Michael Harper headed up the Fountain Trust in the seventies before Tom Smale took over. It helped many Anglicans like me to believe in the charismatic gifts as biblical gifts for today.

[6] Francis MacNutt, *Healing* (Indiana: Ave Maria Press 1974), p. 128.

I didn't know a lot about it at the time, but I did like the idea of a 'word' from God informing the ministry – having faith in what God says he is doing rather than faith in my faith.

During my time in Nottingham, I was extremely fortunate to be sent on placement to St Margaret's Aspley, where John Finney was the vicar. They had a monthly healing service on Wednesday nights, fasted and prayed all day and then laid hands on all who came forward, having first instructed the ladies to remove their hats. On one occasion, I was invited to join John in doing the ministry, along with Felicity Lawson, another student from St John's.[7]

'What do I say as I lay hands on the sick?' I asked naïvely.

'Whatever God tells you to say!' came the reply.

I'll make it up, I thought. *No one will know.*

I had a blinding headache with all this fasting stuff, and as I went along the line of people who were kneeling at the communion rail I simply spoke whatever came into my head. Power came on some; others were reduced to tears, and yet more people came up to me afterwards with questions like, 'How did you know?'

But it only worked in Aspley. I was ordained in 1976 and didn't get a sniff of another healing or a 'word' from God until I went to hear John Wimber in Sheffield, in 1985.[8] In the meantime, I began reading books about Smith

---

[7] Canon Felicity Lawson and Bishop John Finney are at present assisting Martin Cavender in his new job as ReSource Director. Sounds like a terrific team to me. Details from office@resource-arm.net. Website:www.resource-arm.net

[8] I attended the Signs and Wonders and Church Growth Conference, Part 1, at Sheffield in the autumn of 1985, where John Wimber was the main speaker.

Wigglesworth, the healing evangelist from Yorkshire who died the year I was born, and I couldn't help wondering why we'd not been told about him at theological college.[9] Apparently, he raised 14 from the dead, was used by God to heal thousands of others, and led many to faith in Christ. A few years ago, I met two of his granddaughters; they told me how most of Smith's family lived well into their eighties, but also how Grandfather had not been able to pass on to anyone else the specially anointed ministry God gave to him. Food for thought, I felt.

I tried very hard myself to get words from God, and I never ducked out of any opportunity which came my way to pray for the sick. However, after I left Aspley I did not encounter any more supernatural healings until I heard and met John Wimber. I was one of a congregation of about 4,000 people, in front of whom the big American modelled how to pray for healing. People were picked out of the crowd with 'words of knowledge'; they came on the stage for the laying-on of hands, and then testified into the microphone to being healed. It was all a bit like T. L. Osborn really, except this was not on film but live, and in England. To go with the practice of healing that was modelled, they also emphasised John 5:19 throughout the week: 'Jesus gave them this answer: "I tell you the truth, the Son . . . can do only what he sees his Father doing." '

It looked like Osborn, sounded like MacNutt, and I liked

---

[9] In recent times, I have come across two helpful books on the life of Smith Wigglesworth: Jack Hywel-Davies, *Baptised by Fire* (London: Hodder & Stoughton 2001); Julian Wilson, *Wigglesworth* (Milton Keynes: Authentic Media 2002).

it because Jesus really did seem to be doing the stuff amongst us that he'd done when on earth.

We had a go in our own church when I returned home, and this time we met with some success. We experienced a few healings and many more 'words of knowledge' from God, which encouraged us, and at times proved to be life-changing experiences.

During this time, some Australians turned up in our church and liked what was going on. When they returned to the Antipodes they wrote to me in enthusiastic mode and sent me some of their magazines, which taught me a new phrase: 'covenant right'. According to them, we had a 'covenant right' to physical healing, because of the work of Jesus on the cross, and all we had to do was to 'name it and claim it'. It came across a bit like a Christian Science shop steward to me, and I wasn't at all sure I preferred it to what MacNutt or Wimber taught, but it was another idea to add to my confusion.

After we'd been doing this stuff for a while in and around Birmingham, I was invited to attend a fortnight's residential course for vicars.[10] Some well-known canons in the Church of England were teaching on all things charismatic, including healing, and I went along for a very enjoyable ride where I made many new friends and heard some interesting things, like this: 'Healing in the New Testament is in the atonement.'

It sounded to me like going back to T. L. Osborn rather than going on with John Wimber, so I dared to ask a

---

[10] The Changing Church course was held in Birmingham at Queen's College, August 1986.

question: 'Excuse me, sir, but have you noticed how Jesus did healing *before* he died on the cross?'

'Ah yes,' he replied, 'but the cross can work backwards as well as forwards.'

Indeed, I thought. *Like Dr Who, the time traveller.*

I had a million other questions to ask, but there never seemed to be quite enough time. I liked the practice of Osborn, the teaching of MacNutt, the combination of the two I'd met in Wimber, and the absolutely mind-blowing inspiration of Smith Wigglesworth, but fitting it all together theologically with the New Testament was proving to be a little troublesome. I wondered too about the 'Third Wave' of the Holy Spirit, which Wimber identified as coming after the Pentecostal movement and the charismatic movement,[11] even though he taught and modelled the healing ministry as if it were a 'for all time' kind of teaching. Experience seemed to suggest that God did more healings during the 'Third Wave' than before or after it, which strangely enough fitted to some extent with what the lecturer at St John's had said during my interviews: 'At different times, God does more healing than at others.' Interestingly, John Wimber also wrote a lengthy book called *Power Healing*, in which he didn't mention the cross once and took some stick for it, all of which led me to less clarity and greater bewilderment.

People who loved Jesus and saw him heal the sick from time to time were now rolling around in my brain, assuming

---

[11] The Third Wave is well documented by Kevin Springer in *Riding the Third Wave* (Basingstoke: Marshall Morgan & Scott, Marshall Pickering 1987).

contradictory positions on the healing issue, and I was finding myself perplexed. I was determined, if at all possible, to try to sort it out in my own mind just as soon as I could find the time, and I hoped the two-week course in Birmingham might give me that opportunity.

I was assigned a tutor, who asked me to write him a 10,000-word essay.

'Healing?' I enquired tentatively. 'I'd like to write about Healing and the "Third Wave", T. L. Osborn, Francis Mac-Nutt, Smith Wigglesworth, John Wimber, Dr Who and the Bible.'

'Everyone writes about healing,' he replied, in a careful and dignified manner. 'We all know quite a bit about that subject, but wherever I go people keep coming out with these "words of knowledge", and I don't know anything about them. Why don't you write about "words of knowledge" instead of healing? I think we'd all find that much more helpful.'

I asked around among the learned canons, and they all agreed with my tutor, so I did what I'd been advised to do. Later, others came across my essay and persuaded me to use it as the basis of a book for Kingsway, called *The Hot Line*.[12] It was hard work, but many people liked it and it sold quite well. However, after the learned canons I knew had all retired, when many years had gone by, my children had grown up and I had a bit more time, I decided to write my book... the one they had advised me not to write – the one I had always wanted to write – in an attempt to find and

---

[12] Peter H. Lawrence, *The Hot Line* (Bristol: Terra Nova 1997). Used by permission.

present New Testament answers to all my questions on healing. These are the questions I asked the New Testament to answer for me:

a) Is physical healing linked directly to the cross/atonement of Christ?
b) If not, what does the New Testament teach about physical healing?
c) What are the implications of what the New Testament teaches for Christians today?

This book seeks to answer these questions.

However, when I reached the halfway point in writing it, the Holy Spirit came upon me during my prayer-time and seemed to say: 'Peter, I want you to put all your best healing stories into this one book, to encourage others and inspire them to have a go for themselves.'

In a brief moment, in the twinkling of an eye, the size of the book doubled and its character was transformed. Suddenly, it became as much God's book as my book, and the aim was no longer to satisfy my own curiosity but to help, equip and inspire others to heal the sick. If biblical theology is not quite your thing, I suggest you read the summary at the beginning of each chapter and then flick from story to story. They are numbered from one to forty-six. But I do hope church leaders and those who enjoy Bible study will read it all, because knowing the biblical basis for healing may just help and motivate those who know and love the Bible to have a go as well.

I finished the first draft of this book in the early part of 2005 and then in the last week of April headed for the Toronto Airport Christian Fellowship with ten others from our church. It turned out to be a mind-boggling experience, and one which tested my biblical discoveries to the limit.

What I discovered, by reading every verse of the New Testament, is that it is only in the New Jerusalem that healing comes to us as a direct consequence of the cross. Until then, between the first and second comings of Jesus, in the age of the Spirit, it is the Spirit who heals. I now brought this thesis to the 'Glory' conference, which was being held in Toronto at one of my favourite churches.[13]

On our first Sunday evening, Pastor Duncan Smith spoke about healing, during which he shared some wonderful stories about his trips to South Africa and elsewhere. He had seen a pastor from Malawi totally healed of cancer, blind eyes being opened, and the Holy Spirit guiding him to help someone out of a wheelchair. At a training day for 300 pastors in the predominantly Muslim country of Turkmenistan, the Lord led Duncan to spit on his hand and put it on the tongue of a lady who was mute. She had never spoken before but, at 45, was healed and spoke her first words to a gobsmacked mum. 'What are we having for lunch?' she enquired, as if she had been speaking all her life. The pastors present gave all the glory to Jesus for her complete healing.

Duncan told us that the will of Jesus is to heal everybody; then he asked all those who were ill and wanted to be healed to stand. We prayed for everyone – several times – and were encouraged to cast out the spirit of infirmity, in Jesus' name, if it wasn't going too well.

---

[13] The conference was entitled: Show Me Your Glory; it was held at the Toronto Airport Christian Fellowship from the 27th to the 30th April 2005.

Of the hundred and fifty or so of those who stood, about five or six testified to being healed while I was there. An elderly man was healed right in front of where we were sitting. He came into the meeting with what looked like very stiff joints and poor mobility, hobbled about in some pain with the aid of a stick, and seemed to be suffering virtually all over his body before he was gloriously healed. His face shone and he leaped around like a newborn lamb, stick above his head, with no apparent discomfort, in front of several from our church, who were thrilled to witness his healing and rejoice with him.

Later in the week, John Arnott, the senior pastor, led us in a beautiful time of healing. He invited the Holy Spirit to move among us in healing power while he and his wife Carol gave words of knowledge about those the Holy Spirit was specifically touching that night. This made the teaching that went with it seem a little strange.

'Say after me,' John said to everyone who wanted healing, "Lord Jesus, this healing belongs to me because of the work you did on the cross."

'Faith has already been exhibited', John continued, 'when you turned up for the meeting, when you lifted your voice to him in worship.'

Several times, John repeated: 'I want you to know it is the will of God to heal you.'

And a few testified to being healed. Wonderfully, John gave a 'word' from God about a tightness around the stomach which caused pain and made breathing difficult – he said there were two people present who were suffering from this condition, whom God was healing. A lady came on the stage and said she had just been healed of the exact condition John described, and a young man came up and said he was one-quarter healed – so he received more prayer.

The ministry was done with such sensitivity and love it was a joy to be there, and the testimonies were inspiring to hear. The practice fitted what I had discovered in Scripture perfectly – it is the Spirit who heals – even though the teaching that went with it was harder to understand from a New Testament point of view.

Later still in the week, the other senior pastor, Steve Long, invited everyone who wore glasses or needed contact lenses to stand. Steve himself was wearing glasses and so was I, so up I got. Out of the 3,000–4,000 present, Steve said there were about 85 per cent standing. We took off our spectacles, laid hands on our eyes, prayed our best prayers for some time, put our spectacles back on and sat down. One lady came forward to say she could now read words on the sheet without her glasses, which she hadn't been able to do before, and we praised Jesus for what he did for the one lady. People came on stage and prayed for Steve; he took off his glasses, and went over in the power of the Spirit. Power came all over him and blessed him, but he still put his glasses back on in order to conclude the meeting.

And then there was Heidi Baker.[14] To watch Heidi in action in Toronto is to give the critics of the 'Toronto Blessing' a field day. She twitches, jerks, collapses, laughs and

---

[14] Heidi Baker and her husband Rolland are the directors of Iris Ministries in Mozambique. They lead a growing ministry to the orphans of Maputo, oversee more than 5,000 churches and train existing and emerging pastors. One of her books is a bestseller: Rolland and Heidi Baker, *There is Always Enough* (Tonbridge: Sovereign World 2003).

shrieks out uncontrollably. 'Not quite our cup of tea,' said a few of my Anglican friends when I showed them the DVD. For three years during the nine years she has been coming to Toronto, Heidi just collapsed on the floor, unable to move, and needed to be carried everywhere. Her testimony is this: 'Nine years ago, when I came to Toronto, I was undone – and I haven't been done up since.' The word she often used was 'wrecked'.

'This can't be of God,' say the critics. 'This must be of the devil.' However, if this is so, then the devil has led tens of thousands to Christ so far in 2005, and healed thousands in the process. The story goes like this . . .

In January, while in one of her collapsed-totally-possessed-by-Jesus states, the Lord took her to heaven. There, in a vision, she saw chariots of fire with God holding all the reins. 'Come with me,' said God. 'Get into the chariot and let me take you for a ride.' And Heidi said, 'Yes.'

In the first three months of 2005, Heidi shared with us how God had taken her to places in Mozambique (where she is based as a missionary), Malawi, South Africa, Brazil, Sierra Leone and Chicago. Guided by the driver of the chariots, Heidi frequently used children, who believe God does things, and asked them to hug the sick and the dying. Blind eyes were opened; the lame walked; the deaf heard; cancerous tumours fell away, and the dying were restored to life. Villages, towns and cities have started to believe in Jesus because of the word of God she preaches with signs following. It doesn't look like Satan to me.

In January, Heidi was specially called and anointed by the Holy Spirit for this phenomenal chariot ride, and this is what revival seems to look like in 2005. The revivalist jerks, twitches, laughs, collapses on the floor and from time to time shrieks out uncontrollably, and then helps tens of thousands to know Christ and be healed by him.

I said to John Arnott while I was there, 'The prophets are claiming that the tide is turning back home. Revival may be coming to Britain.'

'Ask them what it will look like,' he commented instantaneously. 'Ask them what it will look like.'

Those who are praying for revival in Britain and want to know what it will look like may need to read the historical accounts of revivals carefully and then buy the DVD of Heidi Baker speaking at TACF on Wednesday 27th April 2005.[15] That's what I believe revival may look like, as it has done ever since the disciples appeared to be drunk on the Day of Pentecost.

And what did I make of all I saw and heard in Toronto regarding healing? This is my summary of the teaching I received during the week I was there:

a) Healing belongs to me now because of the work Jesus did on the cross.

b) It is the will of God to heal me now.

c) I have already exhibited enough faith to be healed by turning up at the meeting and lifting up my voice to God in worship.

As 1 of 2,500 out of 2,501 who were not healed of impaired vision, I don't think so. Something seemed to be wrong somewhere. I admire Steve Long enormously for having

---

[15] Toronto Airport Christian Fellowship, website: www.tacf.org; email: mail@tacf.org

the courage of his convictions; it's just that after all I have read in the New Testament, coupled with what I experienced in Toronto, it looks to me as if his convictions may need a little tweaking. At the very least, he probably needs to ask a question about the difference between disease and decay. Positively, wonderfully, this is what I experienced or heard about while I was there:

- Duncan Smith was led by the Holy Spirit to help someone out of a wheelchair, and to heal a lady mute from birth. Others were healed when the Holy Spirit came upon them.
- When Duncan led a time of ministry in Toronto, an elderly man was beautifully healed of stiff joints and pain right in front of us, when the Holy Spirit came upon him.
- When John and Carol Arnott discerned that the Holy Spirit was present to heal the sick, and were led by the Spirit to give discerning words about what he was doing, one or two significant healings took place.
- When the Spirit of God came on one lady who could not read without her glasses, she was healed.
- When the Holy Spirit came powerfully upon Heidi Baker, she saw in the spirit what God was doing. When she went where he went, and did what he did, large numbers of people were healed and saved by the Holy Spirit working through her.

What I experienced, and the testimonies I heard during my week in Canada, seemed to me to match exactly what I'd just read in the New Testament. It is the Spirit who heals. But if you want to know how and why I think some of their teaching on healing does not always match what the New

Testament teaches and needs a little tweaking, you'll have to read the rest of the book.

It was a privilege to be in Toronto, to feel the love and to experience the power of God at work among us. It was a thrill to see the Holy Spirit move among us and heal some, though my heart did go out to those who came in wheelchairs and left in wheelchairs after what was taught from the front.

It was wonderful being there for a week, and it was inspiring to take part in real worship with thousands of others. It was encouraging to see a few people being healed, virtually everyone being blessed and to hear of the healing and revival stories taking place elsewhere in the world. Our God is a big God. That's why I love asking him to come, waiting for him to come and seeking to respond to his coming – letting him know he can do whatever he wants to do, whenever he wants to do it, in any way he chooses.

I hope all of you will enjoy the stories in this book and take inspiration from them. I am afraid those that include me are not quite in the same league as those of Heidi Baker but they may encourage those of you who, like me, feel somewhat inadequate most of the time. I also hope many of you will use it as a way of checking out what the Bible really does say about healing for today, and risk having a go. It really does say it is the Holy Spirit who heals – and the really good news is that all believers can ask him to come.

Please forgive me if at times I may sound a little repetitive. It is partly due to having been a teacher who became a clergyman, partly due to my enthusiasm about what the Bible teaches, and partly due to the sheer weight of scriptural evidence which to my mind seems to endorse my findings. If I just say it once or twice and include only one or two verses to back it up, you may not fully appreciate the weight of Scripture that emphasises the healing work of the Holy Spirit.

What I discovered when I studied the New Testament is that it is the Spirit who heals. What I experienced in Toronto, both live and second-hand through testimonies, is that it is the Spirit who heals. What I struggle with is the belief that God offers healing to everyone of everything always, right now, because of the cross, practically, experientially and theologically, as I cannot find such teaching in the New Testament.

I have never met anyone with more faith in Christ's healing than Heidi Baker, but sadly in October 2005 even she was taken seriously ill and needed hospital treatment for a while.

See what you think. Remember: a summary of what I discovered is included at the beginning of every chapter (except the last one, which is for all), while the healing stories are numbered from one to forty-six for those who, like my wife Carol, prefer stories to theology.

Whatever you think as you read it, I pray that like T. L. Osborn, Francis MacNutt, Smith Wigglesworth, John Wimber, Heidi Baker and the team from Toronto, you will all have the thrill of seeing God at work, coming among us with healing in his wings.

2

The Anointed Jesus Heals the Sick

A look at the Gospels

Most of the healings recorded in the New Testament are found in the Gospels and Acts of the Apostles, so I began my search for biblical truth by reading the four Gospels. I would recommend them to anyone. I simply read the text carefully in the NIV version, believing the plain sense to be the main sense, and this is what I found:

- Physical healing in the Gospels is seen as the work of the Holy Spirit.
- Jesus Christ healed the sick because he was perfect man full of the Holy Spirit.
- His disciples healed the sick when they were given the same authority and power by the same Holy Spirit who anointed Jesus.
- Nowhere could I find Jesus, or the Gospel writers, saying that Jesus could heal the sick because he was going to the cross, or that the cross works backwards.
- Nowhere could I find Jesus, or the Gospel writers, saying that Jesus died for sicknesses as well as sins, or that it is our covenant right to be healed.

In short, in the Gospels, it is the Holy Spirit, working through Jesus and his disciples, who heals.

1. The Spirit heals in Penzance

One Saturday evening, a few years ago, I was invited to speak at a parish church near Penzance. The church was comfortably full and as usual I spoke from the Bible and illustrated it from daily life, with a touch of humour now and again to keep people awake. Afterwards, I invited people to stand while I asked God the Father through Jesus Christ to send his Holy Spirit upon us, to do whatever he wanted to do.

I couldn't see very clearly from the front but, apparently, a lady called Yvonne crashed over quite dramatically in the back row early in the proceedings and ended up lying flat out on the pew. This is what she wrote to me afterwards:

> I knew about people 'falling in the Spirit', but not a down-to-earth person like me. *No way* was I going to embarrass myself and everybody else. When it came to the time to ask the Holy Spirit to come, time I think stood still for me. I was aware, yet not aware, there but not there, my mind clear and open yet with no real concept of what was going on around me. I was to crash down, quite suddenly I've been told, but I really have no (or hardly any) recollection of that part, and certainly there was no embarrassment.

At the end of the time of ministry, as people began to drift out, I made my way to the back of the church where Yvonne was still horizontal, eyes closed with face beaming.

We enjoyed her countenance for some time until, eventually, her eyes opened as she returned to the upright position and made her way home. The letter continued:

> I came away feeling, oh – totally in awe of the power that was in me – the peace – yes – and the stillness.

I didn't know at the time that Yvonne had cancer. Three or four years previously she'd undergone four operations within nine months and now it had returned. She was due to see her surgeon the following Tuesday. She described their encounter like this.

> The surgeon looked at me – looked at the notes – at me again – shook his head and said, 'Good Lord!' So I said, 'Yes, he is, isn't he?'

It took several subsequent X-rays at frequent intervals and a second opinion before she was finally declared to be fully healed. We believe God, the Holy Spirit, did it.

A few years later, I was back in Cornwall again, this time in a different parish church, where I shared this story as part of my talk. 'Does anyone know Yvonne?' I asked a little hesitantly, 'Or know how she is getting on?'

'Yes!' another lady called out. 'She's getting ordained next summer.'

Jesus Christ

The New Testament begins like this: 'A record of the genealogy of Jesus Christ' (Matthew 1:1).

When Jesus Christ was registered for the junior school at Nazareth, he had a different surname from the one by which he has been known, even by blasphemers, for nearly 2,000 years. The title 'Christ', which means 'the anointed one', only came to him at his baptism, when he was anointed with the Holy Spirit. The people wondered if John the Baptist might be 'the Christ' but John pointed them to Jesus (Luke 3:15–16; John 1:29–34).

'And as he [Jesus] was praying, heaven was opened and the Holy Spirit descended on him in bodily form like a dove' (Luke 3:21–22). This was a fulfilment of Isaiah's prophecy:

> A shoot will come up from the stump of Jesse;
> from his roots a Branch will bear fruit.
> The Spirit of the Lord will rest on him –
> the Spirit of wisdom and of understanding,
> the Spirit of counsel and of power,
> the Spirit of knowledge and of the fear of the Lord. . .
> (Isaiah 11:1– 2; see also Isaiah 42:1)

Jesus accepted the title 'Christ' from Peter (Matthew 16:16–17), and later Peter went on to link the anointing of Jesus with Jesus' ability to heal.

> God anointed Jesus of Nazareth with the Holy Spirit and power, and . . . he went around doing good and healing all who were under the power of the devil, because God was with him. (Acts 10:38)

The Christ (Greek), the Messiah (Hebrew), is the anointed one – the one who is anointed by the Spirit of God to do the work of God – and this anointing is recorded in all four Gospels before Jesus has healed anyone. All of the signs and wonders which are described in the Gospels, including the physical healings, come after Jesus has been anointed with the Holy Spirit.

In the Gospel according to the physician Luke, this anointing is emphasised at the start of Jesus' ministry: 'Jesus, full of the Holy Spirit, returned from the Jordan and was led by the Spirit in the desert' (Luke 4:1); 'Jesus returned to Galilee in the power of the Spirit' (Luke 4:14). And then in Luke, on the lips of Jesus, this anointing with the Holy Spirit is linked directly to physical healing:

> The scroll of the prophet Isaiah was handed to him [Jesus]. Unrolling it, he found the place where it is written:
> The Spirit of the Lord is on me, because he has anointed me to preach good news to the poor. He has sent me to proclaim freedom for the prisoners and recovery of sight to the blind . . .
> (Luke 4:17–18)

Jesus claimed it for himself by adding: 'Today this scripture is fulfilled in your hearing' (Luke 4:21). And lest anyone seek to interpret Jesus' quotation of Isaiah as meaning just 'spiritual sight to the spiritually blind', Jesus used this and other parts of Isaiah later in the Gospels when replying to a question from John the Baptist.

> [John sent disciples to ask:] 'Are you the one who was to come, or should we expect someone else?' Jesus replied, 'Go back and report to John what you hear and see: The blind receive sight, the lame walk, those who have leprosy are cured, the deaf hear, the dead are raised, and the good news is preached to the poor. Blessed is the man who does not fall away on account of me.' (Matthew 11:3–6; cf. Isaiah 35:4–6; 61:1)

People had asked John if he was the Christ, the Messiah, the anointed one, but he had led them to Jesus (Luke 3:15; John 1:19–34). Now in prison, he wants to check that he has got it right – and Jesus not only confirms John's prophetic understanding, but also gives him evidence to help him believe. The evidence given, to prove that Jesus is the anointed one, is that he is healing the sick as prophesied by Isaiah. There is also a corollary to this statement: if healing the sick is the evidence of being anointed by the Holy Spirit then it follows that the anointing of the Holy Spirit is what enabled Jesus to heal the sick. This is the understanding of Jesus' ministry as outlined by all four Gospel writers.

2. The Spirit heals in Birmingham

One morning, as I was working in my study, a wave of heat swept over me and I sensed God may be calling my number. I stopped work, began praying, and this thought came into my head. 'I want you to go and visit Janet and John [not their real names], right now.' This was a married couple in their twenties who'd been to our church a few times, though I didn't know them well.

I'll give them a ring and check they're in, I replied to the thought in my head, knowing the importance of checking out on earth words that appear to come from heaven.

They're not there, replied the other end of the dialogue.

I was puzzled. *They're not there but God wants me to visit them?*

They will be there when you arrive, came the next 'word', as if God could read my mind.

Unfortunately, Janet and John lived several miles from our church, and I didn't fancy wasting an hour or so, not to mention worrying what the treasurer might say if I asked him for expenses. What would you do? I went – slowly – through the heavy city traffic, knocked at the door loudly several times, and found there was no one there. Of course not. It was mid-week, and both of them would be out at work. How silly! I got into my car without, I'm sorry to say, displaying any of the fruits of the Spirit I was supposed to be growing.

'Told you so,' I said, loudly, as I clunk-clicked and put the key into the ignition.

Stay where you are, said the next thought. *They'll be here in two minutes.*

I was not keen. I paused. 'OK,' I said, 'you've got two minutes.'

I stared hard at the second hand on my watch for two minutes, then started the engine, put the car into reverse, looked into the rear-view mirror and saw Janet and John driving in.

'What are you doing here?' they asked simultaneously, when we all emerged from our cars.

'God sent me,' I said, and smiled.

They were amazed. Having been married several years, this was the first time they'd ever been home together mid-week, and God sent the vicar.

It transpired that after many embarrassing tests, the medical profession had told them they would not be able to have their own children, due to his low sperm count, and had advised them to apply for adoption. They were now on their way to meet the authorities and a little girl who was available for adoption, calling in at home for just five minutes to change and grab a sandwich. It was lovely to be there at such an important moment in their lives and to pray with them.

'Sorry, God!' I said on the way home. 'It was you after all.'

And then I got to thinking and praying and realising that God seemed to be on their case in a special sort of way. So I invited myself back one evening the following week, with a lady called Patricia from our church. Yes, the interview had gone well, and no, they didn't mind if we prayed for them.

We invited them to stand together in front of their own sofa and then asked God the Father through Jesus to send his Holy Spirit upon them. Janet started shaking almost immediately and then collapsed into the sofa but John stood firmly rooted to the spot. Slowly his arms were lifted high above his head in a position of adoration as his hands began to shake uncontrollably and wouldn't stop.

'How long is this likely to go on?' John eventually asked me, in a rather shaky kind of voice.

'I've never known it last more than three weeks,' I commented with a smile.

After the time of ministry, Janet, Pat and I chatted together while John tried to get me some supper, but he spilled my cornflakes all over the floor. He shook for over an hour, which was awesome to behold and great fun for the three of us, who enjoyed watching it. But I was even more delighted to find myself baptising their own son within a year, a younger brother for the girl they adopted.

The Spirit of God came powerfully upon John, and he was healed.

Why did Jesus need the Holy Spirit?

If Jesus is God, why did he need to be anointed by the Holy Spirit?

Whenever I suggest to theologically trained audiences that in the Gospels it is the Spirit who heals, they always ask me what I believe about the divinity of Jesus. Here are my biblical thoughts.

John's Gospel starts with this claim about Jesus: 'Through him all things were made; without him nothing was made that has been made' (John 1:3). The same Gospel comes to its climax after the resurrection with this affirmation from Thomas: 'My Lord and my God!' (John 20:28).

I agree with Scripture and believe that Jesus is God, but in between these two verses Jesus 'became flesh', meaning that he became fully human (John 1:14). In fact, the early church, the New Testament church, rejected as heresy the Gnostic/Docetist belief that Jesus was not fully human. In his letters, John wrote: 'Many deceivers, who do not acknowledge Jesus Christ as coming in the flesh, have gone out into the world. Any such person is the deceiver and the antichrist' (2 John 7); 'Every spirit that acknowledges that Jesus Christ has come in the flesh is from God' (1 John 4:2).

Unlike holy angels, who only appear as human from time to time on the earth, Jesus actually became human and was born of the flesh. To become flesh, or fully human, meant inevitably to lay aside his majesty when he was born at Bethlehem, and this can easily be proved from Scripture:

• Not omnipresent: 'He is not here' (Luke 24:6).
• Not omnipotent: 'I tell you the truth, the Son can do

nothing by himself; he can do only what he sees his Father doing' (John 5:19).

- Not omniscient: 'No-one knows about that day or hour, not even the angels in heaven, nor the Son, but only the Father' (Matthew 24:36).

If there are places where Jesus is not, things he cannot do and information he does not know, then I suggest that, while on earth as a human being, Jesus must have laid aside his majesty. He did not, however, lay aside his holiness or righteousness.

> For we do not have a high priest who is unable to sympathise with our weaknesses, but we have one who has been tempted in every way, just as we are – yet was without sin. (Hebrews 4:15)

The perfect man Jesus, who is God, allowed himself certain limitations when he became flesh, in order to be like one of us. This is why he is the perfect model for us, as well as our Saviour.

In relation to healing, we can see how Jesus – having laid aside his majesty – now needed the **authority** and **power** from the Father, conveyed by the Holy Spirit, in order for him to heal the sick.

The authority of God the Father

In John's Gospel, the *authority* of God the Father working in Jesus is seen as vital to his healing ministry. In John 5, Jesus visits the hospital in Jerusalem (the Pool of Bethesda), where 'a great number of disabled people used to lie – the blind, the lame, the paralysed' (v. 3). Jesus heals 'one who was there', a man who had been an invalid for 38 years. The sick man wasn't a particularly good man but rather something of a moaner and a groaner. When Jesus asked him if he wanted to get well, he complained, didn't answer the question and afterwards was not seen to be praising God like most other people healed by Jesus. Not surprisingly, when Jesus saw him later, he said to him, 'See, you are well again. Stop sinning or something worse may happen to you' (v. 14).

He wasn't a good man, and he wasn't a man full of faith in Jesus either. When asked who healed him, we are informed: 'The man who was healed had no idea who it was' (v. 13). I am therefore bound to ask: as the one who was healed was neither good nor full of faith, why did Jesus choose to heal him? In the discourse that follows, Jesus explains it: 'Jesus gave them this answer, "I tell you the truth, the Son can do nothing by himself; he can do only what he sees his Father doing"' (v. 19). God the Father seems to have said: 'That one!', so Jesus healed 'that one', and says that by himself he could not heal any other, because he could only do what the Father was doing. John the Baptist, speaking about Jesus, describes how Jesus could know and speak the words of God which carry the authority of God: 'For the one whom God has sent speaks the words of God, for God gives the Spirit without limit' (John 3:34). Jesus speaks the words of God and knows the mind of God because he is filled with the Spirit of God, 'without limit'.

When Jesus says that he can do 'only what he sees his Father doing', it would seem right to assume that when the Father is not doing healing, Jesus cannot do it either. At the pool, there were many sick people present, but John records Jesus healing only 'one who was there' (John 5:5). Although the divinity of Jesus is declared most strongly in John's Gospel, the dependency of Jesus on his Father is also a strong theme in John, and the suggestion throughout is that Jesus did, said and taught whatever the Father gave him the authority to do and say through the Holy Spirit (John 5:30; 7:16; 8:28; 12:49–50; 14:10, 24). Jesus was always completely obedient to the Father, so whenever the Father revealed his will to the Son, through the Holy Spirit, then Jesus did it, and whenever that will was healing, Jesus had his Father's authority to heal, and he healed.

3. The Spirit heals in Merley

On Easter Day 2004, I asked God the Father through Jesus to send his Holy Spirit on our evening congregation at the Lantern. God seemed to come beautifully on everyone present, so I was able to relax at the front and enjoy watching him work peacefully and joyfully on his precious bride. We had, of course, already confessed our sins, praised and worshipped him for his glorious Easter triumph and listened attentively to his word. Now we waited in the stillness for him to do whatever he wanted to do, before we headed off towards the Bank Holiday.

As I waited myself, somewhat relieved in the knowledge that my tense Easter exertions were now at an end, an economics teacher from the local grammar school made his way cautiously and carefully to the front. Everyone else had their eyes closed, so I met him off-stage, where he whispered to me.

'I think there is someone present', he began in an apologetic tone, 'who has arthritis in one hand. A lady, I think.'

Previously, David had sometimes been right and sometimes been wrong when giving words he thought were from God, but he is greatly loved and respected by all in our church. Apparently, he'd seen a picture in his mind of a bird, and the Holy Spirit had drawn his attention to one of its feet, especially the curved claws. It reminded David of an arthritic hand, so he passed it on to me unobtrusively, in case I wanted to act upon it.

'Go on letting God come,' I said into the microphone, 'but if someone here has arthritis in one hand, could you wave it at me?'

I made the decision to give this word for three reasons:

a) David had been right before.

b) Arthritis in *one* hand is unusual.

c) It wouldn't do any harm or disturb people if wrong.

Instantly, one lady waved her right claw at me, so I sent David to her while everyone else carried on undisturbed, letting God work with them.

David laid his hand gently on the lady's shoulder and almost immediately her right hand began shaking violently, accompanied by a strong pumping motion. I'd seen this before when another person was healed, and wondered if I should encourage everyone to open their eyes and watch God healing someone, but . . . I am British; I didn't want to disturb others, and I didn't want to embarrass the lady. Afterwards, I regretted not doing so.

Jane wrote to me later in the week to inform me of her healing, giving all the glory to Jesus. Thirty-five years earlier she'd been a professional singer and trumpeter, but suffered violence at the hands of her professional manager and as a result her right hand was badly damaged. She could no longer play her trumpet and had given up her career. The medical profession later used the term 'arthritic hand'. In her letter, Jane described how very painful it had been for 35 years, how she had needed painkillers, but now, since Sunday night, she'd become pain-free, didn't need any tablets and could bend all her fingers. Jane was also able to play her trumpet again. Over a year later, her hand is still fine.

It seemed good to us all that God the Father through Jesus sent his Holy Spirit on Easter Day, conveying to us his authority to heal, and Jane was healed. To God be all the glory!

The power of the Holy Spirit

Doctor Luke wrote this:

> One day as he [Jesus] was teaching, Pharisees and teachers of the law, who had come from every village of Galilee and from Judea and Jerusalem, were sitting there. And the power of the Lord was present for him to heal the sick. (Luke 5:17)

The implication of Luke's phrase 'the power of the Lord was present for him to heal the sick' is that there were times when the power was not present for Jesus to heal; otherwise, Luke would not have mentioned it. In this particular story, Jesus' discernment that the power of the Lord was present to heal enables him to prophesy that the man is going to be healed, and to link it to the authority of the Father:

> 'But that you may know that the Son of Man has authority on earth to forgive sins . . .' He said to the paralysed man, 'I tell you, get up, take your mat and go home.' (Luke 5:24)

As the man is healed, we note that Jesus not only has authority to forgive, when the circumstances are right, but also to heal.

Similarly, there were other times when the power of the Lord to heal was present. In chapter 6, Luke commented:

> A great number of people . . . had come to hear him [Jesus] and to be healed of their diseases . . . and the people all tried to touch him, because power was coming from him and healing them all. (Luke 6:17–19)

More particularly, when healing a woman subject to bleeding Jesus said, 'Someone touched me; I know that power has gone out from me' (Luke 8:46).

The suggestion in Luke's Gospel is that when 'the power of the Lord was present for him to heal the sick', then Jesus could do it, and it was this power coming from him which brought physical healing. In the Bible, 'the power of the Lord' is normally equated with 'the power of the Holy Spirit', especially when it refers to supernatural power. The Spirit of the Lord came upon Samson in power to give him supernatural strength (Judges 14:6, 19; 15:14), and on Saul to enable him to prophesy (1 Samuel 10:10). Isaiah prophesies that the Spirit of the Lord will give the Messiah the Spirit of power (Isaiah 11:2). Peter preaches about Jesus being anointed with the Holy Spirit and power (Acts 10:38), and Paul writes about 'signs and miracles, through the power of the Spirit' (Romans 15:19). But it is in Luke's own writings that we see power associated with the Holy Spirit most commonly: the angel said to Mary, 'The Holy Spirit will come upon you, and the power of the Most High will overshadow you' (Luke 1:35); 'Jesus returned to Galilee in the power of the Spirit' (Luke 4:14); 'Stay in the city until you have been clothed with power from on high' (Luke 24:49); 'You will receive power when the Holy Spirit comes on you' (Acts 1:8).

It seems reasonable to suggest that the 'power of the Lord . . . to heal' (Luke 5:17), the power which flows through Jesus to heal (Luke 6:19; 8:46), is the power of the Holy Spirit, who is, after all, the Lord (2 Corinthians 3:17–18). The power to heal seems to come and go according to the will of the Father even though the presence of God, who is with Jesus through the Holy Spirit, remains with him constantly. There is always a difference between the presence of God and the activity of God. (The 'presence' of God and the 'activity' of God is discussed more fully in Chapter 10.)

The people also saw deliverance as an act of power, and Jesus linked his work of deliverance to the Holy Spirit: 'If I drive out demons by the Spirit of God, then the kingdom of God has come upon you' (Matthew 12:28; cf. Luke 4:36). I think we can assume, as is implied, that Jesus was not driving out demons by Beelzebub and therefore was driving out demons by the Spirit of God. Once more, we note that the power of the Holy Spirit in Jesus, working through Jesus, was the power to heal.

4. The Spirit heals in Bearwood

David and Tina are regular members of our St Barnabas congregation in Bearwood. Since 1986, they have cared for about 80 children as foster parents, including some mother and baby placements. In 2001, Eathan, aged ten weeks, came to them with his 26-year-old mother, in considerable need and distress. He was her fifth child; the other four had all been adopted, and while they were both with David and Tina, Mum agreed that Eathan should be handed over for adoption as well. She was unable to care for this very needy baby, being in great need of care herself.

Eathan could only see things about a foot away, had very poor hearing, a crooked little body, was unable to turn his head around, and after developmental tests the hospital suspected cerebral palsy. David's and Tina's house group prayed regularly for Eathan, and many sensed in the Spirit that God wanted to heal him.

One Sunday morning, at the church of St Barnabas, Geoff, the team vicar, knelt down and laid hands on Eathan. He asked God the Father, through Jesus, to send the Holy Spirit on him and do whatever he wanted to do. Unusually, the little baby showed no signs of worry but smiled as God's healing power came upon him.

That day, God opened Eathan's eyes so that he could see and react to people and things at the far end of a room. Gradually, his hearing and mobility reached full normality, and eventually the hospital released him as 'completely healed'. By the time he was ten months old, he was crawling around and getting into all kinds of mischief, as normal children do. But God had not finished yet.

A lovely Christian couple who'd tried for eleven years to have their own children, without success, were allowed to adopt him as their own. Tina said, 'A perfect match truly made in heaven,' as they seemed to relax immediately in one another's company. And then a second healing took place. A month after the official adoption, Eathan's new mum discovered that she was pregnant; she eventually gave birth to Eathan's brother, who looks just like him. As I write, Eathan has just celebrated his fourth birthday and is about to start school as a perfectly normal, well-adjusted child.

The house group continued to pray for Eathan after he left David and Tina, and as they did so it seemed to them that God was saying he'd allowed his new mum's womb to be closed for eleven years so that they would adopt Eathan. With hindsight, we can look back at the wonderful works of the God who delayed one healing for eleven years in order to facilitate another. To him belong all our thanks and praise.

Jesus did not heal before his anointing

After Jesus was anointed by the Holy Spirit, and whenever the Spirit of God gave Jesus the authority and the power to heal the sick, then Jesus did healing. On the other hand, the New Testament suggests that before Jesus was anointed he did not do any healing.

> Coming to his home town, he began teaching the people in their synagogue, and they were amazed. 'Where did this man

get this wisdom and these miraculous powers?' they asked. 'Isn't this the carpenter's son? Isn't his mother's name Mary, and aren't his brothers James, Joseph, Simon and Judas? Aren't all his sisters with us? Where then did this man get all these things?' And they took offence at him. (Matthew 13:54–57)

The people who knew Jesus well were obviously taken by surprise when he started healing the sick at the age of 30. 'Where did this man get all these things?' they asked. His relatives also seemed a little shocked. In Mark 3, his family are so upset with Jesus 'they went to take charge of him, for they said, "He is out of his mind"' (Mark 3:21).

Subsequently, surprise turned into hostility. In Luke 4, after Jesus has announced in Nazareth that the Spirit of God is on him to proclaim 'recovery of sight for the blind' (v. 18), he senses the hostility of his own people and says to them: 'Surely you will quote this proverb to me: "Physician, heal yourself! Do here in your home town what we have heard that you did in Capernaum"' (v. 23). Jesus goes on to explain that Elijah and Elisha did not perform miracles on demand but only as directed by God, and they respond by trying to throw him down the cliff (v. 29).

It doesn't appear that Jesus' time in Nazareth during his first 30 years had been jam-packed with signs and wonders, miracles and healings, for which the Nazarenes were truly grateful. Rather, the people who knew Jesus well, including his own family, were surprised and hostile when he began healing the sick. And if this is a rather general comment, there does appear to be biblical evidence of a specific person whom Jesus was not able to heal – Joseph. Joseph is alive when Jesus is twelve years old (Luke 2:41–52), but after that he is not mentioned as still being alive anywhere in the Gospels.

In John 2, Jesus' mother, Jesus and his disciples are present at a wedding in Cana, and Mary assumes authority. In Mark 3, 'Jesus' mother and brothers arrive' to take Jesus home because they said, 'He is out of his mind' (Mark 3:21, 31). Surely, on both occasions, if Joseph had been alive, it would have been his role to take authority in the situation, and not Mary or the brothers. But the clearest indication of Joseph's whereabouts is found at the cross:

> When Jesus saw his mother there, and the disciple whom he loved standing near by, he said to his mother, 'Dear woman, here is your son,' and to the disciple, 'Here is your mother.' From that time on, this disciple took her into his home. (John 19:26–27)

It seems most likely, from reading the Gospels, that by the time Jesus began his ministry and was baptised in the Holy Spirit, Joseph, his earthly guardian, had died. Although he may have been older than Mary, it does look as though Joseph died before he reached the biblical 'norm' of three-score-years-and-ten. I believe this was a person whom Jesus would have wanted to heal, but apparently Jesus had neither the authority nor the power to do so. It appears from the Gospels that if the Father was not doing healing, and the healing power of the Holy Spirit was not present, then Jesus could not heal the sick, even Joseph.

When Jesus laid aside his majesty, particularly his omniscience and his omnipotence, it looks as if he needed the authority and the supernatural power of God the Father that the Holy Spirit brings, in order to do supernatural healing.

By the end of the Gospels, after the resurrection, all

authority in heaven and on earth is given to Jesus and in the book of Acts, after his ascension, Jesus is the one who sends the Holy Spirit from heaven. This is the exalted Jesus, the Jesus whom we know and have known for nearly 2,000 years as the one who heals, but we must be careful not to read our experience of the exalted Jesus back into the earthly Jesus of the Gospels. What the New Testament teaches consistently is that Jesus, who was perfect man full of the Holy Spirit, could only do signs, wonders, miracles and healings when the Spirit was doing them through him. Though in nature Jesus is and always has been God, the New Testament informs us that when Jesus was born on earth he became flesh and laid aside his omnipresence, his omnipotence and his omniscience. The 'go-between' Holy Spirit not only provided Jesus with the authority of God to heal, but also the power of God to heal.[1]

5. The Spirit heals in Canford Magna

On the morning of the 10th April 2005, John and Jean were undecided about where to go to church. John, a psychotherapist and clergyman, wanted to come to Canford Magna, to our ancient royal chapel beside the Stour.[2] Easter had come and gone, and a time of refreshing away from his own parish, on a Sunday when he had no parochial duties, seemed like a good idea at the time.

---

[1] *The Go Between God* is the title of a most excellent book by John V. Taylor (London: SCM 1972).

[2] Before Canford Manor was owned privately, it belonged to the monarch. In those days, people like King John, Edward IV, Henry VII, Henry VIII and Edward VI used our church as their chapel.

Jean had planned to worship in one of the three churches that John helps look after, to see some friends, but at five minutes past ten, rather late in the day for the distance involved, they agreed to go together to Canford Magna.

At five past ten a few faithful souls were gathered in the side chapel to pray, and I was one of them. It was the weekend of the televised American Masters golf tournament, which had continued until almost one o'clock in the morning due to bad weather, and I was feeling very tired. I'd already done the 8 o'clock holy communion service, and my presence owed more to duty than inspiration. Tony, the parish treasurer from the Lantern, had come to preach about money from a biblical perspective, and healing was simply not on our agenda that morning.[3]

Pauline, the treasurer's wife, joined us for prayer. At five past ten, she sensed the words 'right ear' come into her mind, and shared them. *Yes*, I thought, somewhat cynically and wearily, *I expect there will be someone in church with a right ear.*

John and Jean arrived in mufti just in time for the start of the service, and slipped in amongst the rest of the congregation, unnoticed. Tony spoke well about money and giving, and John puzzled in his mind over what God might be saying to him. 'How may I bless you, Lord?' he prayed inwardly when the sermon came to an end.

'It is the other way round,' God seemed to say. 'This morning I want to bless you.'

At the end of the service, the leader reminded everyone

---

[3] In December 2004, I moved from the Lantern Church, Merley, to the parish church at Canford Magna.

there was an opportunity for prayer in the side chapel; he gave out the word concerning someone with a problem in the right ear, whereupon John recognised it as a word for himself and decided he would go forward for prayer after the final blessing.

At the age of eight, John lost most of the hearing in his right ear. The medical profession felt the loss was due to mumps, which had affected the nerve, and said there was nothing they could do. John remembers from his school-days having to ask for a special seat in the front on the right for his aural examinations in French and German, so that he could hear it all with his left ear. Three or four times, John had received prayer for his right ear without noticing any marked improvement, and for several years he'd not been able to hear anything on his right-hand side.

Cecilie (a member of our ministry team) prayed, asking God the Father through Jesus to send his Holy Spirit on John, and then waited quietly. In the stillness, with his eyes closed, our visiting clergyman began to hear a man's voice. He assumed the person was on his left-hand side but when he opened his eyes he was amazed to see that it was Geoff, on his right, who was speaking.

Very graciously, John went to the microphone in church and shared with those of us who were drinking coffee that he could now hear in his right ear for the first time since he was eight years old.

I rang John the next day to see how he was. 'It's marvellous!' he said. 'To God be all the glory. I can now hear in stereo.' I'm pleased to record that a couple of months later, John's hearing continues to improve. He also reports a more immediate awareness of God's presence with him and an encouragement to step out in faith in whatever God has next in store for him and Jean.

Jesus' disciples heal the sick

One of the strongest reasons for believing that Jesus Christ was able to heal the sick due to the anointing of the Holy Spirit rather than his divinity is that he was able to pass the healing ministry on to his disciples. The authority and power of God came to them from God through Jesus; first the Twelve, then the seventy-two were also able to heal the sick (Luke 9:1; 10:1). If Jesus had healed the sick because he was God, rather than perfect man anointed with the Holy Spirit, then his disciples would not have been able to do what he did, but Luke writes this:

> When Jesus had called the Twelve together, he gave them power and authority to drive out all demons and to cure diseases, and he sent them out to preach the kingdom of God and to heal the sick. (Luke 9:1–2)

The parallel passage in Mark informs us how they got on: 'They drove out many demons and anointed many sick people with oil and healed them' (Mark 6:13).

Once more, we note the words 'authority' and 'power' connected to healing, which we have already identified as the authority of God the Father conveyed by the Holy Spirit, and the power of the Spirit, who is the Lord. Anointing with oil is an outward and visible biblical symbol for being anointed with the Holy Spirit (see my comments on the book of James in Chapter 4). The Twelve and the seventy-two could heal the sick and cast out demons because Jesus was able to pass on to them the same authority and power that had been given to him. It looks as though these were specific moments in time and particular places when Jesus could encourage his followers to have a go. Between the sending out of the Twelve and the seventy-two, Jesus is rejected in a Samaritan village as he had been rejected in his own town of Nazareth, and as Jesus addresses the second group he bemoans his rejections at Korazin, Bethsaida and Capernaum (Luke 9:53; 4:28–30; 10:13–15). It looks as though the Father gave a word to Jesus that he was willing to do healing and provide the power in the places to which Jesus was sending them where the 'harvest was plentiful', and he passed it on to his disciples (Luke 10:2). There is no indication in the Gospels that the harvest was plentiful everywhere Jesus and his disciples went.

In John 14:10–17, clarified later in John 16:15, Jesus said that anyone who believed in him would be able to do the miracles he had been doing, in his name, once he had ascended to the Father and asked him to send the Holy Spirit. In the Gospel of John, there are seven signs, of which four are healings and all are described as miracles (John 4:54; 6:2; 10:38; 11:47; see also 14:11). It is therefore quite clear that Jesus promises that when he goes to the Father, and the Father sends the Holy Spirit, the disciples and all other believers will heal the sick. It is important to note that Jesus does not say that when he goes to the cross the disciples will heal the sick, but when he goes to the Father and sends the Holy Spirit. This, we shall see in the next chapter, is exactly what happened.

Jesus 'gave them power and authority . . . to cure diseases . . . and to heal the sick' (Luke 9:1–2). He told the seventy-two to 'heal the sick' (Luke 10:9). Jesus also promised that when the Holy Spirit comes, after he has ascended, 'anyone who has faith in me will do what I have been doing. He will do even greater things than these, because I am going to the Father' (John 14:12). All of which leads me to the very definite belief that physical healing in the Gospels is seen as the work of the Holy Spirit, either through Jesus or through the disciples, but either way it leads to the same conclusion: it is the Spirit who heals.

Three problems

When I read every word in the four Gospels, and noted again and again that it is the Spirit who heals, I failed to find any reference to Jesus dying for sicknesses, the cross working backwards, or that Christians have a New Covenant right to healing. There are, however, three places where others have claimed to find them, which need to be addressed. As a former English teacher, I have been careful to look at the context in each case.

1. 'He took up our infirmities and carried our diseases' (Matthew 8:17)

This reference is the one often quoted as Jesus taking our infirmities upon himself, or dying for our sicknesses, to confirm the beliefs of people like T. L. Osborn and John Arnott.

> When evening came, many who were demon-possessed were brought to him, and he drove out the spirits with a word and healed all the sick. This was to fulfil what was spoken through the prophet Isaiah: 'He took up our infirmities and carried our diseases.' (Matthew 8:16–17)

Here, Matthew is quoting Isaiah 53:4 (from the Greek version of the Old Testament, called the Septuagint), but the context in Matthew is vital in understanding how he is using this Old Testament verse.

Jesus has driven out demons and got rid of sicknesses. He has not become demonised himself, nor sick. So Matthew is not saying that Jesus has taken upon himself their demons or their sicknesses but rather he has got rid of them. He healed the sick just as Isaiah prophesied the Messiah would do, in the same way as Jesus quoted Isaiah to convince John the Baptist that he was the Christ. Matthew uses 'took up' our infirmities and 'carried' our diseases to mean 'took them away' and 'carried them off'.

After Isaiah 53:4, the prophet goes on to portray the Suffering Servant dying for our sins. After Matthew 8:17, the Gospel writer goes on to show Jesus dying for our sins. Neither of them proclaims that Jesus died for sickness, or that believers have a right to healing; Matthew simply states that Jesus healed the sick as Isaiah prophesied the Messiah would do. The relationship between sin and sickness will be looked at in Chapter 7, and the relationship between the cross and healing as declared in Isaiah 53 will be studied in Chapter 6. For now, we simply note that this verse does not link the healings of Christ directly with the cross of Christ – neither the cross nor the death of Jesus is mentioned here.

2. Jesus healed everyone he met who was sick

One of the reasons some healing-evangelists claim that Jesus wants to heal everyone today is because Jesus healed everyone he met who was sick, while on earth, and 'Jesus Christ is the same yesterday and today and for ever' (Hebrews 13:8). I am sure that Jesus does want to heal more people today than we see at present, but hopefully our study of the Gospels may motivate us to give a more careful approach to the text and a little more caution with our claims. In response, here are a few pointers to ponder:

a) Such a claim is an argument from silence and not one the Gospel writers make for everyone of everything, always. Jesus may have said no on some occasions that were simply not recorded.

b) Jesus did not heal 'many' at Nazareth (Matthew 13:58).

c) Jesus only healed for three years out of thirty-three, and only then when he was anointed to do so by the Holy Spirit. It is possible that Joseph died in Jesus' presence.

d) In the presence of Jesus on Good Friday, three men (including Jesus himself) died – and they did not want to do so (Luke 22:42 – 23:46).

e) As in the days of Elisha, there were many lepers in Israel when Jesus walked the earth, but he only healed a few of them. The day after a healing-revival broke out in Capernaum, the crowd looked for Jesus and found he had been praying since the early hours. 'They tried to keep him from leaving them' records

Luke (4:42) and, judging from the sick man they had waiting for him when he came back to Capernaum, it looks as if they wanted Jesus to do more of the same (Mark 1:29 – 2:12). It seems right to say that on this occasion Jesus said no to the sick in Capernaum and went somewhere else. The implication is that Jesus healed those to whom God sent him and by so doing said no to a lot of other people.

f) At the Pool of Bethesda, the local hospital, Jesus healed 'one who was there' (John 5:5). John is silent about any others.

g) Peter and John healed a man 'crippled from birth' at the Beautiful gate in Jerusalem (Acts 3:1–10). Luke's comment is worth noting: 'When *all* the people saw him walking and praising God, they recognised him as the same man who used to sit begging at the temple gate called Beautiful' (Acts 3:9–10; my italics). This suggests quite strongly that Jesus would also have known about him and walked past him several times.

h) Jesus did not heal Lazarus before he died, despite an urgent request leading to two subsequent complaints (John 11:1–44). Instead, he did what the Father told him to do, which included saying no for at least four days.

i) *Jesus only did what the Father was doing, and seems to have healed whenever the power of the Lord was present for him to heal. Because he is the same yesterday, today and for ever, and is present in believers by his Spirit, we who have faith in Christ can do the same.*

3. *Sozo*

Whenever people preach, speak or write about healing in the atonement, one word which always seems to crop up is the New Testament Greek word *sozo,* which is usually translated 'I save' but can mean 'I heal'. The simple argument goes that as Jesus died to save us, and the word 'save' can also mean 'heal', then Jesus also died to heal us. It is an argument that is often used, but in truth it is an argument coming out of a dictionary rather than the Bible. The dictionary often gives us more than one English translation for Greek words, and it is only the context in which they are being used that enlightens us as to which of those meanings is intended at any one time. The Gospels do not suggest that *sozo* always means save and heal whenever it is used. We need to consider a few examples.

> Just then a woman who had been subject to bleeding for twelve years came up behind him and touched the edge of his cloak. She said to herself, 'If I only touch his cloak, I will be *healed.'*
>
> Jesus turned and saw her. 'Take heart, daughter,' he said, 'your faith has *healed* you.' And the woman was *healed* from that moment. (Matthew 9:20–22; my italics)

Three times, derivations of the word *sozo* are used here (indicated by my italics), and are translated as 'healed' in the NIV, or 'made whole' in the King James Version: 'I will be healed' (v. 21); 'your faith has healed you' (v. 22); 'the woman was healed' (v. 22).

There are five other healing stories where *sozo* derivatives are also used (Mark 10:52; Luke 8:36, 50; 17:19; 18:42). So the word *sozo* can mean 'physical healing' and in six Gospel stories is used in that way, but the word *sozo* is also used when physical healing cannot be implied from the context:

a) The disciples went and woke him, saying, 'Lord *save* us! We're going to drown!' (Matthew 8:25; my italics)

b) Then Peter got down out of the boat, walked on the water and came towards Jesus. But when he saw the wind, he was afraid and, beginning to sink, cried out, 'Lord *save* me!' (Matthew 14:29–30; my italics)

c) Jesus said to him, 'Today salvation has come to this house, because this man, too, is a son of Abraham. For the Son of Man came to seek and to *save* what was lost.' (Luke 19:9–10; my italics)

d) Then Jesus said to her, 'Your sins are forgiven.' The other guests began to say among themselves, 'Who is this who even forgives sins?' Jesus said to the woman, 'Your faith has *saved* you; go in peace.' (Luke 7:48–50; my italics)

Twice the disciples are saved from drowning, and Zacchaeus and the woman are saved from their sinful lives. Whatever the details, the people in these four stories are not saved from sickness and disease but something else. So, the word *sozo* can be used to mean physical healing but it can also be used when the context does not imply physical healing in any way. And this means that if the New Testament says we are *saved* by the death of Christ we need to check with the context to see if physical healing is included or implied by the use of the word *sozo*; otherwise, it just means 'saved', as with Zacchaeus, and not physically healed (cf. Romans 5:8–9; 10:10; 1 Corinthians 15:2). As Wittgenstein, a philosopher of language, used to say, 'A word means what it is used to mean', i.e. not necessarily what a dictionary says it can mean.[4] I can find no contexts in the Gospels where *sozo* is used in connection with the cross to suggest that physical healing as well as spiritual salvation is part of the atonement.

In *The Illustrated Bible Dictionary*, an article on salvation by B. A. Milne and G. Walters states this:

> Salvation is moral and spiritual. Salvation relates to a deliverance from sin and its consequences and hence from guilt (Rom. 5:1; Heb. 10:22), from law and its curse (Gal. 3:13; Col. 2:14), from death (1 Pet. 1:3–5; 1 Cor. 15:51–56), from judgement (Rom. 5:9; Heb. 9:28), also from fear (Heb. 2:15; 2 Tim. 1:7, 9f.) and bondage (Tit. 2:11 – 3:6; Gal. 5:1f.). It is important to indicate the negative implication of this i.e. what Christian salvation does not include. Salvation does not imply material prosperity or worldly success (Acts 3:6; 2 Cor. 6–10), nor does it promise physical health and well-being. One must be careful not to overstate this particular negative, as clearly remarkable healings did and do take place and 'healing' is a gift of the Spirit to the church (Acts 3:9; 9:34; 20:9f.; 1 Cor. 12:28). But healing is not invariable, and hence is in no sense a 'right' of the saved (1 Tim. 5:23; 2 Tim. 4:20; Phil. 2:25f.; 2 Cor. 12:7–9).[5]

---

[4] Most of what Wittgenstein said is contained in *Lectures and Conversations on Aesthetics, Psychology and Religious Belief,* which is a record by students rather than Wittgenstein's *ipsissima verba,* but this quote was often used by the lecturers on the philosophy of religion that I heard when I was at university.

[5] *The Illustrated Bible Dictionary, Part 3* (Leicester: Inter-Varsity Press) p. 1375.

So far, I have checked the 89 chapters in the Gospels and not found any context which suggests that Jesus died for sicknesses as well as sins. On the other hand, I have found many verses which inform me that it is the Spirit who heals. I can now summarise my findings in the Gospels.

Jesus is the Christ, the Messiah, the anointed one, anointed by the Holy Spirit to heal the sick, from time to time. Having laid aside his majesty in order to become flesh, he could only do what the Father was doing. The Spirit coming is the Father working, so when the authority of the Father and the power of the Holy Spirit were present for Jesus to heal the sick, then he healed them – but only then. The same was seen to be true of the Twelve and the seventy-two, who also healed the sick when the authority of God the Father and the power of the Holy Spirit had been passed on to them to do so, by Jesus. In the Gospels, supernatural physical healing is not linked directly to the cross because it is the Spirit who heals.

6. The Spirit heals in Illogan

At the church in Cornwall, where I shared the story of the lady who was healed of cancer, I then asked God the Father through Jesus to send his Holy Spirit on the whole congregation and do whatever he wanted to do. It was a very special time for many people and the worst they got was blessed. Towards the end of the ministry, as I noticed the covers being taken off the delicious-looking sand-wiches and cakes at the back of church, I asked people to raise a hand if they would like specific prayer. Our team members then attended to everyone's needs but, as I left them to it and made for the goodies, I noticed one lady still with her hand up, and no one was with her. She was sitting at the back in her own specially padded reclining chair, as the church pews were too uncomfortable for her. Her condition was later described like this in their parish magazine:[6]

> Iris has been receiving specialist treatment for the past five years. Three years ago she had a hip operation that sadly was not a success and she described her condition like this: 'I had pain in my neck and back, and even in my hands; I couldn't knit or sew. Recently I got completely stuck at the end of my road and needed help to get home. My doctor was very forthright about my condition; "Don't expect it to get better," he said. "It'll get worse!"'

I felt led to tell Phil, our floor manager and the only ministry team member still available, to have a go on this lady while I moved on into the dining area to have a go on something else.

Phil laid hands gently on Iris and then asked God the Father through Jesus to send his Holy Spirit in healing power on her, and God did. Power, shaking and especially phenomenal heat were experienced by both of them, followed by peace, at which point Phil was led away to minister to others.

While I was partaking of earthly delights in the dining area, shrieks of heavenly joy were suddenly heard coming from the aisle of the church, where Iris was leaping

---

[6] The article about Iris, with an accompanying picture, is on the front page of *The Link between Illogan, Portreath and Trevenson* (October 2001). It is the newspaper of St Illogan Parish, and is published monthly.

about in a most non-Anglican way. This is how the people of Cornwall recorded what happened in their magazine, alongside a picture of Iris holding her stick in the air:

> The evening service on Sunday 23rd September was led by Revd Peter Lawrence, who was visiting with a team from Canford Magna in Dorset. At the end of the service Peter asked anyone who especially wanted prayer for healing to raise their hand. One of the team members then prayed with Iris. 'He placed his hand on my head,' she relates. 'I've never shaken so much in my life, then I felt this heat going down my head and through my body, and as it went all my pain went with it.'

Iris arrived in pain at the parish church and left with her stick under her arm, walking unaided for the first time in years. 'It's absolutely wonderful,' she said. 'When I woke up on Monday morning I still could hardly believe it. The Lord has healed me, and I can't stop thanking him. I feel so well.' Interestingly, the headline on the front page of the magazine read, 'Touched by the Power of God.' To him be all the glory.

3

The Anointed Disciples Heal the Sick

A look at the Acts of the Apostles

If the New Covenant, sealed by the blood of Christ, offers physical healing for all who believe in Jesus, then the Acts of the Apostles is the book in the New Testament where I would expect to read about it. This is the book that contains all the healing stories recorded in the New Testament after Jesus' death on the cross, and the one that reports on the first 30–40 years or so of the early church. Those who had lived with Jesus and been taught by him both before and after the resurrection were still around, and 30–40 years is enough time to assess new experiences, new benefits and new teachings in the important area of healing.

Luke, the physician (Colossians 4:14), always showed a special interest in healing, and he took considerable pains to write out several of the apostles' sermons, some of which explained how they were able to heal the sick. Luke could so easily have included material on the atonement and how it was linked to physical healing if he had considered it to be relevant, particularly if there was now a significant change from the way Jesus and the apostles were seen to do healing in his first book. In Luke's Gospel, it was the Holy Spirit who healed the sick, first through Jesus, and then through the disciples; if the cross of Christ had changed the way the disciples could now heal the sick, then this is where I would expect to read about that change. What I found, however, when I read the Acts of the Apostles, was exactly the opposite. This is what I discovered:

a) Physical healing in the Acts of the Apostles is seen as the work of the Holy Spirit.

b) The disciples were able to heal in the same way as Jesus healed, in the name of Jesus, because they were filled with the same Holy Spirit.

c) Nowhere could I find the disciples, nor the writer of Acts, saying that as Jesus died for sicknesses as well as sins all may now be healed; rather, physical healings are seen as exceptional events, signs, wonders and miracles.

d) Many of those healed in the Acts of the Apostles were not yet Christians, and had no New Covenant rights.

e) Responding in faith to what Jesus has done on the cross puts us right with God, making it possible for Jesus to baptise us in the Holy Spirit, but it is the Holy Spirit who heals.

7. The Holy Spirit heals a bad back

I first saw the Holy Spirit heal someone in church early one Sunday morning. As I entered our church in order to prepare for the 8 o'clock communion service, I came across our churchwarden, who was in distress. He was trying to put out the bread and the wine on the Lord's table, but his body language and the agony which was written all over his face showed there was something seriously wrong.

'Peter,' I said, 'you're suffering. What's the problem?'

Our 65-year-old churchwarden explained how he'd been struggling for the last three months with a trapped sciatic nerve and torn muscles down the right-hand side of his body, which had become so bad his wife now needed to help him get dressed.

'I cannot stand, sit or lie down without being in pain,' Peter continued. He told me he'd tried his GP, the hospital, a physiotherapist, an osteopath and a chiropractor, but no one had been able to solve his problem. At first, the prescribed painkillers had brought some relief, but now their effectiveness had diminished as his body became used to them.

'Would you like us to pray for you?' I asked, and Peter said he would be most grateful.

So, after the service had finished, Peter stood in front of the bishop's chair behind the communion rail while I asked God the Father through Jesus to send his Holy Spirit on him. I placed my hand on his back where the pain seemed to be worst and Susan, a member of the congregation who had stayed behind after the service to help, put her hand on his forehead.

After a while, Peter's face began to shine, indicating the activity of the Holy Spirit; then, all of a sudden, he was thrown back quite violently into the bishop's chair.

The large carved-oak throne, comfortably padded with soft cushions, had never seen anything quite like this. The churchwarden now lay prostrate across it, eyes still closed, while his face continued to register a powerful engagement of the Holy Spirit. Susan and I were watching carefully to see if we could discern what was happening when, just as suddenly as before, Peter's right leg began twitching in spasm-like movements. It looked to us as if some unseen person had grasped hold of his right foot and was jerking it powerfully up and down, even though by this stage no one was touching him.

'Thank you, Lord,' I said, hoping it was the Lord. 'Bless you, Father, for whatever it is you are doing,' I continued. And, after 15 minutes, I prayed, 'Lord, please don't forget there is an 11 o'clock service this morning.'

Nothing I said, however, made the slightest bit of difference, as the Lord continued doing what he wanted to do. Eventually, the leg stopped kicking, the power faded and Peter opened his eyes. He stood up gingerly and walked around as if he was trying on a new pair of shoes.

'Yes,' he commented. 'That'll do. That'll do nicely.'

Peter was completely healed, and the next day he came over to dig the church gardens. When the Spirit heals it is a very special moment in a person's life, and for those privileged to be present it is glorious to behold.

The disciples are filled with the Holy Spirit

In the four Gospels, we noticed how Jesus was filled with the Holy Spirit at his baptism, after which supernatural activity (including healing) took place through him. Jesus himself linked the two events (Luke 4:18–21). This pattern is now repeated in the Acts of the Apostles. The followers of Jesus are told to wait in Jerusalem until Jesus sends the Holy Spirit to them, clothing them with power from on high (Luke 24:49; Acts 1:4–5, 8). They had already been told by Jesus that when he went to the Father and asked him to send the Holy Spirit, they would be able to do the works he had been doing (John 14:12, 16). This is now possible because Jesus has received all authority in heaven and on earth and assumed his rightful place in heaven (Matthew 28:18).

On the Day of Pentecost, there was the sound of a violent wind; tongues of fire came to rest on the disciples, and all of them were 'filled with the Holy Spirit and began to speak in other tongues as the Spirit enabled them' (see Acts 2:1–4). Following on from this, 'many wonders and miraculous signs were done by the apostles' in the name of Jesus, including the healing of a man crippled from birth (Acts 2:43; 3:1–10).

When I read the complete Acts of the Apostles at one sitting, it all seemed to fit together as a single piece, following very closely the pattern of the four Gospels. Indeed, reading the whole book in one go made me wonder (though I am not the first) whether it ought more properly to be entitled: The Activity of the Holy Spirit Working Through the Apostles. We need to examine the evidence in a little more detail.

The disciples heal the sick in the name of Jesus

When Peter was asked to explain what was happening on the Day of Pentecost, this is what he said:

God has raised this Jesus to life, and we are all witnesses of the fact. Exalted to the right hand of God, he has received from the Father the promised Holy Spirit and has poured out what you now see and hear. (Acts 2:32–33)

Jesus obviously receives the Holy Spirit from his Father in a new and different way from when on earth – in a way in which he can now give/send/pour/baptise in the Spirit – and this is the fulfilment of what God prophesied would happen:

a) John the Baptist said that Jesus would baptise people in the Holy Spirit (John 1:33).
b) Jesus said he would send the Holy Spirit to the believers (Luke 24:49).

Peter confirms that the Day of Pentecost events fulfil these promises and shortly afterwards goes on to heal – in the name of Jesus Christ of Nazareth – a man 'crippled from birth' (Acts 3:1–8). This fits exactly what Jesus predicted would happen (John 14:12, 16). We can now summarise the story so far:

a) Jesus said that Peter would heal the sick, in Jesus' name, when the Holy Spirit came to him.
b) Jesus fills Peter with the Holy Spirit.
c) Peter then heals a man in the name of Jesus.

We note, however, what Peter did not say, either to the crippled man or to those who questioned him afterwards. He did not say, 'Jesus has died for sicknesses as well as sins, so you can now walk.' It also looks as though the healed man is not yet a believer and so does not claim his New

Covenant right to healing but receives it as a free, unmerited gift of grace.

There seems to be a case for arguing that in the beginning of the Acts of the Apostles it is the Holy Spirit who heals. It is a case that will get stronger.

8. The Holy Spirit heals shingles

A few months after our churchwarden was healed of a bad back by the Holy Spirit, he gave me a ring.

'Hello, Peter! It's Peter,' said Peter.

'Hello, Peter!' I replied. 'How yer doin'?'

'I've got the shingles,' he continued.

Now I'm not at all medical and as this was the churchwarden ringing the vicar at a time when we were laying a new path at the back of the church, I responded rather naïvely, thinking the gravel had arrived.

'I'll come and help you move it,' I said, somewhat prophetically.

'No,' said Peter. 'It's an illness. Like chickenpox, only worse. I'm in a lot of pain, and I wondered if you'd come and pray for me again. . .?'

'I'll be there right away,' I said, apologetically.

Our vicarage was on one side of the church, and Peter and Peggy lived on the other side, so I was there in a few moments. Once more, it gave me no pleasure to see the pain which was registering on Peter's face as he lifted up his sweater and shirt to reveal a six-inch band of red which went all the way round his stomach region. There was no bishop's chair in the house, so Peter stood in front of a big armchair as I prayed, 'Father God, we ask you through Jesus to send your Holy Spirit on Peter and do whatever you want to do.'

Immediately, Peter fell backwards into the chair so, remembering what happened last time, Peggy and I had a cup of tea while we waited and watched what God was doing. There was no jerking or twitching on this occasion, but after about 15 minutes the eyes in the middle of Peter's now shiny face opened. Slowly he rose from the chair, saying, as he did so, 'That'll do. That'll do nicely.'

He lifted his sweater and shirt again, revealing to us, and to himself, that the red band had totally disappeared. Once more, the Holy Spirit had moved in power on Peter, who had been completely healed – and I was thrilled to be there.

The Holy Spirit does signs, wonders and miracles through the believers

In the Acts of the Apostles, there are a number of noteworthy signs, wonders and miracles described by Luke as the work of the Holy Spirit.

- The Holy Spirit enables the followers of Jesus to speak in many languages (Acts 2:4).
- The Holy Spirit gives prophecies, visions and dreams to believers (Acts 2:17–18).
- The Holy Spirit helps the disciples to speak the word of God boldly (Acts 4:31).
- The Holy Spirit reveals liars to Peter and terminates them (Acts 5:3, 9).
- Stephen, full of the Holy Spirit, does great wonders and

miraculous signs and sees heaven opened while facing death with courage (Acts 6:5, 8; 7:55).

- The Holy Spirit comes on believers with visible effect when Peter and John lay hands on them (Acts 8:17–18).
- Philip is guided by the Holy Spirit and transported by him (Acts 8:29, 39).
- The Spirit gives knowledge to Peter (Acts 10:19).
- The Holy Spirit enables the Gentiles to speak in tongues (Acts 10:44–46).
- Agabus predicts a famine through the Holy Spirit (Acts 11:28).
- The Holy Spirit empowers Paul to predict and give blindness to Elymas (Acts 13:9).
- The Holy Spirit enables the Ephesians to speak in tongues and to prophesy (Acts 19:6).
- There are other references that also imply it is the Holy Spirit doing miracles from the context in which we find them (e.g. Acts 2:43; 9:17–18).

It is obvious from this list that the Holy Spirit does signs, wonders and miracles in the Acts of the Apostles. There are also two references to 'God' doing miraculous signs and wonders:

a) God did miracles, wonders and signs through Jesus (Acts 2:22).
b) God did miraculous signs and wonders through Barnabas and Paul (Acts 15:2).

It is not difficult, however, to establish from Luke's second volume that the Holy Spirit is God. In Acts 5:3, Peter said, 'Ananias, how is it that Satan has so filled your heart that

you have lied to the Holy Spirit . . .?' and in the next verse
Peter said, 'You have not lied to men but to God.' As the
Holy Spirit and God are seen as interchangeable, we can
add these two examples to our list. God, the Holy Spirit,
does many signs and wonders and miracles in the Acts of
the Apostles.

Interestingly, by the time we reach chapter 16 we can also
add Jesus to the Trinity. In Acts 16:6, Paul and his compan-
ions are 'kept by the Holy Spirit from preaching the word',
and in the very next verse, the 'Spirit of Jesus' stops them
entering Bithynia. Just as God and the Holy Spirit are interchangeable, so Jesus and the Holy Spirit are seen here to be
interchangeable. Everybody wants to know how, along with
a thousand other questions about the Trinity, but the Acts
of the Apostles is basically a descriptive piece of writing and
not a theological textbook, and does not answer such questions. For now, I merely record that the experience of the
early church in Scripture was of a God who was Father, Son
and Holy Spirit (Acts 2:33). For the purposes of this book, it
is the role of the Holy Spirit that is important, and in the
Acts of the Apostles he is definitely the one who does signs,
wonders and miracles, including healing, here on earth.

The Acts of the Apostles sees healings as signs, wonders and miracles

Luke writes his second book in such a way that healings are
seen to belong to the category of signs, wonders and miracles, just the same as in the Gospels. Here is the relevant
evidence:

a) 'Jesus of Nazareth was a man accredited by God to you

by miracles, wonders and signs, which God did among you through him, as you yourselves know' (Acts 2:22).

In John's Gospel, there are seven 'miracles' or 'signs', of which four are healings (John 4:54; 6:2; 10:38; 11:47; see also 14:11; I am assuming that a four-day-old corpse is a serious illness). We can at least argue that the New Testament sees the healings Jesus did as miraculous signs and wonders which Peter says, in the Acts of the Apostles, God did through Jesus by anointing him with the Holy Spirit (Acts 10:38).

b) 'Everyone was filled with awe, and many wonders and miraculous signs were done by the apostles' (Acts 2:43).

Having been filled with the Holy Spirit, the apostles are enabled to do signs and wonders, and then five verses later Luke gives us an example:

> One day Peter and John were going up to the temple at the time of prayer – at three in the afternoon. Now a man crippled from birth was being carried to the temple gate called Beautiful . . . (Acts 3:1–2)

And the man is healed. 'One day' suggests that a follow-on example is being given of a 'miraculous sign', and this is clearly how everyone who saw the healed man understood the event. The Sanhedrin said, 'Everybody living in Jerusalem knows they have done an outstanding miracle, and we cannot deny it' (Acts 4:16). It is also how Luke saw it: 'For the man who was *miraculously* healed was over forty years old' (Acts 4:22; my italics).

> c) The apostles performed many *miraculous signs and wonders* among the people. . . As a result, people brought the sick into the streets and laid them on beds and mats so that at least

Peter's shadow might fall on some of them as he passed by. Crowds gathered also from the towns around Jerusalem, bringing their sick and those tormented by evil spirits, and all of them were healed. (Acts 5:12, 15–16; my italics)

There is a gap of three verses between the signs and wonders and the healing but, as in the previous point, the amazing shadow-healings all look like examples of miraculous signs and wonders.

d) Similar wording is used about Philip's visit to Samaria. He was, we are informed, a man 'full of the Spirit' (Acts 6:3):

When the crowds heard Philip and saw the *miraculous signs* he did, they all paid close attention to what he said. With shrieks, evil spirits came out of many, and many paralytics and cripples were healed. (Acts 8:6–7; my italics)

And: 'Simon himself believed and was baptised. And he followed Philip everywhere, astonished by the great *signs and miracles* he saw' (Acts 8:13; my italics).

In the case of Philip, the description of healings as miraculous signs is even more certain as this time there are no verses in between; this adds a degree of confirmation to the previous examples as well. Everything we read about healings, signs, wonders and miracles in the New Testament has a distinct unity about it.

e) As with the apostles and Philip, so Paul and Barnabas continue the anointed work: 'Paul and Barnabas spent considerable time there, speaking boldly for the Lord, who confirmed the message of his grace by enabling them to do miraculous signs and wonders' (Acts 14:3). A few verses later, Luke gives an example, reminiscent of Peter and John, as if he is keen to show that Paul is as anointed as Peter: 'In

Lystra there sat a man crippled in his feet, who was lame from birth and had never walked. He listened to Paul as he was speaking . . .'(Acts 14:8–9). And he was healed.

f) In Ephesus, the link between extraordinary miracles and healings is seen very clearly. Again, if we replace shadows with handkerchiefs, Luke presents his friend Paul in a similar way to his presentation of Peter. 'God did extraordinary miracles through Paul, so that even handkerchiefs and aprons that had touched him were taken to the sick, and their illnesses were cured and the evil spirits left them' (Acts 19:11–12).

These particular verses confirm how the Acts of the Apostles sees healings as miraculous signs and wonders, as indeed does John's Gospel. This means that physical healing in both the Gospels and the Acts of the Apostles is not seen as a covenant right for all believers in all places at all times, but as an extraordinary event – a sign, a wonder, or a miracle. We also note that all *godly* signs, wonders and miracles referred to in the Acts of the Apostles are seen as works of God, the Holy Spirit. While Simon from Samaria and demons from Philippi and Ephesus appear to be capable of doing some wonders as well as the Holy Spirit, Luke never links their activities to physical healing.

As this book is primarily about God's healing, as revealed to us in the Bible, I shall not be looking at supernatural healing from other sources except to comment that as Satan and demons can give sickness, they can also take it away. In my limited experience, a person who seeks supernatural healing apart from Jesus sometimes finds the physical symptoms are alleviated for a while, but then gradually he or she begins to resemble someone under oppression, who belongs to another. This merely illustrates the importance of entering into a New Covenant relationship with God through Jesus, as described in God's word, and then as children of God asking God the Father through Jesus to send his Holy Spirit to do whatever he wants to do. Jesus assures us that if we do this we shall not receive snakes or scorpions – picture language for evil spirits or the power of the enemy (Luke 11:11–12; 10:18–19).

As godly miraculous signs and wonders are seen as the work of the Holy Spirit, and healings are seen as godly signs, wonders and miracles, it seems right to suggest that in the Acts of the Apostles it is the Holy Spirit who heals.

9. The Holy Spirit heals the lame and disabled

A few weeks after helping Peter to move the shingles, I heard rumours of strange goings-on taking place in his home. Apparently, he was running Bible studies followed by the laying-on of hands on a Tuesday night, and some people were being healed. As vicar of the parish I thought I ought to check this out, so at the first convenient opportunity I joined the Tuesday night session.

As I approached Peter's and Peggy's house, a car drew up beside the gate. Two big, rather tough-looking, wouldn't-want-to-meet-in-a-dark-alley-at-night type of people got out of the car and extracted an equally tough-looking lady from the front passenger seat. They then dragged her along the path with massive under-armpit leverage, lifted her over the threshold of the property and dropped her into a large, comfortable armchair.

'Right,' said the older one, whom I took to be the lady's husband, 'we're off to the pub then. We'll pick you up at half-past nine!' And they disappeared into the darkness, leaving the lady to unbutton her own coat and smile at the gawping onlookers.

There were about seven or eight others gathered in the small lounge, and after coffee and biscuits the Bible study began. It was a real struggle and an eye-opening experience to see ordinary folk trying to find their places in old Bibles from which the dust had only recently been blown away. But Peter persevered, beamed at everyone and finally arrived at the point in the meeting to which they had all been looking forward.

The lady whom I had observed creating furrows up the garden path like an ox-drawn plough insisted on being first, and no one felt led to challenge her. As she was unable to stand, she leaned forward in the chair while Peter put his hand gently on her forehead and Peggy put her hand on the lady's shoulder. We already knew she wanted to be able to walk again unaided, so Peter prayed, 'Father God, we ask you through Jesus to send your Holy Spirit and do whatever you want to do.'

As we watched and prayed, power came all over her from the tip of her head, where Peter's hand was delicately resting, to the soles of her feet. For a while, it seemed as if she was struggling with a kind of power that for the first time in her life she was unable to handle, but in the end the struggle gave way to a peaceful, tearful kind of joy. Eventually, she opened her eyes and then, encouraged by Peter, got to her feet unaided and cautiously took a few steps before moving seamlessly into a non-Sadler's-Wells, non-dignified type of leaping and dancing. It wasn't pretty, but it was wonderful to behold. Thus encouraged, we moved on to the next patient.

If our churchwarden Peter was a golfer or a cricketer, rather than someone who prayed for the sick, I would have said he was on a roll or hitting a purple patch of good form when so many people were being healed. In the spiritual realm, however, we need a different kind of language, but inevitably we run into the difficulty of being precise about the unseen world. Some talk about waves of the Spirit or a move of God, while others speak of thin air, thick air, renewal or revival. Whatever language we use, the truth is that at this moment in time God was with Peter, and as the Holy Spirit stirred within him he sensed when the authority and power of Jesus was present to heal the sick.

A 30-year-old man was the next one to receive prayer that night – a man who had not managed an upright position at any time during the evening. He explained to us all how he used to be a hospital porter but had damaged his back while lifting a patient 'in an incorrect manner', as a result of which he'd lost his job and been unable to work at anything else since. He stood in the middle of the room and helped Peter to find the spot in his back which was the centre of his trouble.

'Oh yes!' said Peter. 'There's a lump there.'

Having come to check things out, I put my hand on the lump myself and felt something like a small triangular pyramid of bones sticking out. I'm not at all medical, and nobody else bothered to find out what medical words describe this particular condition, but it was definitely not right, gave considerable pain, and helped my critical faculties because it was tangible.

Despite protestations from Peter, I withdrew to the side of the room so that he and Peggy could do the business. They both very correctly and sensitively laid hands on the ex-porter while at the same time Peter asked God the Father, through Jesus, to send his Holy Spirit on him. Initially, the face of the man with a bad back screwed up with tension and discomfort as his entire frame bent over, causing his eyes to face the ground, but gradually, as we waited in prayerful silence, his face relaxed, his eyes came off the floor and his back began to straighten up. Ultimately, the young man found himself in a perfectly upright position, opened his eyes and testified that the pain had gone completely.

Immediately, I leapt forward, put my hand on his back and felt around for the pyramid which had been there a few moments before, only to find that the whole area was now as smooth as the sand on the seashore. A wave of God's Holy Spirit had healed him, and to God be all the glory.

Meanwhile, as this was taking place, the healed lady kept fidgeting with the curtain and looking out of the window, as if she was planning her big moment. At the appointed time, she spotted the car arriving, leapt out of her chair, did up her coat and stood in the hallway ready to pounce. As the garden gate opened, so did the front door, but the two escorts were stopped in their tracks by what they saw coming towards them. The lady skipped in their direction, flung out her hand in a dramatic gesture and announced, 'I've been healed. I'm walking home. I don't need you any more,' and with that, she swept past them, flung wide the gate and vanished into the night.

Authority and power

In the Gospels, we noted how Jesus healed the sick whenever authority and power were given to him by God the Father through the Holy Spirit to do so. When Jesus sent out the Twelve to heal the sick, he passed on to them the same authority and power that had been given to him (Luke 9:1). At the transition from the end of the Gospels to the beginning of Acts I couldn't help noticing that the words 'authority' and 'power' appeared again just as prominently as before: 'Then Jesus came to them and said, "All *authority* in heaven and on earth has been given to me"' (Matthew 28:18; my italics); 'I am going to send you what my Father has promised; but stay in the city until you have been clothed with *power* from on high' (Luke 24:49; my italics); 'You will receive *power* when the Holy Spirit comes on you' (Acts 1:8; my italics).

From this point onwards, everything comes through Jesus, who has been given 'all authority' and is now the one who sends the Holy Spirit. He is able to do this because his death puts his followers right with God, creating a righteous channel to the Father through himself, along which the Holy Spirit can flow. On earth, Jesus could receive the Holy Spirit directly from the Father because he was righteous; we can now receive the same Holy Spirit from the Father through Jesus because his death makes us righteous before God. The principles are therefore the same for us as they were for Jesus. To heal the sick, we need the authority of God and the power of God that comes to us from Jesus through the Holy Spirit; then we can do the same things as he did, the same way he did them.

When Peter and John were used by God to heal the man crippled from birth, 'all the people were astonished and came running' (Acts 3:11). Peter then asked them this question: 'Why do you stare at us as if by our own *power* or godliness we had made this man walk?' (Acts 3:12; my italics). Lying behind Peter's question is the assumption that power has been necessary in order to heal the man. Later, the rulers and the teachers of the law asked:

> 'By what *power* or what name did you do this?' Then Peter, filled with the Holy Spirit, said to them: '. . . It is by the name of Jesus Christ of Nazareth, whom you crucified but whom God raised from the dead, that this man stands before you healed.' (Acts 4:7–8, 10; my italics)

In asking how the man was healed, the members of the Sanhedrin were wanting to know by what *power* and by what *authority* (name) he was healed. They knew the key to healing was power and authority, and Peter, filled with the Holy Spirit, did not disagree with them in his answer. Peter obviously believed that the authority and power to heal the man came from and through Jesus.

In chapter 9, Peter meets Aeneas at Lydda, 'a paralytic who had been bedridden for eight years. "Aeneas," Peter said to him, "Jesus Christ heals you"' (Acts 9:33–34). This is glorious. Once more, Peter believes that Jesus has authority and power to heal this man and is willing to do so. But this is not a formula which will work for all people for all time, as is illustrated by the next healing.

Peter goes straight from Lydda to Joppa at the request of the disciples because Tabitha has died, and this is what he did:

> Peter sent them all out of the room; then he got down on his knees and prayed. Turning towards the dead woman, he said, 'Tabitha, get up.' She opened her eyes, and seeing Peter she sat up. (Acts 9:40)

Faced with a corpse, and a group of people wanting him to raise her from the dead, Peter goes down on his knees and prays. It may be possible to argue that we can go round expecting to heal everyone who is sick but it is very difficult to argue that we can go round expecting to raise everyone from the dead (the number of people alive today from the time of Peter is a very round figure). Peter cannot raise anyone from the dead, nor can he ask Tabitha if she has enough faith to be healed; this can only be done if he who has all authority gives that authority to Peter. And this can only be done if Jesus, who sends the Holy Spirit to his disciples, sends the power. I suggest, therefore, that this was probably an asking and listening prayer that may have gone something like this: 'What are you doing, Lord? What authority do I have? What power will you send?'

Notice, however, that Peter then rises and says, 'Tabitha, get up', which is an exercise in faith: faith in what Jesus has just said through the Holy Spirit he will do; faith in the healer and not in the healing. Interestingly, when Paul was used by God to heal Publius's father, he prayed first and then 'placed his hands on him' (Acts 28:7–10). This also looks like an asking and listening prayer.

On the Day of Pentecost, the Holy Spirit came with great power and spoke through the believers (Acts 2:1–4). This is power and authority. Peter then said that now the Holy Spirit has been sent by Jesus from heaven, all God's servants – young and old, male and female – will be able to hear God's voice and speak God's words (Acts 2:17–18). This is authority. When the believers prayed for God to stretch out his hand to heal, 'the place where they were meeting was shaken. And they were all filled with the Holy Spirit and spoke the word of God boldly' (Acts 4:31). This is power and authority.

'Stephen, a man full of God's grace and power, did great wonders and miraculous signs', and 'they could not stand up against his wisdom or the Spirit by whom he spoke' (Acts 6:8, 10). This is power and authority. Peter prophesied that Sapphira would drop down dead, and she did (Acts 5:9–10); Paul prophesied that Elymas would become blind and he did (Acts 13:11). This is authority and power. Paul saw in 'a man crippled in his feet' a work of God going on that enabled the man to be healed, and his discerning of an evil spirit in a slave girl at Philippi enabled her to be set free in the name of Jesus (Acts 14:8–10; 16:16–18). This is authority and power.

Power and authority – spiritual gifts of healing, miracles, faith and words from God – can be seen peppering the Acts of the Apostles whenever the Holy Spirit was at work. Authority and power are needed to heal the sick; the Holy Spirit provides authority and power; in the Acts of the Apostles it is the Holy Spirit who heals. And one story of healing that Luke must have heard being told over and over again brings it all together most clearly.

Ananias (not the one who dropped down dead) is getting on with his little Christian life, minding his own business, hoping and praying that the persecuting pagans will not come knocking on his door, when all of a sudden the phone rings – in his spirit, that is. It's Jesus.

'Ah yes!' says Jesus. 'Ananias. Got a job for you. Damascus. Straight Street. House of Judas. A blind man. Name of Saul.'

'Excuse me, Jesus,' interrupts Ananias, somewhat alarmed. 'Did you say Saul?'

'Yes, Ananias. Saul,' replies Jesus. 'I want you to lay hands on him and. . .'

'But, Lord!' blurts out Ananias. 'Perhaps you haven't heard. He's not a nice man. He's. . .'

'Go!' commands Jesus. *That's authority.*

So Ananias goes.

Placing his hands on Saul, he said, 'Brother Saul, the Lord – Jesus, who appeared to you on the road as you were coming here – has sent me so that you may see again and be filled with the Holy Spirit.' Immediately, something like scales fell from Saul's eyes, and he could see again. (Acts 9:17–18)

That's power. When Jesus says, 'Go!' and we go, he sends the power to accomplish his will.

10. The Holy Spirit heals a blind eye

Peter, our churchwarden, full of the Holy Spirit, had the same privilege as Ananias of seeing a blind eye restored. His near neighbour and good friend was the caretaker at the local school and, being 65, was due for retirement. He and his wife were very much looking forward to this and began to make plans accordingly when, quite out of the blue, tragedy struck. Peter's friend suddenly became blind in one eye.

The caretaker went to his GP, who referred him to the hospital where, after numerous tests, he was given the bad news. The blindness was caused by a haemorrhage at the back of the eye; there was nothing the hospital could do, and it was unlikely to right itself significantly. The very bad news was that they would now have to take his driving licence from him.

This information was devastating to both of them, as driving was very much a part of their plans for retirement. The school caretaker poured it all out to Peter, who immediately sensed the authority of Jesus welling up inside him, encouraging him to have a go.

As before, Peter laid his hands gently on his friend's forehead near to his blind eye and asked God the Father, through Jesus, to send his Holy Spirit. By now, Peter was not at all surprised when power came upon his neighbour, removing the signs of stress and discomfort from his face and replacing them with a beatific smile.

When he opened his eyes, Peter's friend could now see clearly through both of them and the Lord's name was praised.

The caretaker kept his next appointment at the hospital, and the doctor, after looking into his 'bad eye' and getting him to read a card with it, assumed the notes had put down the wrong eye by mistake. He checked again, and found that not only had Peter's friend been healed but he could now read the smallest letters on the card, which he'd been unable to read even before the blindness. His driving licence was returned to him, and he and his wife went on to enjoy a happy retirement together for nearly 20 years.

The cross and the covenant in Acts

We have noted that the Gospels and the Acts of the Apostles do not link the death of Christ directly to physical healing, nor do they state that healing is a covenant right because of the cross. The idea that Jesus died for sicknesses as well as sins is not found in the Gospels or Acts. However, what is to be found in connection with the cross is very important for those wanting to heal the sick in the name of Jesus. In my survey, I came across two things on offer from God as a result of Jesus' sacrificial death:

a) The forgiveness of sins.
b) The gift of the Holy Spirit.

Here is some of the evidence.

> [Peter said,] 'God has made this Jesus, whom you crucified, both Lord and Christ.'
>
> When the people heard this, they were cut to the heart and said to Peter and the other apostles, 'Brothers, what shall we do?' Peter replied, 'Repent and be baptised, every one of you, in the name of Jesus Christ for the forgiveness of your sins. And you will receive the gift of the Holy Spirit. The promise is for you and your children and for all who are far off – for all whom the Lord our God will call.' (Acts 2:36–39)

In the Acts of the Apostles, the cross is most frequently mentioned as part of the package – lived, died, rose, ascended – as a result of which God offers forgiveness of sins and the gift of the Holy Spirit to all who repent of their sins and believe in the Lord Jesus (see Acts 3:19; 4:11–12; 5:30–32; 10:39, 43–44; 13:38–39, 52; 20:28; 26:18; also see Luke 24:45–49). The importance of baptism in water is sometimes included as an outward and visible sign of that belief.

The New Covenant is not mentioned in Acts, but the forgiveness of sins and the gift of the Holy Spirit are prophesied in Isaiah, Jeremiah and Ezekiel as New Covenant promises (see Isaiah 59:20–21; Jeremiah 31:31–34; Ezekiel 37:14, 26–27). Isaiah's prophecy is particularly important in confirming Peter's statement that God's offer is to us as well as to the people of his day, just as with Joel's prophecy (Acts 2:17–21).

We are on very firm scriptural ground when we claim that through the work of Christ, including the cross, those who repent and believe in Jesus can be put right with God and receive the gift of the Holy Spirit. This is only one step away from saying we can be physically healed because of the cross, but it is an important step. It looks like this.

a) All believers are put right with God through the cross of Christ.
b) This enables God to send his Holy Spirit through Jesus to all believers, as he promised.
c) It is the Holy Spirit who heals.

Our aim, then, in seeking to be healed by God is to repent of our sins, believe in the Lord Jesus Christ (which may include baptism), and ask him to fill us with his Holy Spirit again and again. God's promise is to give us the Holy Spirit who heals, not necessarily the healing.

11. The Holy Spirit heals thrombosis

As soon as Peter and Peggy retired, they moved to Cornwall, where they caused a lot of trouble. They attended their local parish church after they'd arrived but made the mistake of telling the vicar that God had used them in the past to heal the sick, and asked him if they did the laying-on of hands in their new church. This produced a no-no. No they didn't and no they couldn't.

But the churchwarden became ill; Peter and Peggy prayed for him, and he was healed. A nearby curate also became ill, and then a lay reader, and then. . . all were healed. So Peter rang me up. 'How about coming down for a few days,' he asked, 'and doing a couple of meetings while you are here?'

'What about the vicar?' I asked cautiously, being one myself.

'Oh, that's all right,' replied Peter. 'He'll be away on holiday.'

I insisted on full permission being granted first, and then agreed, despite major trauma and trepidation leaping around inside me, as Peter had a much higher opinion of my faith in God for healing than I had. I started praying like mad. I was just beginning to wonder how on earth I was going to live up to Peter's hopes and dreams when Peggy phoned. Peter was seriously ill – he'd suffered thrombosis! If there was one person I believed God might heal when I laid hands on him in Jesus' name, it was Peter. Initially, it was sad news, but eventually God turned it into good news.

Our first meeting was on the Tuesday night at Trelowarren Christian Fellowship; I expected 10 people to turn up, but about 200 came.[1] They sat in the chapel, the lounge and the library, and the sound was relayed throughout the house, but nobody seemed to know if Peter had come as he'd been very ill. At first, I began to feel guilty and then weak and wobbly at the thought of addressing all these people who would be expecting so much after Peter had told them about. . . when all of a sudden, I saw his distinctive bald head at a distance. Manna from heaven had arrived.

I rushed over straight away and got the two no's I was hoping for: no, he wasn't well, and no, he didn't mind being prayed for in front of 200 people. Hallelujah!

After the worship and my talk, I invited Peter to the front and interviewed him about his thrombosis. He stood on a chair, rolled up his trouser leg and showed us the large swelling covering his right ankle, which meant the outline of his ankle bone couldn't be seen.

I invited two ladies, whom I'd met briefly, to come out and pray for Peter. They were very apprehensive, never having done it before, but they didn't know Peter like I did. As one of them put her hand on his forehead, and the other one held hers close to his ankle, I asked God the

---

[1] Trelowarren Christian Fellowship is situated near Helston, in Cornwall. They still run courses and welcome people to stay. It's a great place. Email: trelowarren@fellowshipt.freeserve.co.uk

Father through Jesus to send his Holy Spirit on Peter and do whatever he wanted to do.

Within seconds, Peter fell backwards; the ladies caught him neatly and laid him down gently as I began to waffle into the microphone:

'Sometimes when the Spirit comes, people fail to remain standing, so we catch them, put them down gently and carry on in our new position as if nothing has happened. Kay has her hand on Peter's ankle and as it was a thrombosis Beth is laying her hand gently on his heart. We just wait and watch and bless what the Father is doing. . .'

. . . when suddenly Beth interrupted me, *sotto voce*, off-piste. 'Pssst! Peter,' she whispered, trying to get my attention, 'I think he's just died.'

This was an unexpected blow. We'd done John Wimber's beginners' course, when we visited a hospital and had a go on the patients, but I hadn't done the advanced course, when we all go to the morgue.[2]

'Are you sure?' I whispered back.

There was a pause. And then. . .'Hang on a minute. There's still a pulse,' said Beth. 'I think it was just the thumping palpitations giving way to a more normal heartbeat,' she suggested. 'Yes it's OK. He's still breathing.'

A few moments later, Peter opened his eyes, looked around, was helped to his feet and then said: 'That'll do. That'll do nicely.' He felt fine. Then, without being asked,

---

[2] John Wimber with Kevin Springer, *Practical Healing* (London: Hodder & Stoughton 1987). The advanced course, you'll be glad to know, is a joke and doesn't exist!

he rolled up his trouser leg so that everyone could see how the swelling had disappeared completely and the outline of his ankle bone was now clearly visible.

It may not surprise you to learn that it was Peter who brought Yvonne to the church in Cornwall on the Saturday night a few days later while the vicar was away, where she was healed of cancer.

Normally, when we ask God the Father through Jesus to send his Holy Spirit, people are blessed, and sometimes a sign or a wonder or a miracle takes place and they are healed. To God be all the glory.

4

Healing Is a Gift of the Holy Spirit

A look at the Epistles

In the Acts of the Apostles, we read a lot about the Holy Spirit, quite a bit about healing and very little, comparatively speaking, about the cross. In the Epistles, we read a lot about the cross, a fair bit about the Holy Spirit and very little, comparatively speaking, about healing. Surprisingly, we read more about Christians in the Epistles being ill and dying than being healed. Even so, though there are no healing stories, the teaching on healing is very relevant. This is what I found:

- Healing in the Epistles is seen as a gift of the Holy Spirit.
- We are encouraged to pray to God for him to heal.
- There is evidence that faithful Christians became ill and some died.
- There is considerable material about the cross of Christ and the New Covenant sealed with his blood, but I found nothing to link the cross of Christ directly with physical healing, or to see it as a New Covenant right.

In contrast to the Gospels and Acts, the focus in the Epistles switches from the evangelists to the evangelised, from the healers to the healed, as they are written to Christians. The question being addressed is this: 'Having received the gospel of Jesus Christ, how shall we now live and what shall we do?' The Epistles are about discipleship – the new life and lifestyle of those who have now entered the kingdom of God.

Cynthia is a disciple of Jesus Christ, and the following story tells how Jesus healed her, by his Spirit.

12. No more mobility allowance

Cynthia was over 80 per cent disabled and for some time had been deteriorating physically. She had a chronic degenerative spinal condition with neurological disorders and functional impairment, which meant that the whole motor system of her body did not work properly. She saw double through very narrow tunnel vision, but at times even this was lost through muscle spasms. Cynthia had little use of her limbs and needed a specially stabilised electric wheelchair. There was no known cure for her illness, and the doctors said all they could do was to make her as comfortable as possible and support her all they could. One doctor gave her only two years to live 'at the outside'.

Many Christians prayed constantly for Cynthia, without any evidence of physical improvement, until one night she was left on her own in the house. The family saw she was comfortable with Bible, book, drink and a snack very close by, and then at about 7.40 pm they went out. At 8.30 pm, Cynthia prayed, 'Oh Lord, forgive my weakness of faith. I believe; help my unbelief. If there is anything you want me to do for you with the rest of my life, here I am.'

Shortly after this, the Spirit of Jesus began to fill the room most powerfully. With head bent, Cynthia was aware of a glow which grew stronger and caused a tremendous brightness but she experienced no fear. Expecting to see a great light shining through the window, she looked up, but saw instead a vision of Jesus, who himself was the source of the light inside the room by the far wall. The overwhelming feeling was one of extreme cleanliness.

Jesus moved towards Cynthia and then very gently touched her head, wrists and ankles. A wonderful cleansing glow spread throughout her body, giving the sensation of padlocks and chains being sprung loose. Instantly, her sight was restored and her hands, feet, legs and body were straightened and could now be moved without pain. Gradually, the vision of Jesus faded, whereupon Cynthia leapt out of the wheelchair and spring-cleaned the house from top to bottom, ready for when the family returned. They were obviously overjoyed when they did, and a little fearful it would not last, but they need not have worried. When I last saw Cynthia, years after the incident, she was still fit and active.

Cynthia's healing, however, caused the authorities a few problems: at the time, she was receiving a mobility allowance; now she had to be investigated and examined by doctors. In due course, she received notification that 'due to a relevant change of circumstances' they were withdrawing her mobility allowance. It is good to know and worship a Jesus who can bring a relevant change to circumstances! What a wonderful gift of healing for Cynthia, her family and friends and church to receive from the Spirit of Jesus. I have known Cynthia for several years, and it has always been a great thrill to see her clambering over seats as a member of a ministry team to pray for others. She loves to give away everything that God has given to her – to be used by him for his glory.

Romans

Romans is our longest epistle (by three verses); it therefore comes first and is probably the most systematic one to follow. For seven chapters, Paul argues how Jesus makes it possible for us to be put right with God through faith in Christ and principally by what he has done for us on the cross. 'God presented him as a sacrifice of atonement, through faith in his blood' (Romans 3:25). In chapter 8 he argues that if we belong to Christ we have the Spirit of Christ – the Spirit of God – living in us (Romans 8:9–10, 14), and this can bring healing and wholeness to Christians in spirit, emotions, mind, will and body. It works something like this.

The right *image* of God is restored to our spirit, healing the wrong image of God which came to us through the Fall (Genesis 3:8). 'By him we cry, 'Abba, Father' (Romans 8:15). The *Spirit* himself testifies with our *spirit* that we are God's children (8:16). As we are now 'in Christ Jesus' (v. 1), which means having the 'Spirit of Christ' within us (v. 9), it becomes possible to live 'according to the Spirit' (v. 4) and be 'controlled . . . by the Spirit' (v. 9). This leads to harmony and wholeness. Our *spirit* comes alive (v. 11); fear (*emotions*) is replaced by sonship (v. 15), and we are now free to choose (*will*) life rather than death (v. 13), a share in God's glory (v. 17) rather than sin (v. 12). The Spirit of God also brings life to our bodies:

> And if the Spirit of him who raised Jesus from the dead is living in you, he who raised Christ from the dead will also give life to your mortal bodies through his Spirit, who lives in you. (Romans 8:11)

In other words, health and wholeness come to our spirits, souls and bodies through the presence and activity of the Holy Spirit in us. These are the same steps we noted towards the end of Chapter 3. Our response to the cross of Christ puts us right with God, which allows him to fill us with his Holy Spirit, who is the one who heals.

But, we are bound to ask, is perfection achievable – or, if not, how much healing and wholeness can we expect before Jesus returns? Paul makes two important comments.

a) 'All have sinned and fall short of the glory of God' (Romans 3:23); 'What I do is not the good I want to do; no, the evil I do not want to do – this I keep doing'(Romans 7:19). What Paul describes in Romans 8:1–17 is not so much healing, though this may take place when we first become Christians, but how to stay well. It is more about health and wholeness than the removal of symptoms. Sadly, we all continue to sin, even after we become Christians, and the corollary of this passage is that sin can cause dysfunction, disharmony and disease. The Holy Spirit continues to convict us of sin and to bring God's forgiving, healing love to us when we repent of our sins, but the battle between sin and forgiveness, sickness and healing seems to continue. Those whom I have seen God heal supernaturally usually become ill again, of something else, from time to time. Jesus said that sickness and sin are not always connected but the consequences of sin – e.g. in my case over-eating – often lead to physical problems. The Holy Spirit, and in this passage our response to the Holy Spirit, can bring healing to spirit, emotions, mind, will and body, but not easily or automatically for everyone of everything, always. It is not a right to claim but a path to tread.

b) In Romans 8, Paul continues like this:

> I consider that our present sufferings are not worth comparing with the glory that will be revealed in us. The creation waits in eager expectation for the sons of God to be revealed. For the creation was subjected to frustration, not by its own choice, but by the will of the one who subjected it, in hope that the creation itself will be liberated from its bondage to decay and brought into the glorious freedom of the children of God.
>
> We know that the whole creation has been groaning as in the pains of childbirth right up to the present time. Not only so, but we ourselves, who have the first-fruits of the Spirit, groan inwardly as we wait eagerly for our adoption as sons, the redemption of our bodies. For in this hope we were saved. But hope that is seen is no hope at all. Who hopes for what he already has? But if we hope for what we do not yet have, we wait for it patiently. (Romans 8:18–25)

If this passage is read carefully, I think it is reasonably obvious that Paul sees freedom from decay as a future hope.

This I believe was the simple mistake made in Toronto when those who wore spectacles or contact lenses were encouraged to claim their healing from Jesus. Now that I am nearly 60, I do not see as well as I did when I was 20, but I do not have a disease. I am suffering from decay, or what my children describe as old age. Paul writes that freedom from decay is a future hope – one I am looking forward to immensely.

In Romans chapters 1 to 8, we note how the Spirit brings the 'first-fruits' of what is to come. This 'foretaste', plus Paul's teaching on decay, means there is no offer here of complete healing for everyone of everything yet, but the more we are controlled by the Spirit, the more health and wholeness we can expect.

Right or request?

If there is money in my bank account, no matter who put it there I have the *right* to draw it out and use it whenever I choose to do so. It is mine; I own it, and I have the right to it.

If I want the bank to cancel Third-World debt, to donate money to charity, or to give me a loan for a new car, I have to make a *request*. The money is not mine; I have no rights, and therefore I make my request known.

There is a major difference between a *right* and a *request*.

All over the world, Christians of virtually every denomination regularly pray and make their requests known to God for healing. Even non-churchgoing non-Christians will sometimes ask us to pray for them if they are unwell. There are good New Testament reasons for asking God to heal, and they are to be found in the Epistles: 'Pray for each other so that you may be healed,' exhorts James (James 5:16); 'I pray that you may enjoy good health and that all may go well with you,' comments John (3 John 2); 'And pray in the Spirit on all occasions with all kinds of prayers and requests. With this in mind, be alert and always keep on praying for all the saints,' instructs Paul (Ephesians 6:18; see also Philippians 4:6 and 1 Timothy 2:1).

In contrast, there are no good New Testament reasons for claiming healing as a right for all people, of everything, always, right now, and it is not a belief to be found in the Epistles. Paul, John and the writer to the Hebrews have a lot to say about the cross of Christ, and the many benefits which are available to believers because of it, but automatic physical healing is not one of them.

Healing is a gift of the Holy Spirit

The author of the letter to the Hebrews writes about the gifts of the Holy Spirit:

> This salvation, which was first announced by the Lord, was confirmed to us by those who heard him. God also testified to it by signs, wonders and various miracles, and gifts of the Holy Spirit distributed according to his will. (Hebrews 2:3–4)

In the light of all I have written so far, these verses could be seen as the theme of this book. It is God who does all these things, through his Holy Spirit, 'according to his will'.

In Paul's first letter to the Corinthians, he lists nine gifts of the Holy Spirit, one of which is miracles and another one is healing: 'Now to each one the manifestation of the Spirit is given for the common good. To one there is given . . . gifts of healing by that one Spirit, to another miraculous powers' (1 Corinthians 12:7–12). In Paul's list, healing and miracles come next to each other and – according to John's Gospel and the Acts of the Apostles – are similar. We have already seen that there are seven miracles in John's Gospel, of which four are healings. Here are the other three:

a) Jesus turns water into wine (John 2:1–11).
b) Jesus feeds five thousand plus with 'five small barley loaves and two small fish' (John 6:1– 14).
c) Jesus walks on the water (John 6:16–21).

Now some of the Christians I know have seen God heal the sick and do other miracles, but I don't know any who do the following:

a) Order a jug of water in a restaurant with the intention of turning it into wine.
b) Put out five small loaves and two small fish at the Harvest Supper and expect the vicar to do the rest.
c) Walk to the Isle of Wight from Canford Magna without using a boat.

Please don't get me wrong. I do believe in the God of miracles and I'm well aware that in the Indonesian revival of the sixties God regularly turned water into wine for use at holy communion. The point is that we do not have miracles in our own bank accounts that we have a right to draw out and use whenever we choose. Miracles are given as a gift of the Holy Spirit 'just as he determines' (1 Corinthians 12:11).

Assuming the gift of tongues in this list is not the individual, personal, private gift but a public anointing for a public message, then all these spiritual gifts operate in the same way. (The context of this teaching is 'when you come together', which seems to confirm this interpretation – 1 Corinthians 11:20, 33; 14:26; see also 11:17; 11:34; 12:7; 12:12; 14:23.)

This is how it might look in church today. All these examples have actually happened to us, and some are mentioned elsewhere in the book.

When we came together, our musical worship leader asked God through Jesus to inhabit our worship with his presence and power, by his Holy Spirit. After three songs, he paused and said, 'I believe God wants to share a *prophetic* word with us,' and waited in silence.

Nervously, after two minutes of waiting, a lady from the congregation began to speak. 'My children, I am indeed present among you today in power. Seek my face, listen to my voice, obey my promptings and I will do special things among you.'

A second person approached me and whispered in my ear, 'I think the Lord wants me to give a message in tongues!' Knowing the person and sensing God's Spirit on him, I led him to the microphone where he spoke briefly in *tongues* for all to hear.

After this I nodded to the worship leader, who prayed, 'Lord, please give us the *interpretation* of this word.'

Almost immediately, a lady, trembling a little, spoke out a suggested *interpretation*: 'We praise you, Lord, for your presence and your power. We give you all the honour and the glory. We love you, Lord,' and sensitively, appropriately, the group led us in two more songs of adoration, into which, encouraged by the words, the people entered fully.

After some prayers and the preaching of God's word, I asked God the Father to do amongst us whatever he wanted to do by his Spirit. Most people were engaged and filled as God moved amongst us. David came to the front and gave *a word of knowledge* about a lady with arthritis in one hand. As David approached the lady who claimed it, and he saw the power of God already at work on her, the gift of *faith* rose up inside him, and he knew she was going to be *healed*. When he laid hands on her shoulder, more power came, her arm shook up and down violently, and the lady was *healed*.

The rest of the ministry team moved among the congregation, gently blessing what the Father was doing. One lady developed a headache in the presence of a female member of the team, who *discerned* the presence of a demon. Another member of the team came to help, sensed God giving her the *wisdom* to take the lady into the side room, where, after the confession of sin, a demon was cast out and the headache went.

A rather hurting person collapsed on the floor as the Spirit came on her. As a member of the team knelt down beside her and laid hands on her, she was *miraculously* covered in gold dust. When the lady saw it herself, she knew God really did love her and wept tears of joy before the light flakes melted away. Only a few saw it, but that was enough.

When we came together and welcomed the Holy Spirit, he gave certain gifts to certain people. Healing is one of those gifts of the Holy Spirit with which he sometimes blesses us when we come together and welcome him to do whatever he wants to do.

The following week, God may do something totally

different and use different people, 'according to his will' (Hebrews 2:4). Some of these gifts convey God's authority, some convey his power, but all enable his will to be done amongst us.

Healing, then, is a gift of the Holy Spirit, just the same as miracles. When the Spirit moves amongst us, giving us God's authority and power, then we can do miracles and healing, the ones he chooses, 'just as he determines' (1 Corinthians 12:11). Healing is not a right but a gift; we may request such gifts, indeed we are encouraged to do so, but God chooses what to give and when to give it. This is what they did when I visited Toronto and as God gave gifts of healing, here and there, it was wonderful to behold.

The disabled in church

The word 'healed' is used once in Hebrews: 'No discipline seems pleasant at the time, but painful . . . "Make level paths for your feet," so that the lame may not be disabled, but rather healed' (Hebrews 12:11, 13). It comes across as an athletic metaphor about perseverance and discipline but it may also be suggesting that ramps should be provided for wheelchairs in our churches. Leon Morris comments:

> Clearly the idea is to put paths into better order to facilitate travel, specifically for the lame. The writer is mindful of the fact that Christians belong together. They must have consideration for the weak among their members, i.e., the 'lame.'[1]

---

[1] Leon Morris, Commentary on Hebrews, *The Expositor's Bible Commentary,* edited by Frank E. Gaebelein (Michigan: Regency Reference Library, Zondervan Publishing House 1981), p. 139.

I've always believed that if our church is to be known as a 'healing' church then the disabled should be made to feel welcome and that they belong. Can you imagine sitting in your wheelchair while the preacher gives the weekly invitation for those with faith to be healed to come forward? It was not too bad for the first 52 weeks but now you are into your second year at the church, it is no longer a comfortable place to be. You already feel a burden. Big people have to be found every week to lift you up the steps, as there is no ramp. You desperately want to go to the loo, but the chair won't fit in. You did go before you came out but you had to arrive earlier than the others for the long service, to make sure of a car-parking space.

Your church has the reputation of being a healing church but sometimes it makes you sick. Perhaps the non-charismatic church down the road with better facilities and no pointing fingers might make you feel more whole. After all, your mind and spirit are not crippled, and you do want to contribute.

In my opinion, and as suggested in Hebrews, a healing church will always make the disabled feel welcome, allow for it in their budget, and give opportunity for mind and spirit to be exercised, if their theology will allow them to do so.

The sick and the dead

In the Pauline epistles, there is evidence of four sick believers and a number of dead ones:

a) Paul

As you know, it was because of an illness that I first preached the gospel to you. Even though my illness was a trial to you,

you did not treat me with contempt or scorn. (Galatians
4:13–14)

How embarrassing! I know how Paul might have felt. I once
went to Vancouver to speak on healing and people paid
good money to come and hear me. I made it to the lectern
but then collapsed and had to be taken to hospital in an
ambulance, where it was discovered I had hepatitis. The
delegates had to be given their money back, and I felt awful.

Galatians 4:13–14 is descriptive and not prescriptive, so
we cannot argue that Paul was ill because of lack of faith or
because God was not doing healing, but it is strangely com-
forting to know that Paul, who had a ministry of signs and
wonders in a church which experienced miracles, was ill
(Galatians 3:5). Commentators have suggested such illnesses as malaria, epilepsy or poor eyesight (see 4:15), but
unlike the 'thorn in my flesh' of Corinthians (2 Corinthians
12:7), which some think may not be a physical ailment,
'infirmity of the flesh' is generally agreed by scholars to be
an illness.

b) Epaphroditus

The illness and healing of Epaphroditus mentioned in Paul's
letter to the Philippians is just as interesting and relevant to
us as Paul's own sickness described in Galatians. This is
what Paul wrote:

> For he [Epaphroditus] longs for all of you and is distressed
> because you heard he was ill. Indeed he was ill, and almost
> died. But God had mercy on him, and not on him only but also
> on me, to spare me sorrow upon sorrow. (Philippians 2:26–27)

Paul also writes, 'Do not be anxious about anything, but in everything, by prayer and petition, with thanksgiving, present your requests to God' (Philippians 4:6).

Paul was obviously anxious about Epaphroditus, as indeed were the Philippians, because he became ill and almost died. Paul seems to suggest that in such situations we should present our requests to God in prayer. In the end, Paul believed it was God who healed Epaphroditus, while he had to admit that his teaching, theology and practice had not been able to stop his friend from becoming seriously ill. His healing did not come by claiming rights, but by the mercy of God. This, I would suggest, is significant. It was God and his mercy that healed Epaphroditus, and Paul makes no direct reference to the cross or the New Covenant in relation to it.

c) Timothy

As well as Paul and Epaphroditus, Timothy is another person in Paul's writings who became sick. Paul wrote to him: 'Stop drinking only water, and use a little wine because of your stomach and your frequent illnesses' (1 Timothy 5:23). This one really fascinates me. Paul offers wine as a solution rather than prayer or ministry in the Holy Spirit, and he doesn't suggest that Christ died for his stomach and frequent illnesses. Given the likely state of water in those days, it sounds like good advice, but perhaps there is something of greater significance here. I cannot imagine that if Timothy had been sitting in the shadows of Peter (Acts 5:15–16), or been present at Samaria when Philip was used by God to heal so many (Acts 8:6–7), or even been the recipient of one of Paul's special hankies (Acts 19:11–12), Peter, Philip or Paul would have said to him at that time, 'Take a little wine for your poorly tummy.' In this later letter of Paul, we do seem to be living in somewhat different times.

Some Christians believe it is lack of trust in God to use medicine, injections or operations instead of just prayer. Wine may not be a very sophisticated medicine but here Paul recommends its use as well as prayer. He also honoured his friend, Luke the doctor (Colossians 4:14).

d) Trophimus

In the final greetings of his second letter to Timothy, Paul writes, 'I left Trophimus sick in Miletus' (2 Timothy 4:20). I don't think this was because Paul didn't like him, but rather because he had tried to bring healing to him and failed. Once more, the hankies and aprons of former times were no help at this time, and Paul left his friend unhealed.

e) The departed in Thessalonica

Paul's first letter to the Thessalonians refers to people who have died:

> Brothers, we do not want you to be ignorant about those who fall asleep, or to grieve like the rest of men, who have no hope. We believe that Jesus died and rose again and so we believe that God will bring with Jesus those who have fallen asleep in him. (1 Thessalonians 4:13–14)

This is probably Paul's first biblical letter to be written, and possibly the first book of the New Testament, maybe not much more than 20 years after Christ's ascension. The situation is that people are expecting Christ's return but some Christians have already died, and they want to know if the deceased will miss out. Paul, by using the term 'those who fall asleep', seems to be expecting more deaths to take place (1 Thessalonians 4:13). Of equal significance to us are those who have already 'fallen asleep', i.e. not died through persecution but of natural causes (1 Thessalonians 4:14). Their deaths have brought concern, suggesting that their friends would probably have done all they could to heal them, and failed. We can add them to those in the Epistles who became ill, or infirm through age, but who, this time, were not healed.

That makes four sick Christians in Paul's letters, and a number of dead ones in Thessalonica.

Paul wrote a lot about the cross of Christ being the only way to salvation which, if taken on faith, enables believers to be filled with the Holy Spirit. He was familiar with miracles being done by the Holy Spirit and saw physical healing as a gift of the Spirit. Paul was also familiar with sickness and death and did not always suggest that they could be supernaturally taken away. Nowhere does he write that physical healing is a covenant right as a result of the cross, or that Jesus died for sicknesses as well as sins. According to Paul, it is the Spirit who speaks and guides and heals, as Olive discovered.

13. A bishop at the bottom of the garden

When Olive was 13, she fell off a beam in the gymnasium and damaged her spine, causing her to be paralysed for a while. Eventually, she recovered but from then on was in constant pain with her back. In due course, osteo-arthritis attacked both knees, and Olive became a wheelchair person, only able to walk 25 yards with crutches on a good day, with a following wind.

For over 30 years, the medical profession tried everything: Olive went through three major spinal operations; she was encased in plaster, encased in steel and saw various physiotherapists; they tried all kinds of exercises, massages and manipulations, but nothing could take away the pain or restore her mobility.

One day, her consultant, a member of our congregation, asked her, 'Are you a Christian?' This was a very God-given word in season but at the time Olive was deeply shocked and angered by this question and could only mutter in reply, 'Yes, but not a very good one.' He then asked if she'd like to join a prayer group he'd started; Olive said she'd think about it.

Her husband Kevin was a no-nonsense, former-RAF, non-churchgoing, professional photographer, who found himself saying rather firmly, 'Don't go unless it's Christian. You're not going unless we have it checked first.'

Although Kevin had hardly been to church since he'd been confirmed in the Church of England as a teenager, he'd witnessed supernatural activity of a dark kind while abroad, which was connected with various other religious beliefs, and consequently he was concerned. Olive asked the deaconess from her own church about it, and she promised to look into it. Even though the lady was a new deaconess and knew little about healing, she did know that Kevin and Olive had a bishop at the bottom of their garden, where he'd lived, since retiring, for seven years, and she made contact with him.

One Saturday, they both came round and though Kevin was not normally at home on a Saturday, being a press photographer, amazingly he was there when the bishop and the deaconess came to call. The bishop sat down and started talking about the weather, whereupon Kevin sat down and started to cry. To hear Olive tell this part of her story is always amusing. 'He was only talking about the weather, for heaven's sake,' she usually says, with a wry smile and a raise of the eyebrows, as she'd only experienced her husband crying once before in their 27 years of marriage.

In truth, Kevin's tears were for the churches he'd attended in England where nobody seemed to believe in the supernatural, whereas all over the world he'd met people of other religions who appeared to have experienced it, in an unhelpful way much of the time. Strangely enough, Kevin hadn't become a non-churchgoer because he didn't believe, but because in his opinion he did believe and they didn't. His weeping, on seeing the godly bishop, was repentance for his anger and unforgiveness against the church.

The bishop turned his attention to Olive and asked her to think back to the time of her accident. 'I believe the Lord has shown me that the gym mistress carried the guilt of your accident for the rest of her life,' he said in a gentle manner. 'Do you think you could ask God to forgive her?'

Olive had never once blamed her teacher, knowing that she'd slipped and no one was to blame, so there wasn't an anger or resentment problem, just a practical one. The theory was fine – but out loud, there and then, in front of her husband, a deaconess and a bishop? Olive had never once prayed out loud in front of others in her entire adult life. But she did it – stutteringly yet sincerely.

Then the bishop turned to Kevin. 'Would you say a prayer?' he asked in a kindly way. Kevin felt it wasn't right to ask God to heal his wife without believing and committing himself to him, so he prayed silently: 'Lord,' he said, 'if you are there, give me the words to say.' The two words 'Our Father' came to mind, and as he started with those he found the rest flowed. Kevin repented of his sins, turned to the Lord in faith and requested his help to do his will. The bishop laid hands on Kevin, asked the Lord to fill him with his Holy Spirit and Kevin was floating about for months to come.

The bishop sensed the power of the Lord was present to heal if Olive wanted to ask God to heal her, and said so. Olive had never dared ask God for anything for herself before but, encouraged by the Right Reverend, she asked for forgiveness and healing. The deaconess prayed; Kevin prayed; the bishop prayed and anointed Olive with oil in the name of Jesus, and the pain left her back, went through her legs and out through her toes. It was some time before anyone spoke. It was an awesome moment.

In due course, Olive removed her steel encasement and found she could move her back and bend it without any discomfort, but the knees were not healed and she still couldn't walk unaided. This was not enough, however, to stop Kevin from coming to church the next day.

For several months, the bishop encouraged Olive to ask God for complete healing, which she did while working through a number of sins and problems. At a special healing conference, Bishop Maddocks laid hands on her and said, 'You're very good at giving but not so good at receiving.' Olive went to a healing service at Salisbury Cathedral, and a young clergyman with his wife laid hands on her and said, 'You're very good at giving but not so good at receiving,' and taught her to turn her hands upwards to receive when praying.

After a rough ride in a pick-up truck, some pain returned to Olive's back, following which the bishop from the bottom of the garden, after prayer, advised her to remove any wrong ornaments from the house. When the dustbin (in which they had thrown the ebony carving of another god) was emptied by the refuse collectors, and not before, the pain in her back went completely. One morning, a short time later, Kevin bandaged Olive's legs to cover her severe sores before leaving to photograph a royal visit, not knowing that Olive was about to receive a royal visit of her own.

It began when Olive sensed in her spirit the need to destroy a photograph of herself touching a ghost-stone for luck; having done that, she sat on the edge of her bed and prayed, with her hands turned upwards. Tears began to flow, as if all her sins and feelings of guilt were being washed away. At about 10 o'clock in the morning, as she stood up to go to the bathroom, Olive realised the pain had gone from her legs; the knees were now straight, and amazingly the sores which Kevin had bandaged a short while before had all gone. Olive walked unaided into the bathroom, then down the stairs, then up again, then spent the whole morning running up and down the staircase making suitable noises as she did so. When Kevin returned home for lunch, he wept and wept, for three months.

Later that day, Olive phoned Bishop Ban It Chiu – the bishop who lived at the bottom of the garden – but before she could speak he did: 'You've been healed, haven't you?' he began. 'At 10 o'clock this morning. I was praying, and the Lord told me.'[2]

It took Olive three years to get rid of her mobility allowance. She kept returning the book with a note of explanation but they wouldn't believe her, and sent another one back every time. Eventually, they wrote to Olive's GP to ask if she was mentally ill, and he confirmed her testimony of God's healing. Years on, we still give God all the glory, as do all the members of Olive's church who remember her in the wheelchair.

---

[2] I got to know Olive when she was the lay pastoral assistants' representative in our deanery. Her consultant was Chris Moran, from our Lantern congregation. Bishop Chiu Ban It is mentioned warmly by Michael Green in his excellent autobiography, *Adventure of Faith* (Harrow: Zondervan 2001), pp. 222–4, 260, 351–2. Ban It was the person who helped Michael to receive the gift of speaking in tongues. Bishop Ban It Chiu is the same person – but when he retired to England, having married an English wife, he kept receiving letters addressed to 'Mr It', so he moved his name around a bit.

James

The letter of James does not mention the death of Christ or the cross, but provides more teaching on physical healing than any other epistle. Here are the relevant verses:

> As you know, we consider blessed those who have persevered. You have heard of Job's perseverance and have seen what the Lord finally brought about. The Lord is full of compassion and mercy. (James 5:11)
>
> Is any one of you in trouble? He should pray. Is anyone happy? Let him sing songs of praise. Is any one of you sick? He should call the elders of the church to pray over him and anoint him with oil in the name of the Lord. And the prayer offered in faith will make the sick person well; the Lord will raise him up. If he has sinned, he will be forgiven. Therefore confess your sins to each other and pray for each other so that you may be healed. (James 5:13–16)
>
> The prayer of a righteous man is powerful and effective.
>
> Elijah was a man just like us. He prayed earnestly that it would not rain, and it did not rain on the land for three and a half years. Again he prayed, and the heavens gave rain, and the earth produced its crops. (James 5:16–18)

Surprisingly, this is the only mention of Job in the New Testament, particularly as it is the one book in the Old Testament which states categorically that not all sickness is due to sin. James reinforces this view when he writes about a sick man whom God heals: 'If he has sinned, he will be forgiven' (5:15). The 'if' is a simple way of saying that not all sickness is due to sin.

We also note that in the story of Job the sick person suffered greatly for a considerable time, and James commends him for his perseverance. It seems to have been the permissive will of God that the righteous Job suffered greatly from sickness, despite protestations from the comforters. God said this to them: 'Who is this that darkens my counsel with words without knowledge?' (Job 38:2); 'Will the one who contends with the Almighty correct him? Let him who accuses God answer him!' (Job 40:2). In other words, God is God and God knows best. This is why we often need a 'word of knowledge' from God in order to do his will, which in Job's case was painful sickness for a long time.

The teaching on healing by James is all about prayer: 'Is any one of you in trouble? He should pray' (James 5:13). The words 'pray', 'prayer' or 'prayed' appear seven times in six verses, and sickness is the main trouble to be addressed. Whenever James writes about prayer in the rest of this letter, it is about *asking* prayer: 'You do not have, because you do not ask God' (4:2; see also 1:5–6). In this passage, the response to the prayer of faith is that 'the Lord will raise him up' (James 5:15). The people pray, and God responds by healing. This sounds like an *asking* prayer as well. James encourages those who are sick to ask God in prayer to heal them, making it a request, not a right, though the writer believes in a God 'who gives generously to all' (1:5), is 'full of compassion and mercy' (5:11) and loves to heal (5:15–16).

As well as praying for healing, the elders are instructed to anoint the sick with oil in the name of the Lord. In the Bible, anointing with oil is the outward and visible symbol for being anointed with the Holy Spirit (James 5:14): 'So Samuel took the horn of oil and anointed him in the presence of his brothers, and from that day on the Spirit of the Lord came upon David in power' (1 Samuel 16:13). James recommends anointing with oil for those who are seriously sick (need raising up) and by so doing teaches the church to ask God the Holy Spirit to come on those who are sick.

Perhaps the biggest problem brought up by James for this study is the prayer of faith: 'And the prayer offered in faith will make the sick person well' (James 5:15). Does this imply that everyone can be healed of everything, always? While remembering Job and his long illness, who was praised by God and James for his perseverance, we now turn to Elijah, who is offered to us by James as the example of a person who uses the prayer of faith; the kind of prayer that will make a very sick man well.

The incident of praying for rain that James quotes helps us to understand the prayer of faith: 'After a long time, in the third year, the word of the Lord came to Elijah: "Go and present yourself to Ahab, and I will send rain on the land"' (1 Kings 18:1). Elijah prayed for rain because God told him he was going to send rain. This is the prayer of faith: praying for what God has said is going to happen, thereby demonstrating our faith in God, his authority and his power. It was 'powerful and effective'.

Praying or anointing in the name of the Lord is not a formula but an act of obedience that demonstrates faith in the Lord. When he says, 'I will send rain,' or 'I will heal,' and we pray for rain or healing, then we are exercising faith in the Lord. James wrote earlier that the person who prays this kind of prayer 'must believe and not doubt' (James 1:6). But if God has not said, 'I will send rain,' or 'I will heal,' as in the case of Job, then we do not have his authority to command healing in Jesus' name, and the prayer of faith is faith in our faith rather than the Lord, or 'words

without knowledge' that led to God's criticism of Job's comforters. Praying what God has told us to pray is the prayer
of faith.

In 1988, I found myself needing to use the prayer of faith
and the perseverance of Job when praying for Sonja in
South Africa.

14. A chronic illness

Johannesburg in May is beautifully autumnal with burn-
ing sun at lunch-time and freezing temperatures at night.
I was there as a member of the ministry team from England at a John Wimber 'Signs and Wonders' conference
held in the NEC (National Exhibition Centre), and I had
a big red badge. It was sleeveless shirts during the day,
with hamburgers and coke for lunch, and warm blankets
in the evening, with hamburgers and coke for tea. They
didn't serve anything else.

In the afternoon, I attended the healing seminar with
about 500 other people. However, before it started, while
I was sitting alone in a chair minding my own business,
God spoke to me. I only know it was God with hindsight;
at the time, it seemed like a lot of intrusive waffle going
on in my head that I couldn't remove.

'Do you see that lady sitting two rows in front of you,
Peter?' the thought seemed to be asking.

'Yes, Lord,' I replied silently.

'She has a chronic illness,' he continued, 'and I'd like
you to minister to her.'

'Fine,' I replied. 'That's why I'm here. I've got a big red
badge.'

The talk was long yet inspiring, with many stories of dramatic healings taking place in the power of the Spirit, but although the teaching was great, the appeal to come forward for healing was, by comparison, awesome. If you needed your toenails clipping, wore a hearing-aid, or were getting a bit thin on top, you would have found yourself leaping out of the chair and rushing forward for prayer.

'Will the ministry team come out first?' the speaker asked, and I knew as he said it that the numbers we had would be inadequate. I began to rise to my feet in order to help when an inner thought restrained me. 'Not you;' it seemed to say, 'stay where you are.'

'But Lord!' I protested in my innermost being. 'I'm a member of the ministry team. I've got a badge. They need me.'

God didn't argue; he just repeated himself, so I sat down and held my Bible in front of my ministerial licence lest someone in authority should commandeer my services.

Everyone in the room seemed to rush forward – first the badges then the delegates – everyone, that is, except me and the lady sitting two rows in front of me. *If she's got a chronic illness,* I began to think to myself, *why on earth. . .?*

'Up you get now,' interrupted the thought. 'Go and offer to pray for the lady. She has a chronic illness.'

At the time, I didn't even know what 'chronic' meant, thinking it was 'serious' rather than 'long-term', but in the end I obeyed the prompting. I thought I'd play the innocent Englishman abroad.

'Excuse me, Madam,' I began hesitatingly, in a Surrey accent, 'so sorry to bother you. I just thought God might be saying there was something wrong with you and you might like some prayer?'

'I have a chronic illness,' she said, 'and I'd love you to pray with me.'

Was God speaking? Was it by his authority, in his name, that the phrase *chronic illness* had slipped through my defence mechanisms? My faith was just starting to rise when, foolishly, I dared to ask another question.

'Hope you don't mind me asking,' I continued, as she began to stand up, 'but if you have a chronic illness, why did you not go forward?'

'It's like this, Peter,' she replied, having read my badge. 'I'm a well-known Christian in South Africa and I've had a pain in my stomach for 20 years. Everyone knows about it. I've been to the hospital four times but no one can find out what is wrong with me, despite numerous tests. All the world-famous healing-evangelists come to do meetings in Johannesburg, and everyone has had a go on me. John Wimber has already tried this week, so I thought I might sit this one out, as the ministry team look rather swamped.'

She looked at my very worried, wish-I-wasn't-here face, and then added, 'But if you'd like to have a go, that's fine.'

The words *No, I wouldn't. Get me out of here* formed in my mind but failed to surface due to fear. My faith level now disappeared six feet under, but sometimes obedience will do. I would have preferred to have a lady with me to help with the ministry, but as none was available I laid my hand gently on Sonja's forehead and asked

Father God, through Jesus, to send his Holy Spirit on her. Nothing happened. Didn't think it would.

'Shall we go and get a hamburger?' asked Sonja, when her eyes eventually opened.

'Shall we?' I responded somewhat rhetorically and tried to smile.

As God would have it, I bumped into Sonja the next day during ministry time and found myself asking her: 'Shall we have another go?'

'Shall we?' asked Sonja, with a smile. So we did. I invited the same Holy Spirit to come as on the previous day and the same nothing happened as before.

As God would have it, Sonja and I met again the following day, the last day of the conference. 'Shall we have one last go?' I asked.

'Shall we?' came the expected response, but with the smile of a fellow-sufferer. I think she was pleased I hadn't given up. Sometimes obedience and perseverance will do.

As I was about to pray, a lady from our ministry team walked past, so I stopped her. 'Could I borrow your hand?' I enquired politely. So, *this time* we put the lady's hand on Sonja's stomach and mine on her forehead, and *this time* the words came out slightly differently.

'Holy Spirit, I ask you to come on Sonja and show her if there is anything she needs to do,' I prayed, and then waited in silence. At last, there appeared to be some engagement with the Spirit, and after five minutes Sonja opened her eyes and said: 'I think there are two people I need to forgive.' This was God's communicated word,

which, when acted upon, gave us his authority for healing – something seemed to be happening this time. It was
no problem for a mature Christian like Sonja to do some
forgiving in her own mind, before I then asked God the
Father through Jesus to send his Holy Spirit in healing
power upon her.

The lady's hand heated up, Sonja's stomach heated up,
the pain went and we all had a hamburger. This is min-
istry-power. We believed God had spoken with a word to
set up the encounter and guide the ministry and then
released his spiritual gift of healing. The conference
finished, and I returned to England, but I received an
interesting letter from Sonja some three weeks later. See
what you make of this.

There was no pain for two days; then it all returned as
bad as it had ever been, but Sonja was encouraged. This
was her first two days free of pain for 20 years, so she
went to the hospital to tell them about it. Sonja had not
seen them for several years, so they took another X-ray
to go with the rest of their collection. The doctor hung
them all up on a line and showed them to his patient,
with occasional comments like, 'amazing', 'unbeliev-
able', 'how did this happen?' etc.

Unbeknown to me, Sonja had curvature of the spine
but in the most recent X-ray the spine was now straight.
'And now,' commented the doctor, 'we can see a little
dark spot which was previously hidden behind your
curved spine. That is your stomach pain. I know what it
is and I can cure it instantly with minor surgery, if you
will let me.' She did and he did.

Praise God for his Holy Spirit, who comes to us through Jesus with authority and power, and praise God for hospitals, doctors and nurses. Together, they make a great team.

Peter

We now come to the oft-quoted 1 Peter 2:24, which requires some attention. It is probably most helpful to look at the larger picture first, before we come down to the fine detail.

So far, we have looked at the first 222 chapters of the New Testament and found much evidence to suggest that it is the Spirit who heals but none to suggest that Jesus died for our sicknesses, or that the cross gives Christians a New Covenant right to healing. If we use Scripture to interpret Scripture, we need to be a little wary about suddenly finding one verse which seems to say the opposite, particularly as it is written by somebody who has already said in Acts that it is the Spirit who heals (Acts 10:38).

As we turn to Peter's letters and read through the whole of 1 Peter and indeed 2 Peter, we find that apart from possibly one word ('healed'), in 1 Peter 2:24, there is no mention of physical healing whatsoever. Unlike the letter of James, Peter's epistles are simply not about that subject. That is the wider context that needs to be borne in mind as we now look at the relevant two verses:

> He [Jesus] himself bore our sins in his body on the tree, so that we might die to sins and live for righteousness; by his wounds you have been healed. For you were like sheep going astray,

but now you have returned to the Shepherd and Overseer of your souls. (1 Peter 2:24–25)

What has Jesus died for? Our sins. Why? So that we might die to sins, live for righteousness and return to the Shepherd and Overseer of our souls. What is the context of these verses? Sin. How then have we been healed? From the penalty of sin, so that we might return to a relationship with God. Where is physical healing mentioned in these two verses? It isn't.

The phrase 'bore our sins' is used in the Bible to mean 'paid the penalty for our sins'. Unlike bearing someone's shopping when we take it from them so that we have it, Jesus did not become a sinner. Like the sacrificial lamb or the scapegoat, Jesus paid the penalty for our sins by dying in our place on the cross. The penalty for sin is separation from God, and the healing we receive, according to Peter, when we accept Jesus' death in our place by faith, is being put right with God. Our relationship with God is healed as we return to 'the Shepherd and Overseer of your souls' (1 Peter 2:25).

As we look in more detail at these two verses, it becomes even clearer that this is what Peter is communicating. Until verse 24 of chapter 2, Peter addresses his letter to '*you*' (all my italics):

- '*You* are a chosen people' (1 Peter 2:9).
- 'I urge *you*' (1 Peter 2:11).
- 'If *you* suffer' (1 Peter 2:20).
- '*You* were called' (1 Peter 2:21).
- '*You* should follow in his steps' (1 Peter 2:21).

Then, surprisingly, the writer uses '*our*' and '*we*' in verse 24: 'He himself bore *our* sins in his body on the tree, so that *we* might die to sins and live for righteousness' (1 Peter 2:24; my italics). There are two good reasons why Peter might have done this:

a) Being conscious of his own sin, like all good preachers he wants to identify himself with his audience. In contrast to Jesus, who 'committed no sin' (1 Peter 2:22), mentioned two verses earlier, he wants to make sure that his readers are aware that 'Peter, an apostle of Jesus Christ' (1:1) is himself a sinner.

b) The verses from Isaiah 53 that Peter is using write about 'our transgressions . . . our iniquities . . . we all, like sheep, have gone astray' (Isaiah 53:5–6), so Peter may simply be quoting Isaiah accurately.

Either way, it is then most interesting to see Peter returning to '*you*' for the second part of verse 24 and verse 25: 'By his wounds *you* have been healed' (1 Peter 2:24). This is particularly significant because it is a deliberate misquote from Isaiah 53:5, which reads: 'By his wounds *we* are healed.' There couldn't be a more direct and emphatic application of a verse: 'This is what has happened to you.' Notice also the change from 'are healed' to 'have been healed'. Scholars noticing the change frequently suggest that because of this the NIV semi-colon is in the wrong place, and the phrase that uses 'healing' really belongs to verse 25. Remembering that the original Greek manuscripts of the New Testament were all written in capital letters without any punctuation or numbered verses, William Barclay's translation of 1 Peter 2:24–25 seems to fit better and make more sense of the switch from '*we*' to '*you*':

He himself bore our sins in his body on the tree, that we might depart from sins and live to righteousness. With his stripes you have been healed, for you were straying away like sheep but now you have turned to the Shepherd and Watchman of your souls.[3] (1 Peter 2:24–25)

This rendering does not change the meaning but makes the plain sense of the verses more obvious. It is also better grammatically, and therefore more likely to be the original intention, i.e. not beginning a sentence with 'For'. The way Peter uses this verse is then clear. Jesus has made it possible by his wounds for the broken relationship with God to be healed.

The reason why many people like T. L. Osborn make so much of this verse is that Isaiah 52:13 – 53:12 does contain references to physical infirmity, as we saw earlier in Matthew 8:17. We shall come to this later in Chapter 6, but for now all I want to do is to register that neither Peter nor Matthew uses Isaiah in this way. In Matthew 8:17, the context is definitely physical healing but Matthew does not link it directly to the cross. In 1 Peter 2:24, the context is spiritual healing and Peter does link it to the cross. In our search we are still looking for a New Testament verse which links physical healing directly to the cross.

I have found that healing in the Epistles is seen as a gift of the Holy Spirit, who gives 'just as he determines' (1 Corinthians 12:11). Nowhere could I find that Jesus died for our sicknesses, or that healing was our New Covenant right because of the cross. Instead, I found in the Epistles that

---

[3] William Barclay, *The Daily Study Bible, Letter of James and Peter* (Edinburgh: The Saint Andrew Press 1958), p. 210.

four leading Christians became ill and some died (eventually all did), even though they and we are encouraged to pray to God for healing and good health. Through the cross of Christ we can be put right with God and receive the gift of his Holy Spirit, who is the one who heals.

In this next story, notice the combination of accepting Christ, repenting of sin, forgiveness, and being filled again and again with the Holy Spirit, with a touch of Job-like perseverance ever-present in the not-so-patient patient.

15. Healed in a broom cupboard

In the cold and the heat of the NEC in Johannesburg, the Lord helped me to find Sonja, and at the same conference the Lord helped Enri to find me.[4] Enri was a distinguished-looking wealthy Argentine, who had made his money in South Africa during its apartheid years, and at the end of one session he approached me and asked for prayer. Now well into his sixties, he had large prominent hearing-aids in both ears but in truth, even with them in place, he could hear very little.

On the same day that I asked Father God through Jesus to send his Holy Spirit on Sonja, I made the same request for Enri, with the same result. Nothing happened. On the next day, Enri found me and asked me to pray again for the healing of his ears, and the same nothing came again.

---

[4] In 1988, we did one week with John Wimber as the main speaker, in Johannesburg, and one week in East London with John Mumford as the main speaker. Happy days.

On the final day of the conference, Enri searched for me amongst the 2,000–3,000 delegates who were present; he couldn't find me, as I was probably praying for Sonja at the time, but he didn't give up. During the final session, while we were all worshipping God, Enri spotted me, walked across to where I was standing and tapped me on the shoulder.

'Peter,' he whispered. 'I've been looking for you all day. Will you pray with me one more time, please?'

'Sorry, Enri,' I replied. 'You're too late. We're not allowed to pray for people during the worship.'

'Oh please!' begged Enri. 'If I find a room for us to pray in, will you come with me?'

'Enri,' I responded. 'There *are* no rooms. We've both been here all week and we know there is just one large hall with no side rooms.'

'Well, if I find one,' persisted Enri, 'will you come with me?'

'Enri,' I said as loudly as I dared, 'there are no rooms, so if you find one I'll come with you.' With that, Enri toddled off to the back of the icy cold chamber to search for his imaginary room while the rest of us continued to worship the Lord.

About 15 minutes later, there was another tap on my shoulder and I sensed Enri was back. 'Peter,' he announced triumphantly, 'I've found one. Will you come with me now?'

What could I say? These days, I'd probably tell him to wait until the ministry time at the end of the meeting, as worshipping God and being under godly authority are very important, but at that moment I didn't feel I could say no to Enri a second time. A lady from our ministry team overheard our conversation and very kindly offered to come with us.

Together, we sneaked to the back, hoping John Wimber would not spot us from the stage, and quite quickly arrived at Enri's door in the corner of the hall.

'Here we are,' announced the wealthy Argentine, as he simultaneously pulled the door open. When he did so, all kinds of brooms and dustpans came clattering out, falling on top of us.

'Enri,' I said, with a quizzical look on my face, 'this is a broom cupboard.'

'I know,' he said apologetically, 'but it's all I could find. I'm sure the three of us will fit in if we squeeze up a bit.'

I was very glad there were no tabloid newspaper reporters observing a vicar getting into a broom cupboard with a rich Argentine and a pulchritudinous young lady at the back of a worship meeting. Who knows what headlines could have been written?

We clambered in and, with a mop up my left nostril and my right foot in a bucket, I asked God the Father through Jesus to send his Holy Spirit on Enri. The lady team member laid her hand gently on his shoulder and God came, and came, and came. People may come and go, but God, from a position of presence, comes and comes.

Enri's face registered the moving of the Spirit, and for something like 20 minutes his head was nodding, tears were flowing down his cheeks while power seemed to be present all over him. When God had finished with him, his eyes opened and there was quite a tale to tell.

'I'd no idea, Peter,' said Enri. 'I'd no idea that I'd hurt so many people in my lifetime. Jesus came and showed them all to me one at a time. On each occasion he asked me to repent, I apologised, Jesus forgave me and tears came down my face. I'm so sorry. So sorry. I'd no idea.' If we had just encouraged Enri to claim his healing because of the cross, Enri would not have received this beautiful ministry from Jesus. That's why I always ask God to do whatever he wants to do.

It seemed to be such a deep and profound time that neither of us asked Enri about his ears as we returned to the meeting. The next day, however, I was stood on a football pitch in Soweto, listening to John Wimber preach at an outdoor gathering, when I spotted Enri coming towards me across the turf with a lady on his arm. As he introduced me to his wife, I couldn't help noticing that Enri's large hearing-aids were missing.

'Good news and bad news,' he announced. 'The good news is that I can hear every word John Wimber is saying. The bad news is that I can hear every word my wife is saying.'

She gave him a friendly dig and a beaming smile as they wandered off arm-in-arm like a honeymoon couple. The forgiveness of sins, made possible by the cross of Christ, opened Enri up to the healing streams of God's Spirit. God is very good, and loves to come and heal us, even in a broom cupboard.

5

The Old Testament

In the Gospels, Acts of the Apostles and Epistles of the New Testament, physical healing is seen as the work of the Holy Spirit. Healing is not seen as a covenant right, nor is it linked directly to the cross of Christ. In the Old Testament, however, it is sometimes a covenant right, so naturally it is from the Old Testament that some preachers extract their verses about claiming our healing from God. We need, therefore, to examine the Old Testament carefully. This is what I found:

- Under the Old Covenant, most sicknesses were prescribed and described as punishments for sin: health and healing came as a reward for obedience, and could be claimed as a covenant right if the laws of the Old Covenant were kept.
- The Old Covenant is over.
- A New Covenant is prophesied in the Old Testament, which will bring:

    a) Forgiveness of sins.
    b) A right relationship with God.

c) The gift of the Holy Spirit.

d) Harmony with the created world, political peace and justice.

• Healing is a covenant right for most sicknesses under the Old Covenant, but under the New Covenant it is only a covenant right for all believers when Jesus returns.

Some of the Old Testament prophets were prophetically guided by God to heal in the power of the Holy Spirit, and so was my friend Marie (not her real name).

16. Ransomed, healed, restored, forgiven[1]

When I first met Marie, she was middle-aged, happily married with children, loved the Lord Jesus and was a pillar of the local church. Everyone loved talking to her and sharing their problems with her because she had two listening ears, a sensitive soul and the love of Jesus in her spirit – but it hadn't always been like that.

When she was conceived, Marie's mother didn't want her. When she was born, Marie's mother didn't want her. When she was old enough to be told, Marie's mother told her she didn't want her. Subsequently, Marie was badly abused and naturally enough grew up hating her family. She once said to me: 'Peter, unless you've suffered as I have, you've no idea how good it feels and tastes to really hate.' And she was right. I had not suffered as she had, and I had no idea.

As an adult, Marie was covered from head to toe with

---

[1] From the hymn 'Praise, My Soul, the King of Heaven', first verse, third line.

arthritis and in pain for all of the day and most of the night. However, also as an adult, Marie became acquainted with some Christians, attended church, and met the love of Jesus in his followers that she'd never met before. It was a real kingdom of God encounter. Marie did not know such a world existed, and she entered it gladly by becoming a Christian.

Some time later, as Marie was worshipping God at a service where the Holy Spirit was moving most powerfully, she sensed God speaking to her in her spirit.

'I'd like you to visit your mother after the service,' God seemed to say, 'and forgive her.'

Marie grew up hating her mother because it was her relatives and friends who had carried out the abuse and, although she knew it was happening, Mum did nothing to stop it. So, when Marie was asked by God to visit her mother and forgive her, it was no small request.

'But Father,' Marie protested in response to God's suggestion, 'you know I've tried before. If I ring, she puts the phone down. If I write, she ignores my letters. If I knock at the door, she shouts at me through the letter-box, and tells me to go away.' God didn't argue; he just repeated himself. 'I'd like you to visit your mum after the service, and forgive her,' he said.

'OK,' replied Marie this time. 'But you'll see I'm right.'

One of the reasons it is helpful to hear God speaking is timing. This time, when Marie rang the bell at her mother's house, the door opened and they fell into each other's arms. Over tea, her mother, now well into her seventies, told Marie that she too had been abused as a child but had previously told no one. Marie forgave her mum, and there were more hugs, tears and kisses before she left.

On the way home, Marie began to feel better as God's peace and power moved all over her. She still felt better several weeks later, everywhere except the big toe on her right foot, so she went to see her doctor. In due course, tests were carried out, and Marie was declared free from all the symptoms of arthritis. 'What about my big toe?' she then asked.

'That's not arthritis,' said the doctor, 'that's something else. I'll give you some cream for that.'

When Marie obeyed God, forgave her mother and the Holy Spirit moved powerfully upon her, she was completely healed of arthritis, but then she chose to do something else. Every morning for six months, when she woke up, Marie said out loud, 'I choose to forgive my mother today.'

When I asked her why she did this, she said to me: 'Having hated Mum so much for so long, I just knew that forgiving her had to be a new lifestyle, and not just a one-off prayer. I sensed in the Spirit that if I went back to hating then the arthritis would return.'

'But after six months you stopped?' I queried.

'I reckoned the new lifestyle was in by then,' she said, 'and the arthritis hasn't returned. I've been clear now for 15 years.'

Having become a Christian and received the Holy Spirit, Marie was able to discern God speaking to her by his Holy Spirit. This led Marie to forgive her mother in a deeper way than before, allowing the Holy Spirit to flow through her in healing power, and she was healed.

Healing in the Old Testament

There are a few healings in the Old Testament that fit the healing pattern we have found in the New Testament, and they mostly involve the prophets. Elijah, Elisha and Isaiah were anointed with the Holy Spirit just as Jesus and his disciples were anointed. They could hear the voice of God in a similar way to Jesus and his disciples, so whenever God chose to do healing and communicated it to the prophets, they experienced God's healing power at work.

A widow's son from Zarephath died of an illness (1 Kings 17:17). Elijah prayed, 'O Lord my God, let this boy's life return to him!' The Lord 'heard Elijah's cry, and the boy's life returned to him, and he lived' (1 Kings 17:21–22).

Elisha was used to restore the son of the Shunammite couple (2 Kings 4:18–37) and then Naaman, a commander in the army of the King of Aram, suffering from leprosy, came to see him. Elisha told Naaman to wash seven times in the Jordan; as the commander obeyed the command, he was healed and gave the glory to God (2 Kings 5:1–15). Unfortunately, this did not stop the Arameans from invading Israel, so Elisha prayed and they all became blind (2 Kings 6:18). Elisha prayed again and they were all healed (2 Kings 6:20).

On the negative side, it is worth noting that Elisha, one of those most used by God to do healing, unlike his predecessor Elijah, died of a disease. 'Now Elisha was suffering from the illness from which he died' (2 Kings 13:14).

King Hezekiah became seriously ill and Isaiah said to him: 'This is what the Lord says: Put your house in order, because you are going to die; you will not recover' (2 Kings

20:1). This is one of Isaiah's prophecies that did not come true because Hezekiah prayed and repented, God changed his mind, and the King of Judah was healed.[2] It is also worth noting that when God told Isaiah to inform the king of the good news, he said, 'Prepare a poultice of figs and apply it to the boil, and he will recover' (Isaiah 38:21). Faith and medicine seemed to go together even in Old Testament times.

The healing of Naaman in 2 Kings 5, referred to by Jesus in Luke, is similar to the healing of the paralytic in John 5. 'And there were many in Israel with leprosy in the time of Elisha the prophet, yet not one of them was cleansed – only Naaman the Syrian' (Luke 4:27). Similarly, at the pool of Bethesda 'a great number of disabled people used to lie – the blind, the lame, the paralysed' (John 5:3). Jesus healed 'one who was there' because he only did what he saw the Father doing (John 5:19), and Elisha healed only one person of leprosy, because that was what God was doing.

These stories fit the New Testament pattern: God's prophetic people hear his voice, pray according to his will, and sick or even dead people recover. The book of Job, mentioned briefly in the letter of James (James 5:11), also fits the New Testament pattern, but in a different way.

Job was a good man and God said, 'There is no-one on earth like him; he is blameless and upright, a man who fears God and shuns evil' (Job 1:8). Even so, Satan was given permission by God to afflict Job 'with painful sores from the soles of his feet to the top of his head' (Job 2:7). After much

---

[2] Some of God's prophecies are not so much about predicting the future as declaring what God intends to do. As in Dickens' *A Christmas Carol*, people can change the future through repentance and prayer. See also the book of Jonah.

suffering, and many false accusations, God eventually healed Job completely. At the end of the book, we are still not allowed to know why God allowed this to happen, other than being told that God is God; this is similar to the healing of the blind man in John 9. 'Who sinned, this man or his parents, that he was born blind?' asked the disciples. 'Neither,' replied Jesus (John 9:3). Neither Job nor the blind man was sick because of sin, and both had to suffer a long time until God healed them.

These are a few of the healing stories in the Old Testament which fit the pattern of healing in the New Testament as practised by Jesus and his disciples. However, under the Old Covenant, you may be surprised to discover, they are not in the majority.

Healing and the Old Covenant

When Moses was called by God to lead his chosen people Israel, God demonstrated to him his ability to use disease as a sign, a weapon or a judgement (Exodus 4:6–7). He then gave boils to the Egyptians who opposed his people (Exodus 9:8–12) and struck the Israelites with a plague when they committed idolatry (Exodus 32:35).

Having experienced God's ability and willingness to use sickness as a punishment, the people of Israel then entered into the covenant with God, and this was the teaching on sickness that accompanied it. 'If you pay attention to these laws and are careful to follow them . . . The Lord will keep you free from every disease' (Deuteronomy 7:12, 15; see also Exodus 15:26; 23:25). On the other hand, if they disobeyed God, this is what was promised to them:

If you do not obey the Lord your God and do not carefully follow all his commands and decrees I am giving you today, all
these curses will come upon you and overtake you: . . . The
Lord will plague you with diseases . . . The Lord will strike you
with wasting disease, with fever and inflammation . . . The
Lord will afflict you with the boils of Egypt and with tumours,
festering sores and the itch, from which you cannot be cured.
The Lord will afflict you with madness, blindness and confusion of mind . . . The Lord will afflict your knees and legs with
painful boils that cannot be cured, spreading from the soles of
your feet to the top of your head . . . these curses will come
upon you . . . because you did not obey the Lord your God.
(Deuteronomy 28:15, 21–22, 27–28, 35, 45)

Most of Leviticus chapters 13 and 14 considers infectious
skin diseases, and what should be done if a man recovers:
'Then the priest is to sacrifice the sin offering and make
atonement for the one to be cleansed from his uncleanness'
(Leviticus 14:19). The suggestion made by this elaborate rit-
ual is that these infectious diseases were a punishment from
God, and atonement was necessary to put things right.

The promise of healing, when sin had been committed
and sickness had come, became more clearly defined during
Solomon's reign:

When I . . . send a plague among my people, if my people, who
are called by my name, will humble themselves and pray and
seek my face and turn from their wicked ways, then will I hear
from heaven and will forgive their sin and will heal their land.
(2 Chronicles 7:13–14)

This is what happened to the Jews under the Old Covenant:
God struck them with a severe plague when they didn't like

the menu he had provided (Numbers 11:33), and God gave
leprosy to Miriam when she sinned against him (Numbers
12:1–15). The Lord struck the Israelites with another plague
when they 'grumbled against Moses and Aaron' (Numbers
16:48–49), and inflicted the people of Israel with poisonous
snakes when 'they spoke against God' (Numbers 21:4–9).
The Philistines were afflicted with tumours when they stole
the ark of the covenant (1 Samuel 5:12), and 70 men from
Beth Shemesh died because they looked inside it (1 Samuel
6:19). Michal became barren when she despised David's
worshipping of God (2 Samuel 6:23); David's newborn son
died when David committed adultery and murder (2
Samuel 12:13–14), and 70,000 people died of plague when
David sinned again by taking a census (2 Samuel 24:15).
God rewarded King Jeroboam with a withered hand for
opposing his prophet (1 Kings 13:4); he gave leprosy to
Gehazi, who sinned against him (2 Kings 5:20–27), and he
gave leprosy to King Uzziah, who also sinned against him (2
Chronicles 26:16–23). In the end, a most severe plague
came to many of God's people, and they were exiled from
Jerusalem because they'd sinned against God (Jeremiah
21:6; Ezekiel 5:12).

In contrast, the plague stopped when David repented of
his sin, prayed and offered sacrifices (2 Samuel 24:25); God
healed Jeroboam's withered hand when the king asked the
prophet to intercede for him (1 Kings 13:6); Naaman was
healed of leprosy when he obeyed God (2 Kings 5), and
King Hezekiah was healed of a fatal illness when he wept
and repented before God (2 Chronicles 32:24–26; see also
Isaiah 38).

In the famous story of Aaron's budding staff, the people

sinned; a plague came upon them; Aaron made atonement for them; the plague stopped, but 14,700 people died (Numbers 16:47–50). The Israelites became sick as a penalty of sin before atonement was made, but after atonement was made the people were no longer punished for that sin by sickness.

The majority of references to sickness in the Old Testament are seen as a penalty of sin from God, linked to the Old Covenant relationship between God and his people Israel. If they obey him, he will keep them free from all diseases, but if they disobey him he will cause sickness to come upon them. If they then repent, God will heal them. Thus, we have a punishment system designed to help the Jews to obey God's rules and remain his people. Under the Old Covenant, some healings, at least, could be seen as a covenant right, as long as the people turned from their sin and did not sin again.

17. The healing of the nations

The heart of God is such that even when nations sin badly against him he always wants to heal them. In 1988, I visited East London, beside the Indian Ocean in South Africa, during its apartheid years, where warm seas with a perfect climate producing lush vegetation made it a far cry from the East London I knew.[3]

While I was there, I visited Mdantsane, the second largest township in South Africa, though very much

---

[3] I was part of a Vineyard team led by John Mumford, doing meetings in East London, South Africa.

suffering at the time under a prejudiced regime. Even so, they entertained us gladly and generously, singing unaccompanied songs in perfect natural harmony whenever requested.

Afterwards, I dined at the house of some Christians in the town, some of the most courageous and sacrificial people I've ever met.

'We pray every day for apartheid to end,' they said, 'and for justice to come to those who live in the townships.'

'But,' I observed, 'the people of Mdantsane outnumber you thirty, forty, or fifty to one. If they are given their freedom, it is likely they'll march in here, take your houses and murder the lot of you.'

'Yes,' they replied. 'We know. It is very likely indeed, but we are prepared for that. What is right is what is right. What Jesus wants is what we pray for every day, and he wants liberation and equality for our neighbours.'

'Why don't you come to England and pray for them from there?' I asked.

'No,' they said. 'We are South African. We were born here; we live here; we work here; we pray here, and we die here. If we are to be martyred for the kingdom of Jesus Christ, so be it,' they concluded, 'but let justice flow like a never-ending stream.' I was deeply impressed.

That night, in their church of about 400 people, I invited the elders to join me on the stage. I believed God had been speaking to me during the afternoon about something special he was going to do, and he wanted the leaders to witness it. It turned out to be an occasion I'll always remember.

I asked God the Father through Jesus to send his Holy Spirit upon them. At that time, they hadn't experienced many people falling in the Spirit, and those who'd gone down had done so gently, as the floor appeared to swallow them up. What happened next was totally different from that. About 200 of the adults were poleaxed – suddenly, instantly, powerfully knocked straight to the floor. A few of the children present were a little alarmed seeing their mums and dads hit the floor as if they'd been shot, but the smile on their faces took the fear away, particularly as the adults were up very quickly in a minute or two. This was not ministry as such, but a demonstration of power.

What was going on? I wasn't too sure at the time, but much later I realised this was probably a revelation of God's presence and power, like the night they came to arrest Jesus when the antagonists were all knocked to the floor (John 18:6). I may be wrong, but I suspect there were a number of holy angels involved in this activity, as well as the Holy Spirit. It was as if God was saying, 'There are more with you than against you, and as you pray for apartheid to cease, my power is with you to help you and strengthen you. Don't be afraid; I am with you.'

History now records that when apartheid did come down, almost as quickly as those who fell to the floor, the people who prayed for justice in East London were not murdered. It is still a difficult and tense situation in South Africa, but God loves those who love him, and justice and freedom for the oppressed is part of his healing work.

The Old Covenant was broken and is over

God said to Noah: 'As long as the earth endures, seedtime and harvest, cold and heat, summer and winter, day and night will never cease' (Genesis 8:22). But God said through Jeremiah:

> I will take away their harvest . . . There will be no grapes on the vine. There will be no figs on the tree, and their leaves will wither. What I have given them will be taken from them. (Jeremiah 8:13)

And the famine came to Jerusalem, and the crops failed, and godly women cooked and ate their own children (Lamentations 4:9–10).

God said to Abraham:

> I will establish my covenant as an everlasting covenant . . . to be your God and the God of your descendants after you. The whole land of Canaan . . . I will give as an everlasting possession to you and your descendants. (Genesis 17:7–8)

This was fulfilled and renewed through Moses and Joshua, who sealed the covenant with blood and took the land (Exodus 24:8; Joshua 8:30–35). However, God said through Jeremiah: 'I will send the sword, famine and plague against them until they are destroyed from the land I gave to them and their fathers' (Jeremiah 24:10). And the Babylonians came, destroyed the Temple that symbolised the presence of God with his people, and took most of the survivors out of Canaan, away from the Promised Land, into exile (2 Kings 25:1–30).

God said to David: 'I have made a covenant with [you] . . . I will establish your line for ever' (Psalm 89:3–4).

But God said through Jeremiah: 'None will sit on the throne of David or rule any more in Judah' (Jeremiah 22:30). And when the Babylonians came, the kings were taken into exile too (Jeremiah 52:1–11).

The Old Testament – the Old Covenant – broke down; the people broke it. They lost the harvest, the Temple, the land and the Davidic king. The Old Covenant was over. Isaiah said it was broken: 'The earth is defiled by its people; they have disobeyed the laws, violated the statutes and *broken* the everlasting covenant' (Isaiah 24:5; my italics).

Jeremiah said it was broken:

They have returned to the sins of their forefathers, who refused to listen to my words. They have followed other gods to serve them. Both the house of Israel and the house of Judah have *broken* the covenant I made with their forefathers. (Jeremiah 11:10; my italics)

Ezekiel said it was broken: 'This is what the Sovereign Lord says: I will deal with you as you deserve, because you have despised my oath by *breaking* the covenant' (Ezekiel 16:59; my italics).

Hosea said it was broken: 'Put the trumpet to your lips! An eagle is over the house of the Lord because the people have *broken* my covenant and rebelled against my law' (Hosea 8:1; my italics).

The book of Lamentations is one of the most harrowing to read in the whole Bible. The city of Jerusalem has been destroyed; the Temple has been destroyed; charred bodies of former leaders are lying everywhere; most of those who survived have been taken away to Babylon, and those who are left are starving to the point of cooking and eating

their own children. Why did God allow such devastation –
double for all Israel's sins (Isaiah 40:2)? The biblical answer
seems to be this: *To declare to the Jews, and subsequently the
whole world, that the Old Covenant is over.*

18. Healed under the New Covenant

In February 2005, my wife Carol and I visited her
mother, Anne, in Spain, where she has lived for 18 years.
In the course of our conversation, my mother-in-law
remarked, 'Heather was healed of cancer in the chair
you're sitting in.'

'Can you give me some more details?' I enquired, as I
was writing this book at the time.

So Anne rang Heather, and this is what she said on the
phone:

> I noticed a round, red patch on the outside of my right calf,
> which I thought might have been a bite, but it didn't go
> away. It became redder, bigger and a hard lump developed
> underneath. A few days later, the skin broke, so I went to
> the doctor and he gave me some cream for three days. After
> that, he gave me some more cream but it became worse,
> looked very nasty indeed, almost ulcerated, so I returned to
> the medical centre. Eventually, the doctor told me it was a
> type of skin cancer that he would have to cut out, but in the
> meantime he applied more ointment and bandaged the
> whole area.

That Thursday afternoon, the local Christian ladies met
in Anne's lounge and prayed for Heather with the laying-
on of hands. 'Holy Spirit, come,' they prayed, 'and heal
Heather's leg.' They waited, and he came – they all felt

his presence, his love and his power. On the Monday, Heather returned to see the doctor, with her husband, and this is what she told Anne: 'In the consulting room, with my husband present, the doctor removed the bandage, and his jaw literally dropped. "But it's nearly healed," he said. "Praise the Lord," I said in Spanish. I told him that some Christian friends had prayed for healing, and he said, "Keep praying."'

'And how is it now?' asked Anne.

'Just a minute,' replied Heather. There was silence for a few moments while Heather had a look at her leg before she spoke again.

'It's fine. No sign. No mark. No lump.'

'Can Peter put it in his book?' enquired Carol's mum.

'Of course!' she said. 'Anything you wish for God's glory.'

The Holy Spirit came in love and power, and Heather's leg was healed.

The implications of the broken covenant

The implications of the broken covenant are vital for understanding healing in the Bible, and especially when applying it to ourselves for today. It means that the punishment system which God put in place to go with the Old Covenant is over. It means that sickness is no longer a punishment from God for sin, and that Old Covenant rights to healing no longer apply.

The writer to the Hebrews wrote that the Old Covenant was over:

> For if there had been nothing wrong with the first covenant, no place would have been sought for another. But God found fault with the people . . . By calling this covenant 'new', he has made the first one obsolete. (Hebrews 8:7–8, 13)

I have heard preachers using verses from the Old Covenant to claim that God wants to heal everyone today, and that we have a covenant right to healing. They probably need to look up 'obsolete' in the dictionary. In mine, it says, 'No longer in use – discarded – out of date.' [4] The Old Covenant was broken, is over and no longer applies. If we want to know what is relevant for today, we need to look instead at the New Covenant.

And the ending of the Old Covenant explains why the writers of the Gospels, Acts and Epistles do not say we have a covenant right to healing; they knew the old system was over. It is also why they were keen to show that sickness was no longer a penalty for sin (e.g. John 9:3; Acts 9:36–37; James 5:11, 15). The blood Jesus shed at the cross is the seal of the New Covenant that renders the Old Covenant obsolete because we now have a new punishment system in place. Jesus has paid the penalty of sin, which means that those who enter the New Covenant through the blood of Christ are forgiven and escape the penalty of sin because the old punishment system no longer applies. After the cross, sickness is no longer seen as the penalty of sin, and nowhere in the New Testament is sickness healed automatically as a result of sins being forgiven (see Chapter 7).

If all illnesses today were a punishment for sin from God, then sick people would need a priest rather than a physician.

---

[4] Collins English Dictionary.

But what we find is that injections, medicines and operations work equally well on saints and sinners. The ending of the Old Covenant prepared the way for the advancement of medical science, and the advancement of medical science confirms that the Old Covenant is over. Sickness as a punishment system linked to God's covenant has gone, and what we need to look at in terms of God's supernatural healing for today is the New Covenant. What we have found is that under the New Covenant, sealed by the blood of Christ, we all have access to the one Holy Spirit, and it is he who heals.

19. Healed from the tablets

On one of the courses we used to run in our church, I asked God the Father through Jesus to send his Holy Spirit upon us and do whatever he wanted to do. During the ministry time that followed, a lady developed a very bad headache and people began to pray with her; however, as they did so and laid on hands, the headache became much worse. When I arrived on the scene, there was obvious distress on her face so I immediately prayed, 'Holy Spirit, please help Lucy to see Jesus.'

I always pray this prayer when a person is in distress, but I stop the ministry if they continue to suffer and do not see Jesus. We never describe to them what they ought to see, as that is a visualisation technique which can be equated with idolatry – i.e. putting an image of 'god', which may not be from 'God', into their minds. On this occasion, however, almost immediately, as the Spirit moved upon her, Lucy began to see Jesus on the cross.

It was a close-up of his face, showing something of the intense agony and suffering our Lord went through as he took our sin upon himself. Slowly, Lucy began to see more of the picture, as if the camera was moving along the beam to where one of his wrists was nailed. There, beneath the pierced flesh, fixed also to the cross by a nail, was a little bottle of tablets. Lucy's husband had suffered from heart trouble, and the day he died (suddenly, of a heart attack), Lucy could not remember giving him his pills.

Being a mature Christian, Lucy knew what God was saying, what needed to be done and what was causing the headache: Jesus had died for her sins on the cross, but she was still carrying false guilt in her own body and suffering from the scars. She gave it to Jesus, accepted his forgiveness, forgave herself and then, as God's Spirit continued to flow upon her, the headache went.

This is as close as I have come to experiencing someone healed by Jesus dying for them, but there are subtle differences between this and the classic claims. Although *psychologically* helped by the cross in a very direct way, *theologically* it looks more like this: Jesus died for Lucy's sins which in turn were the root cause of her headache, and when she accepted Christ's death in her place for her sins and received his forgiveness, she was healed. It was the Holy Spirit, however, who was at work on this occasion bringing the vision of Jesus on the cross to her, showing her that, as Christ had forgiven her, it was a sin not to forgive herself and, as his power and presence helped her to forgive herself, she was healed.

The New Covenant is prophesied in the Old Testament

Jeremiah not only said the Old Covenant was over but that a New Covenant was on its way:

'The time is coming,' declares the Lord, 'when I will make a new covenant with the house of Israel and with the house of Judah. It will not be like the covenant I made with their fore fathers when I took them by the hand to lead them out of Egypt, because they broke my covenant, though I was a husband to them,' declares the Lord. 'This is the covenant that I will make with the house of Israel after that time,' declares the Lord. 'I will put my law in their minds and write it on their hearts. I will be their God, and they will be my people. No longer will a man teach his neighbour, or a man his brother, saying, "Know the Lord," because they will all know me, from the least of them to the greatest,' declares the Lord. 'For I will forgive their wickedness and will remember their sins no more.' (Jeremiah 31:31–34)

These are the benefits of the New Covenant that Jeremiah outlined for us:

- It will be one that cannot be broken (Jeremiah 31:32).
- God's law will be written on our minds and hearts (Jeremiah 31:33).
- We will all have a right relationship with God, from the least of us to the greatest (Jeremiah 31:33–34).
- Our sins and wickedness will be forgiven (Jeremiah 31:34).

Jeremiah is not the only prophet, however, to speak of the New Covenant. Here are the Old Testament prophetic verses I have found that seem to refer to the New Covenant, listed with the benefits that are promised:

Isaiah
- 42:6   Those under the New Covenant will provide 'light to the Gentiles'.
- 54:10   They will receive assurance, love, peace and compassion.
- 55:3   It will be an everlasting covenant of love.
- 59:21   God's Spirit will be on them and his words will not depart from their mouths – for ever.
- 61:8   There will be justice.

Ezekiel
- 16:62   They will know that God is the Lord.
- 34:25   There will be peace and safety.
- 37:26–27 A covenant of peace – God's dwelling-place – will be with them.

Hosea
- 2:18   Peace and safety – harmony with nature.

Malachi
- 3:1   A messenger will prepare the way for the covenant.

Before we look in detail at the way Jesus has fulfilled these prophecies, we need to note that the New Covenant will be made 'with the house of Israel and with the house of Judah' (Jeremiah 31:31). We Gentile Christians are grafted on to the Jewish people who enter the New Covenant; we do not replace them (Romans 11:16–24). Christianity does not fit on to British culture and tradition, or American, African, Greek or Roman, but to the Jewish way of life that was given to them by God. Theirs is the only God-revealed way of life; all the others are man-made and maybe at times even demon-inspired. This is why the Old Testament is so important to us; it not only helps us to understand, receive and explain the work of Jesus, but it also shows us what aspects of our culture and tradition need to be challenged and changed.

Jeremiah promised the New Covenant to the Jewish people but the writer of the letter to the Hebrews quotes his prophecy verbatim and explains how it is for all Christians (Hebrews 8:6–13): 'Christ is the mediator of a new covenant, that those who are called may receive the promised eternal inheritance' (Hebrews 9:15).

We know from the rest of the New Testament that all Christians, Jews and Gentiles, are called by God, as expressed in Paul's letter to the Romans:

> Through him [Jesus Christ our Lord] and for his name's sake, we received grace and apostleship to *call* people from among all the Gentiles to the obedience that comes from faith. And you also are among those who are *called* to belong to Jesus Christ. To all in Rome who are loved by God and *called* to be saints . . . (Romans 1:5–7; my italics)

Therefore, we have scriptural authority for applying Jeremiah's prophecy to believing Gentiles as well as to believing Jews (see also Isaiah 42:6). Here is my understanding of the way Jesus has fulfilled the Old Testament prophecies about the New Covenant:

An everlasting covenant from both sides

A covenant that cannot be broken is very helpful. The Old Covenant was an everlasting covenant from God's side only – his people broke their side of the bargain – but the New Covenant is made between God and the perfect man Jesus. As the letter to the Hebrews explains to us, the New Covenant is everlasting on both sides of the fence because it does not depend on us. The New Covenant cannot be broken because Jesus has offered the perfect life and perfect sacrifice on our behalf, once and for all time. If we trust in Jesus and not in ourselves we cannot lose – for ever.

Forgiveness

Malachi predicted that a messenger would prepare people for the New Covenant. This was fulfilled by John the Baptist, who told people to prepare for the coming Messiah by repenting of their sins (Luke 1:76–77; Matthew 3:1–3). Jeremiah does not seem to have foreseen the sacrifice of the Suffering Servant which we find in Isaiah 53, but without understanding how, he speaks about the forgiveness of sins and a right relationship with God, which we now know is made possible by the cross of Christ. Jesus himself links his death on the cross to the New Covenant and the forgiveness of sins: 'This is my blood of the covenant, which is poured out for many for the forgiveness of sins' (Matthew 26:28).

The Holy Spirit

The Spirit promised in Isaiah 59 is obviously the way God's Law will be written on our minds and hearts, and also the way we will all know God, from the least to the greatest.

According to the Acts of the Apostles, and Paul's letters, it is the Spirit who initiates the taking of light to the Gentiles, and gives assurance, love and peace. It is also worth noting that Ezekiel's word about the covenant in chapter 37 comes immediately after the vision of the dry bones, when God says: 'I will put my Spirit in you and you will live' (Ezekiel 37:14).

Jesus' second coming

Some of the prophecies about harmony with nature, political peace, safety and justice will be fulfilled when Jesus comes again. For now, we live in the times when Jesus prophesied there would be 'wars and rumours of wars' (Matthew 24:6). It is, however, the New Covenant that secures our eternal future in a place of peace, harmony and justice (Revelation 21:1–8).

The cross

The Old Covenant was sealed with blood, and so was the New Covenant, and the cross of Christ is the place where sinners can receive the forgiveness of sins. According to the New Testament, what is offered to us through the cross is the forgiveness of sins, a right relationship with God, and the gift of the Holy Spirit – the same things the prophets foretold would come with the New Covenant, hundreds of years before Christ.

Isaiah

The book of Isaiah is the one book in the Old Testament that prophesies physical healing as part of the New Covenant, and requires our special attention.

I will keep you and will make you to be a covenant for the people and a light for the Gentiles, to open eyes that are blind, to free captives from prison and to release from the dungeon those who sit in darkness. (Isaiah 42:6–7; see also Isaiah 49:8–13)

This is similar to Isaiah 61:1, and particularly the Septuagint version quoted by Jesus.

The Spirit of the Lord is on me, because he has anointed me to preach good news to the poor. He has sent me to proclaim freedom for the prisoners and recovery of sight for the blind, to release the oppressed, to proclaim the year of the Lord's favour. (Luke 4:18–19)

As we have already seen, this healing is linked to the coming and anointing of the Holy Spirit. It is a prophecy that these things will happen rather than a promise of healing for all, but there is more than just this in Isaiah. If we abandon the idea of looking solely for the places where the word 'covenant' appears, we can find two other places where the benefits of the New Covenant are promised. In Isaiah 53, physical healing is linked to the sacrificial death of the Suffering Servant, and Isaiah 65 promises healing for all who believe – the glorious climax of the work of Messiah.

Do we then have a promise of New Covenant healing for all in the book of Isaiah? Indeed we do, but we need to notice where it comes in the scheme of things. Look at these messianic prophecies from Isaiah, and note particularly the order in which they come. (Preachers may feel a sermon series coming on.)

• The Christ is conceived (Isaiah 7:14).
• The Christ is born (Isaiah 9:6–7).

- The Christ is anointed (Isaiah 11:2).
- The Christ heals the sick (Isaiah 35:5–6).
- The Christ dies for our sins (Isaiah 53:8).
- The Christ is raised from the dead (Isaiah 53:10–11).
- When the Christ comes to Jerusalem, the Spirit will come, and they shall prophesy (Isaiah 59:20–21).
- The Spirit comes and the good news of the Christ is proclaimed (Isaiah 61:1–2).
- The Christ comes to judge (Isaiah 63:1–4; see also Revelation 19:11–16).
- As a result, there will be new heavens and a new earth, that will look like this:

Behold, I will create new heavens and a new earth.
The former things will not be remembered, nor will they
    come to mind.
But be glad and rejoice for ever in what I will create,
for I will create Jerusalem to be a delight and its people a joy.
I will rejoice over Jerusalem and take delight in my people;
the sound of weeping and of crying will be heard in it no
    more.

Never again will there be in it
an infant who lives but a few days,
or an old man who does not live out his years;
he who dies at a hundred will be thought a mere youth;
he who fails to reach a hundred will be considered accursed.
(Isaiah 65:17–20; see also Isaiah 66:22–24 and Revelation
    21:1–4)

The Isaiah Messiah is linked to healing in Isaiah 35:5–6; 42:7; 53:4; 61:1 (Septuagint), but only in Isaiah 65:17–20 is there healing for all, for ever, as a right. It is the purpose of

God towards which the whole book of Isaiah moves and, indeed, its somewhat upgraded repetition in Revelation makes it the climax of the whole Bible. One obvious upgrade is the fact that Isaiah visualises people dying at a ripe old age, whereas John in Revelation sees the death of death itself. But in both Isaiah and Revelation, all this comes after the judgement – after the return of Christ (Isaiah 63:1–4; Revelation 19:11–16). There are important implications to learn from this.

In the new heavens and the new earth, God makes 'everything new' (Revelation 21:5). 'No more', 'never again', 'no longer' (Isaiah 65:19, 20, 22) will there be any more pain, crying, sickness or death (Revelation 21:1–7). This is our New Covenant right. The clear implication is that as this is 'new' then it will not have happened before. When the judgement has taken place, when the Messiah returns, when the new heavens and the new earth are created, then there will be a New Covenant right to healing for all believers, but not before. Until then, the Holy Spirit enables some to be healed (Isaiah 35:5–6; 42:7; 53:4; 61:1), but not all. This matches the New Testament perfectly. In the Gospels, Acts and Epistles, the Holy Spirit enables some people to be healed, but all eventually die. In Revelation, in the new heavens and the new earth, there will be a New Covenant right for all to be healed when there will be no more death, but not until then.

The Old Testament prophets did not foresee the Messiah coming twice, and this is why John the Baptist began to have some doubts (Matthew 11:2–3). Jesus fulfilled some of the prophecies but not all of them. Consequently, some Jews today have difficulty believing in Jesus – because some of the prophecies, such as Isaiah 65 about the new heavens and the new earth, have not yet happened, and will only be fulfilled when Jesus returns. People who try to claim New Covenant rights to healing for today are making a similar mistake. According to Isaiah 65 and Revelation 21, healing as a covenant right for all believers will only come to pass when they enter the New Jerusalem, after the judgement of Jesus. Then, all who believe and trust in the Lord Jesus Christ will have their robes washed by the blood of the Lamb (Revelation 7:14; 22:14), the seal of the New Covenant, and enter the throne-room of grace by right (Revelation 22:14), where the covenant rainbow that encircles the throne will remind them of God's covenant love (Genesis 9:12–17; Revelation 4:3).

I shall look in detail at the Isaiah 53 passage in the next chapter, but here is a story that has three new creations in one.

20. A new creation

On Sunday 13th February 2005, my friend Geoff preached at St Barnabas Church, Bearwood, one of our three churches. Geoff is a vicar in Wales, and this is one of the stories he told us.[5]

One day, the receptionist at the local doctor's rang up in a state of distress. 'It's Jamsie,' she burbled between sobs. 'He's got lung cancer. . . inoperable. . . just a few months to live . . . could you go round?'

Of course! That's a vicar's job. Terence James was a

---

[5] Geoff Waggett is now the vicar at Ebbw Vale.

heavy-smoking, regular-drinking, fun-loving, soul-of-the-party type in his early forties who'd hardly ever been to church in his life. The X-ray had shown one clear white lung and one completely dark diseased lung, which meant that Jamsie was on his way out, shortly. So Geoff went round.

When he entered the room, there was an atmosphere of death everywhere. Terence's wife, Marilyn, was sobbing in the corner; lifeless dust covered most things, and some brown carnations that had once been white rested in a bone-dry vase that hadn't seen moisture for days.

Terence poured out his sorry tale while Geoff listened and sympathised as best he could. 'Shall I say a prayer with you?' he offered, when there was nothing else he could think of to say, and a weary nod gave him permission. Geoff said a simple prayer, asking God the Father through Jesus to send his Holy Spirit on Terence to do whatever he wanted to do and, after waiting for some time and blessing what the Father was doing, he then left.

As he entered the sunlight once more, the Welsh vicar paused to breathe in new life, allowing the smell of death to fade, before he went on his way with another prayer in his heart for the James family.

A few days later, after several tests at the hospital, Jamsie rang to say that both lungs were now totally clear, and many thanks for the prayer. Geoff was more astounded than Terence and was about to leap over the moon, when his new-found friend continued: 'But that's not the most amazing thing;' he said, 'the best bit was waiting for us when we came downstairs, the morning after your prayer. The carnations are now white again,' he declared, 'standing upright and full of life.'

Terence came to the Lord through his healing and is still alive today, 13 years later. I suppose a burglar could have broken in during the night and replaced the dead flowers with new ones, but Terence and Geoff and I think God did it. A new lung, a new heart, and a renewed bunch of flowers. To God be all the glory!

6

The Isaiah Messiah

In Matthew 8:17, the writer quotes Isaiah 53:4 to show that the Suffering Servant deals with sickness, but there is no mention of the cross. In 1 Peter 2:24, the writer quotes Isaiah 53:5 to show that the death of the Suffering Servant deals with sin, but there is no mention of physical sickness. But here in Isaiah 53 (by which I always mean Isaiah 52:13 – 53:12), sickness and sin, healing and the death of Christ, come together.

This is the passage of Scripture most often quoted by those who proclaim that Jesus died for our sicknesses, or that we have a covenant right to healing because of the cross. I therefore looked at the whole passage very carefully, and this is what I found.

- Jesus fulfilled the role of the Suffering Servant.
- The Suffering Servant takes away the penalty of sin.
- The Suffering Servant takes away sicknesses and pains that are a penalty for sin.
- There is a place in the New Testament which links physical healing directly to the cross of Christ, and those who

enter the New Covenant by the blood of Christ have a right to that healing, when Jesus returns.

Life after death

Most people live and die, but Isaiah informs us that the successful Suffering Servant will die and live: 'my servant will succeed in his task' (Isaiah 52:13 GNB); 'after the suffering of his soul, he will see the light of life' (53:11); 'he will be raised and lifted up and highly exalted' (52:13). The life, death, resurrection and sending of the Holy Spirit from heaven accomplished by Jesus Christ is the greatest success story ever told, and it is continued today by his Spirit. Every time someone is healed or raised from the dead in the name of Jesus, by the Spirit of Jesus, then Jesus is lifted up, highly exalted and our faith in him is increased. It helps us to believe that Jesus has power over life and death, he is still alive, his Spirit is with us, and that he is seeing the 'light of life' (Isaiah 53:11). That is why I have put all my raising-from-the-dead stories in this chapter – to help us believe in the success of Jesus, the Suffering Servant, in whose name and by whose authority and power they were raised. Please note that these are resuscitations from death and not resurrections: like Lazarus and Jairus's daughter, they came back from death rather than going through it as Jesus did.

21. Raised at two-and-a-half

In November 1981, while living in South Africa, Mike and Linda attended a conference led by Bill Burnett, then the Archbishop of Cape Town. It was a time of great blessing when both of them were prayed for to be filled with the Holy Spirit for the first time.

The next day, friends came to visit them for a barbecue which took place on the far side of the house and, after lunch, the children went off to amuse themselves while the parents were busy chatting. The adults assumed the older ones were looking after the younger ones, not knowing that someone had failed to close the door which led to the swimming-pool. Quite unexpectedly, a strange kind of hush came over the whole place, and Linda sensed something was seriously wrong. Suddenly, there was a scream; instinctively, they raced to the pool.

Courtland, aged two-and-a-half, had been lying on the bottom of the pool for something like half an hour when the older children spotted him there. His mother Linda was a trained Red Cross swimming instructor; she knew that whenever oxygen is withheld from the brain there is very little time before damage occurs, and she knew such time had long since passed.

The adults helped the other children to pull Courtland from the pool and lay him on the side, but the little body was cold, grey, hard and clammy. Mike joined Linda but they couldn't get Courtland's mouth open to try resuscitation, so Linda ran off to ring for help; on the way, she silently mouthed a very brave prayer: 'Lord Jesus, take him or heal him completely.'

Mike eventually forced his little son's mouth open and for 15 minutes tried breathing into him without any sign of success, before giving up for a short while. Linda returned and, with Mike, prayed that God would restore

Courtland to them. Mike began breathing into Courtland again, and suddenly his son started to breathe. They wrapped the little body in a towel but, disappointingly, the only sign of life in their son was an incoherent sound gurgling from his mouth, like those that come from the most severely brain-damaged children.

They took their little boy to the hospital, and while the medical practitioners pumped the water out of the child's lungs, Mike called their vicar, Hugh; he asked for Bill and Sheila Burnett and the church to begin praying for Courtland's healing, in the name of Jesus. Hugh took their elder son Matthew to the vicarage and then returned to the hospital, but when he arrived he was greeted with bad news – Courtland's temperature was rising, and they were now afraid of pneumonia. A little while later, a doctor came out and became confrontational, wanting the parents to go home, but fortunately Hugh stepped in, saying they would wait and under no circumstances would they leave until they were ready to do so. It was obvious the doctors didn't think Courtland was going to improve, and were thinking of taking him off the machine which was aiding his breathing.

After much prayer and anxiety and feelings of guilt, the temperature began to drop, and Courtland was taken to the children's ward, where Mike and Linda were allowed to see him. This is what Linda wrote down for me:

> He looked so still and quiet as we came into the ward. He was in a cot with white bedclothes on. I remember leaning over and looking at him through the bars of the cot. I whispered his name. He sort of slightly moved his closed eyes. He

just didn't talk, I am sure, from the suction and the dryness
of his throat. Instead, he held up his little hands to show us
the old children's rhyme: 'Here is the church, here is the
steeple. Open the door and see all the people.' This was a
familiar game we played – Jesus' signature was all over it.
We knew, but knew, that Jesus had saved him and healed
him completely.

At 8 am the following morning, Mike and Linda were
woken by the persistent ringing of a phone, which led
them to think it was important and urgent. It was the
hospital: would they please come and collect Courtland
immediately, as he was tearing up the nursery?

I played chess with Courtland a few years ago, and
found myself up against an intelligent brain; I met him
again in California, where I was able to experience the
joy of seeing how strong, athletic and comfortable he'd
become in the swimming-pool. Sometimes God raises the
dead through Jesus, even today. To him be all the glory!

The relevance of Isaiah 53

There are three clear New Testament references which
make the connection for us between Jesus and the Suffering Servant of Isaiah 53:

> When evening came, many who were demon-possessed were
> brought to him, and he drove out the spirits with a word and
> healed all the sick. This was to fulfil what was spoken through
> the prophet Isaiah: 'He took up our infirmities and carried our
> diseases.' (Matthew 8:16–17)

The eunuch was reading this passage of Scripture: 'He was led like a sheep to the slaughter, and as a lamb before the shearer is silent, so he did not open his mouth. In his humiliation he was deprived of justice. Who can speak of his descendants? For his life was taken from the earth.'

The eunuch asked Philip, 'Tell me, please, who is the prophet talking about, himself or someone else?' Then Philip began with that very passage of Scripture and told him the good news about Jesus. (Acts 8:32–35)

Christ suffered for you . . . He himself bore our sins in his body on the tree, so that we might die to sins and live for righteousness; by his wounds you have been healed. (1 Peter 2:21, 24)

The New Testament quotes Isaiah 53:4, 5 and 7, and applies it to Jesus, so we have scriptural authority for claiming that the role of the Suffering Servant is fulfilled by Jesus. We can also see from these three New Testament quotations that Isaiah 53 is about sickness and healing (Matthew 8:16–17), the death of Christ (Acts 8:32–35, 1 Peter 2:24) and sin (1 Peter 2:24). Isaiah 53 is therefore very relevant to this book.

The context of Isaiah 53

In Chapter 5, I argued that healing is a covenant right under the Old Covenant but not under the New Covenant, until Jesus returns. This is a vital conclusion for understanding Isaiah 53, particularly in relation to healing.

From Isaiah 40 onwards, the people of Israel come back, or are coming back, from exile in Babylon. The Old Covenant is broken and over (Isaiah 24:5), but God has not finished with his chosen people, the Jews (Isaiah 41:9). He now gives his servant Israel two tasks and says that a New Covenant will come into being in relation to these tasks:

> I, the Lord, have called you in righteousness; I will take hold of your hand.
> I will keep you and will make you to be a covenant for the people and a light for the Gentiles. (Isaiah 42:6)

God calls his servant Israel to:

a) be God's people;
b) be a light to the Gentiles.

And he promises to help them: 'But now listen, O Jacob, my servant . . . I will pour out my Spirit on your offspring, and my blessing on your descendants' (Isaiah 44:1, 3). God's servant, Israel, will receive the Holy Spirit to help them be God's people and a light to the Gentiles. Later, God, through Isaiah, links this promise of the Holy Spirit with the New Covenant (Isaiah 59:20–21).

But for now, as we come to Isaiah 53, having worked our way through the other servant passages, we realise that many people have tried to be God's servant and not been successful. The nation of Israel has tried (Isaiah 42:1–7); the faithful remnant of Israel has tried (49:1–7); the prophets have tried (Isaiah 50:4–11) but all have gone astray like lost sheep and failed (Isaiah 53:6). At last, after hundreds of years of trying, a servant appears in Isaiah 53 who will be successful, according to God.

My friend Edmund certainly found that the Suffering Servant was successful.

22. Raised at 19

Edmund had known illness most of his short life, but despite this he came to faith in Jesus Christ and was keen to serve him as best he could, with whatever years God gave to him.

At 19, he was accepted for training in the Church Army and within a year found himself in Manchester, where he stayed with a Christian landlady. During his time there, he was rushed into hospital and died.

'I'd fought illness all my life,' Edmund told me when he stayed in our vicarage, 'but this time my willingness for the fight appeared to have gone and I gave up striving.' At this moment, he found himself separated from his body but still attached by a silver cord (Ecclesiastes 12:6). When his body died, the cord was severed and Edmund at last felt free from pain and suffering.

He watched as the medical staff discovered his death, examined what he'd left behind and then laid out the body behind the screens, but he lost touch with his physical form when they wheeled it away to the mortuary. For some time, he experienced the sensation of floating nowhere in particular, until the sound of voices made him aware he was coming into the presence of others. As his eyes focused on his new surroundings, he recognised members of his family who had already died in the faith of Christ, gathering round him, welcoming him, and affirming him.

After a while, Jesus appeared and walked towards him to welcome him. As he held out his hands and Edmund saw the scars of the Suffering Servant, he remarked:

'They must be the only man-made things in heaven.' Jesus and the saints smiled, and Edmund was delighted to know there was humour in heaven. Interestingly, in this story, Edmund was completely healed when in heaven, but Jesus was not! You could say that Jesus' scars took away Edmund's pain and sickness.

Edmund then saw a dark tapestry depicting his life from beginning to end, which reminded him of certain events that began to make sense for the first time. He noticed particularly how the good moments, like accepting Christ as his Saviour, were very brightly coloured and stood out beautifully against the dark background of his pain and suffering.

As they were chatting about this, the stillness of heaven was dramatically shattered by a rasping voice. It was the voice of his landlady praying, 'Don't let him die, Lord. He's got a work to do for you.' Jesus turned to Edmund and said: 'You'll have to go back.'

Edmund didn't want to go back, but Jesus turned him round, gave him the gentlest of pushes and once more Edmund found himself going through a floating sensation until he came to in his body, in the mortuary. He'd been dead three hours, and his death certificate (which they would allow him to keep) had already been issued. As he sat up, he gave the mortician something of a fright and had to minister to him for a short while.

Such death or near-death experiences are always difficult to validate but, in this case, there was one helpful piece of objective evidence. All the time this had been going on, his landlady had been on her knees beside her bed over a mile away from the hospital, praying out loud, 'Don't let him die, Lord. He has work to do for you.'

Whenever I've told this story before, I've always stopped there but, as this is a book about healing, I will relate what happened next. You'd expect to be informed that Edmund went and got his things, walked back to his digs, and carried on. But he didn't.

When Edmund returned to his body, he was still critically ill, and the mortician had to summon medical help very quickly. For a week, Edmund hung between life and death, but now that his spirit had received ministry he was up for the fight. The body of Christ in the form of his deceased relatives had affirmed him (Scripture forbids us to talk to the dead but presumably when we are dead ourselves it is OK); Jesus had welcomed him; reasons for his suffering had been shown to him, and the love and compassion of his landlady had reached him – she really wanted him to live. All of this now made the battle worthwhile, and eventually Edmund won through.

James wrote that 'the body without the spirit is dead' (James 2:26); when Jesus committed his spirit into God's hands, his body died (Luke 23:46); when the spirit of Jairus's daughter returned to her body, she lived (Luke 8:55). This means that our spirit holds the key to life and death over our bodies, so that ministering to our spirits, as in the ministry Edmund received, is important if we want to be healed when we are sick. It also means that allowing our spirits to be filled again and again with the Holy Spirit is most helpful. This will often bring 'life to our mortal bodies' (Romans 8:11).

When I last saw Edmund, preaching in our pulpit, he was well into his sixties, having done work for Jesus in the Church Army all his adult life, and his spirit was very much alive and full of the Holy Spirit. Since then, he has retired but is still working for Jesus, even in retirement. He kindly checked the details of this story for me and gave me permission to use it. The Suffering Servant is still being successful.

Isaiah 52:13 – 53:12

At the beginning of the famous Suffering Servant passage God is speaking to Isaiah: 'See, my servant will act wisely [some translate: 'will have success']; he will be raised and lifted up and highly exalted' (Isaiah 52:13). 'See' is a very key word for understanding this passage. Isaiah is looking at a vision, and God is explaining it to him. 'See,' says God, 'my servant will be successful.'

This is a good-news start, but if we are thinking of a tall, handsome king like Saul or David, we are in for a terrible surprise:

> Just as there were many who were appalled at him – his appearance was so disfigured beyond that of any man and his form marred beyond human likeness – so will he sprinkle many nations, and kings will shut their mouths because of him. For what they were not told, they will see, and what they have not heard, they will understand. (Isaiah 52:14–15)

People are appalled at the appearance of this servant, who is 'disfigured beyond that of any man' (52:14). Even so, God's task for him to be a light to the Gentiles will be accomplished (42:6; 49:6) and many kings and nations will be affected by him (52:15). The word 'sprinkle' is very significant because it suggests the sealing of a covenant with blood. (Although some – e.g. the RSV – have translated it as 'startle', the literal meaning of the Hebrew word is 'sprinkle', as found in the KJV and the NIV.)

'Moses then took the blood, *sprinkled* it on the people and said, "This is the blood of the covenant that the Lord has made with you in accordance with all these words"' (Exodus 24:8; my italics). The first covenant was sealed with the sprinkling of blood. In these first three verses of the Suffering Servant passage, God is speaking, and he links his servant's appalling appearance with the sacrificial sprinkling: 'His appearance was so disfigured beyond that of any man and his form marred beyond human likeness – *so* will he sprinkle many nations' (Isaiah 52:14–15; my italics). The second 'so' implies the Suffering Servant's disfigurement is connected in some way to a covenant, sprinkling blood over people from many nations, and at the time when Isaiah was viewing the vision, it was yet to come.

In the New Testament this is seen to be fulfilled in Jesus. 'You have come to . . . Jesus the mediator of a new covenant, and to the sprinkled blood that speaks a better word than the blood of Abel' (Hebrews 12:23–24; see also Hebrews 9:13, 19, 21; 10:22; 11:28; 1 Peter 1:2).

In response to God's revelation, Isaiah and his friends were shocked to the core by what they saw in the vision:

Who has believed our message and to whom has the arm
    of the Lord been revealed?
He grew up before him like a tender shoot,
    and like a root out of dry ground.

> He had no beauty or majesty to attract us to him, nothing
> in his appearance that we should desire him. He was
> despised and rejected by men, a man of sorrows,
> and familiar with suffering.
> Like one from whom men hide their faces he was despised,
> and we esteemed him not.
> Surely he took up our infirmities and carried our sorrows,
> yet we considered him stricken by God, smitten by him,
> and afflicted. (53:1–4)

The onlookers were shocked because they believed the disfigured servant in front of them had been stricken by God with sickness (v. 4). A 'root out of dry ground' is a sick plant (v. 2), and the literal translation of 'sorrows' and 'suffering' (vv. 3, 4) is 'pains and sickness'. Even Matthew translated 'sorrows' as 'diseases' (Matthew 8:17). Isaiah wrote: 'We considered him stricken by God, smitten by him, and afflicted' (Isaiah 53:4), and Alec Motyer points out that the Hebrew verb used for 'stricken' is used 60 times in Leviticus 13 and 14 in association with infectious skin diseases.[1]

If we translate the original Hebrew literally, and use Scripture to help us understand Scripture, then the natural conclusion is that the observers were shocked because they believed the picture of the disfigured man they were seeing showed a servant stricken by God with sickness. This was shocking to them because in their eyes sickness was seen as a penalty of sin, and a man stricken by God with a disfiguring sickness was a serious sinner.

---

[1] Alec Motyer, *The Prophecy of Isaiah* (Leicester: Inter-Varsity Press 1993), p. 430.

Sickness as the penalty of sin

Isaiah and his people were shocked by the Suffering Servant's apparent sickness because they had knowledge and experience of the Old Covenant punishment system. As we noted in Chapter 5, sickness, generally speaking, was seen as a punishment for sin, and healing as a reward for obedience. It must have seemed to them as if the whole penal system by which they had lived for hundreds of years was now being changed. John Goldingay, in his commentary on Isaiah, puts it rather neatly:

> He was supposed to be the sinner, they were the righteous. But as they continued to look at him, they found that he was the righteous one and they were the sinners. So he is suffering and they are not, whereas they are the sinners and he is not. Indeed he seems to be suffering for their sin.[2]

At this moment in the history of Israel, the people have returned or are returning from exile (see Isaiah 40). The prophets have declared that the Old Covenant is over, but God has promised his people a new beginning and a New Covenant. Now in this vision, Isaiah sees what is to take place. The suffering and sacrifice of this man will be successful in turning the rules of the Old Covenant upside down. The sprinkling of the Suffering Servant's blood will bring in a New Covenant, where sickness will no longer be seen as a punishment for sin, but where forgiveness of sins and a right relationship with God will come to all who repent and believe.

---

[2] John Goldingay, *God's Prophet God's Servant. A study in Jeremiah and Isaiah 40–55* (Exeter: Paternoster Press 1984), p. 146.

Six chapters later, in Isaiah 59:20–21, the gift of the Holy Spirit, the God who speaks, is also promised as part of the New Covenant. It was the God who speaks who initiated a remarkable healing/raising in Guatemala.

23. Raised at 26

On the 7th December 2004, Alejandra Botzoc, who works with Food for the Hungry in Guatemala, arrived at her local medical centre first thing in the morning to have her cardiac murmur examined by a heart specialist. The doctor, who had studied in France, gave her a four-dimension echograph and then came out with the worst news imaginable. Instead of the suspected murmur, Alejandra was suffering from a rare bacterial disease named after an unpronounceable French doctor. The syndrome is called 'Fethullahaber Barrengerguer', and apparently the bacteria enter the blood when one eats some type of food that has been chemically treated with a product called 'encadece cellulite'. Up to that point, there were only five recorded cases – and the other four were no longer alive.

The bacteria had already eaten 60 per cent of Ale's heart, which meant she had less than two weeks to live. It was far too late to consider a heart transplant, and the doctor had no alternative but to pronounce the death sentence.

On the 7th December 2004, twelve local pastors met in a hotel to pray for Guatemala. It is a wonderful and powerful thing when church leaders come together in unity to pray. At 9.30 am, as they were praying, they heard an audible voice saying to them, 'Pray for Alejandra.' None of them knew anyone of that name, but in total obedience to the God and Father of our Lord Jesus Christ, they all prayed for Alejandra, for some time, in the name of Jesus.

When Ale heard the death sentence, she closed her eyes and said to God: 'Lord, thank you very much for the wonderful 26 years you have allowed me to live. I am very happy to have known you.'

Ale then sang the song 'Come, Spirit, Come', and at 9.30 am her heart stopped; the vital signs disappeared and, having failed to revive her with machines, the doctor began preparing the death certificate.

Meanwhile, the Guatemala pastors were still praying for Alejandra and continued doing so until the Spirit of God told them to stop. He then spoke to them once more, supernaturally giving them a phone number to ring. It was Alejandra's phone number, and this is what she told them:

> At 9.35 am, my heart began to beat again. The doctor and the nurse who were in the room said that when this happened I was talking in a language that neither of them knew, which I imagine was heavenly tongues. They said that a type of electricity came out of me, and when the doctor touched me he received a shock, which caused him to let go quickly.

Apparently, this went on for half an hour before they did another echograph, which showed Ale's heart beating as strongly as a baby's heart, with no signs of anything being wrong. Five further examinations followed before Alejandra was declared to be completely fit and well.

Sometimes when the Spirit of God moves among us and we pray in faith according to his will, people are healed. The New Covenant relationship we have with God through the blood of Jesus enables us to pray, 'Come, Spirit, come,' and usually he does. When we enter the New Covenant, we also become members of a new family that loves us.[3]

By his stripes we are healed

The prophet and his friends believed they were seeing a man disfigured by sickness but the New Testament does not describe Jesus as a sick man. If his form had been marred beyond human likeness by infirmity, I think we would have expected some comment to that effect.

I own ten commentaries on Isaiah – all of them argue that Isaiah 53:2–4 is about a man suffering from sickness (the literal translation of the Hebrew offers no alternative); all of them make the point that in some way or other Jesus is the Suffering Servant, but none of them explain how Jesus is the man disfigured by sickness.

Part of the problem is that Isaiah 53 is a prophetic poem

---

[3] I received the details about Alejandra's new heart from Doug and Jackie Wakeling, who sometimes attend our meetings. Doug is EO of Food for the Hungry in the UK, which is a Christian international relief and development organisation. Alejandra Botzoc works with FHI/Guatemala in their sponsor communications department. Jackie wrote this to me: 'The story was reported to us by an American staff member also in Guatemala that we correspond with occasionally. These are known and trusted people.' May I recommend FHI to you – jwakeling@fhi.net

and as such is not as clear and precise as prose or historical narrative. Is it, for example, a metaphorical picture, like the similar one in Isaiah 1:6, where some accurate detail oozes out occasionally? Is it a visual-aid picture, like Jeremiah's almond tree or boiling pot (Jeremiah 1:11, 13)? How did the prophet know that the servant grew up like a sick plant? Was he guessing from what he saw, or was he in fact mistaken in what he saw? In verses 4 and 5, Isaiah admits that he and his friends have indeed made an error:

> Yet we considered him stricken by God, smitten by him, and afflicted.
> But he was pierced for our transgressions, he was crushed for our iniquities;
> the punishment that brought us peace was upon him, and by his wounds [stripes] we are healed. (Isaiah 53:4–5)

The 'but' with which verse 5 begins suggests a mistake has been made: 'We considered him stricken by God . . . *but* he was pierced for our transgressions' (vv. 4–5; my italics). I think the error could be understood in two ways:

a) We thought God had stricken him for *his* sins but in fact he was stricken for *our* sins.
b) We thought the Lord had given him sickness but it was the piercing, crushing and beating that made him look awful (Isaiah 53:5).

It is possible that both may be true: a) it certainly was *our* sins and not *his* that caused Jesus to suffer, but b) the disfigurement described by God in Isaiah 52:14 was due to 'sprinkling', not disease. A disease like leprosy does not sprinkle others; a blood sacrifice needs to be pierced.

The Jesus I saw in the Mel Gibson film, *The Passion of the Christ*, was disfigured by the brutality of his flogging, and it looks from the first three Gospels as if Jesus was not well enough to carry his own cross all the way (Mark 15:21).[4] Maybe this was the sick figure whom Isaiah saw – he would certainly have looked disfigured by then.

Fortunately, our study of healing does not depend upon knowing if Jesus was ever sick before Good Friday, as it is the suffering and death of the righteous servant on Good Friday that enables God to offer us healing in two ways:

a) Forgiveness of sins.
b) Freedom from the penalty of sin.

As we have already seen, God used sickness under the Old Covenant as a punishment for sin, and this is the sickness that the death of Christ removes for those who believe and trust in Jesus: sickness that is a penalty for sin.

As we look at the death of Christ, described so accurately in Isaiah 53:5–12, we notice why the Suffering Servant is led like a lamb to the slaughter. This fulfils the first of the servant's tasks – putting believing Jews right with God, so that they become God's children.'He was pierced for our transgressions, he was crushed for our iniquities; the

---

[4] Mel Gibson, *The Passion of the Christ*, screenplay by Benedict Fitzgerald and Mel Gibson (Icon Distribution, Inc. 2004). Now available on video and DVD. Although some Protestants find the non-biblical Roman Catholic inclusions unacceptable, I personally feel there is still value in the film, for those who are not squeamish. There is also an edited version which is more suitable for family viewing.

punishment that brought us peace was upon him' (53:5); 'the Lord has laid on him the iniquity of us all' (53:6); 'the Lord makes his life a guilt offering' (53:10); 'he will bear their iniquities' (53:11); 'he bore the sin of many' (53:12).

Jesus Christ did not die for sicknesses; he died for sins. He paid the penalty for our sins so that sickness as a penalty for sin can now be avoided by trusting in Jesus. In what sense has Jesus borne our sicknesses and carried our diseases? In the sense of bringing in the good news of grace to replace the bad news of works. Today, saints and sinners can all be healed by injections, medicines and operations because sickness is no longer a part of God's covenant punishment system. Jesus has taken the punishment for us and by so doing taken away the sicknesses that were due to us because of sin.

In the vision, the onlookers deserved to be sick as a penalty for their sin (53:4, 6), but the Suffering Servant was bearing their sin for them, like the scapegoat on the Day of Atonement and, as a result, they were not sick (Leviticus 16). The death of Christ is how the Suffering Servant brings his people back to God, establishing a New Covenant with God for them sealed by his sprinkled blood, which enables even sinful, unclean Gentiles, from 'many nations', to be put right with God as well. For those who respond in penitence and faith in what Jesus has done for them on the cross, it means the forgiveness of sins, and consequently the end of sickness that is a penalty for sin. The people who saw the vision were not healed from sickness – rather, they did not become sick because the Suffering Servant paid their penalty for them.

Sometimes, people translate the 'wounds' of verse 5 as 'stripes' and argue that it is the flogging of Jesus, not the death, that offers us healing, but Peter includes the cross with the 'stripes' in 1 Peter 2:24, and Isaiah includes the piercing and crushing with the 'stripes' in 53:5. In reality, the execution of Jesus began with his flogging, continued with his crushing (his head was beaten again and again with a rod; a crown of thorns was pushed on his head, and his whole body was crushed beneath the heavy load of the cross he tried to carry – Matthew 27:27–31; John 19:17), and finished with his piercing on the cross. It was a slow and painful death and all of these 'wounds' contributed to it. It was the sacrificial death of Christ, the result of all his wounds, that made atonement for our sins.

Jesus has died for our sin; the penalty has been paid, so God will no longer punish us with sickness if we have faith in Jesus. Those who suffered sickness in the Acts of the Apostles as a penalty for sin were those who were not trusting in Jesus at the time – Ananias and Sapphira (Acts 5:1–10), Simon the sorcerer, nearly (Acts 8:18–24), Saul (Acts 9:1–9), King Herod (Acts 12:21–23) and Elymas the sorcerer (Acts 13:6–12).

The problem for many people who try to use this passage for God's healing today is that they confuse the penalty of sin with the consequences of sin. Christ has died for sin, so sickness that is a penalty for sin can be taken away by believing in Jesus, but sickness that comes as a consequence of sin is totally different. If a person gets lung cancer due to smoking, or AIDS due to their own sexual sin, they are suffering from the consequences of sin, not the penalty of sin. God is not punishing them; they are merely reaping what they have sown. If a person with cancer or AIDS due to the consequences of sin repents of their sin and accepts the death of Christ in their place, they will be forgiven and they will have a place in heaven, but they will still have cancer or AIDS because these illnesses came to them as a result of their sin, not the penalty of sin. They will then need the authority of God the Father and the power of the Holy Spirit coming to them through Jesus to bring physical healing to their bodies.

Understanding how it works

Many parents understand the pain of seeing their child suffering from an illness such as measles. The feeling inside is something like: *If I could suffer measles in your place, I would.* But we all know this is not possible. As I nurse my daughter, I may catch the measles myself, but this is of no use to her; it doesn't take her measles away and it only makes my nursing less effective.

If my child was suffering from a terminal illness, then my pain would be a million times worse. *If I could die for her, I would.* But, as with the measles, my death would only make her suffering worse.

In the normal course of life, I cannot bear my child's measles or my child's death for her – life doesn't work like that. It would only work if measles and death were punishments for misdemeanours, I paid the penalty for her, and the judge acquitted her because the price had been paid.

On the wall of Westminster Abbey is carved a likeness of Maximilian Kolbe, the Christian twentieth-century martyr who died in 1941 at a concentration camp in Poland during

World War II.[5] Apparently, as a result of certain mis-demeanours, several people were chosen at random by the Nazis to be executed as a form of punishment and discipline for the whole camp. Maximilian Kolbe, a single man, offered to take the place of a married man who had been chosen, and was executed instead.

Now, suppose for lesser crimes, the Nazis chose to inject a man at random with measles, and someone's offer to take his place was accepted – *then* it would make sense to talk about bearing his disease for him. Only when sickness and death are punishments does it make any sense to talk about bearing someone else's sickness or death for him – when the person in charge accepts payment from one person for the sake of another.

To summarise, this is how I believe the context of the Suffering Servant passage, the book of Isaiah, the Old Testament and the New Testament helps us to interpret Isaiah 53 in relation to sickness, sin and the death of Christ: *The wounds that caused his death have saved us from sicknesses that were due to us as a punishment for our sins.*

And now we can see why the Gospels, Acts and the Epistles have not applied the cross to sickness. Under the Old Covenant, generally speaking, sickness was a punishment for sin, but the Old Covenant ended in Babylon. Jesus died for sin; therefore, under the New Covenant, sickness as a penalty for sin has been done away with, and something of this was seen by Isaiah and his friends in the vision. They

---

[5] Maximilian Kolbe is one of ten martyrs whose statues are above the west door of Westminster Abbey, and you don't have to pay to see them.

were not literally healed from an actual disease by the Suffering Servant's death, but rather, they did not become ill because of it. They saw and experienced in the vision the coming benefits of the New Covenant, which Jesus sealed with his death.

Sickness still comes to us today as a consequence of sin, or of living in a fallen world where bodies decay and die, but the good news is that the healing Holy Spirit also comes to us when we enter the New Covenant through the blood of Christ and we invite the Spirit of God to come. Isaiah 53 shows us the love of God in Christ Jesus – a love that comes to us again and again today by his Spirit.

24. Raised at 37

James and Pauline had very serious marriage problems. There were sin problems, anger and resentment problems, huge rejection problems and most especially push-it-down-don't-talk-to-anyone-about-it problems, which led to serious depression. They still came to church together, but regularly Pauline would stay with her elderly parents, while James slept alone at the house of his widowed mother, with whom the couple had recently been living.

One Monday morning, while staying with her parents, Pauline felt particularly low. 'I didn't believe you could be angry and be a Christian,' she wrote to me, 'so I just buried my anger again.' Feeling that all hope had gone, Pauline went to the upstairs bathroom, swallowed the contents of a bottle of paracetamol tablets, fixed a shower curtain tie round the window-frame bar, tied the other end around her neck and threw herself out of the window.

Pauline's parents saw the shoes come down first and then the body of their daughter, suspended in mid-air, hanging outside the kitchen window. Satan seemed to have won but then an amazing series of events took place. Two nurses in an upstairs outpatients' block opposite saw the whole incident and rang the ambulance immediately. They also left their duties to run across to Pauline's parents' home, hoping to begin CPR (Cardiopulmonary Resuscitation). In this quiet part of town, a man just so happened to be walking past at the right time and saw the elderly parents struggling to reach their daughter from the upstairs window, in order to support her weight.

He wanted to help but didn't know what to do when, suddenly, another man appeared. The second man asked Pauline's parents if they could see a ladder in a neighbour's garden from their vantage point but they couldn't. The man went away, and amazingly returned carrying a ladder. This helped them, eventually, to get Pauline down to the ground but by this time her breathing and her heart had stopped. Strangely, the man and his ladder then disappeared, never to be seen again, and nobody seemed to know who he was.

The nurses commenced CPR and when the paramedics arrived they resuscitated her but agreed she was probably brain-dead. By the time they reached the hospital, they were sure she was brain-dead.

In casualty, the staff performed a stomach washout and then took her to ITU (Intensive Therapy Unit), where the doctors said there was very little hope. However, it just so happened that Sue, a nurse from our own church, was on duty in ITU that morning, so prayer began in earnest, in the name of Jesus, while key people were contacted on the phone. Monday is my day off, when I don't normally answer the phone even if I am at home, yet somehow that morning they got hold of me immediately.

Sue greeted me in ITU, and told me the paramedics thought Pauline was already brain-dead, but even so I kept going. I held out my hands a few inches above the body so as not to disturb all the complicated tubes and machinery and asked God the Father through Jesus to send his Holy Spirit on Pauline. Unfortunately, despite praying and waiting for some time, I sensed nothing happening within myself and nothing happening to the form that lay before me. In the end, very sadly, I committed Pauline into God's hands and left.

As I was leaving ITU, however, I saw Pete, Sue's husband, a hospital manager and also a member of our church, and felt prompted to ask him to join me in praying once more. Strange, really. Together, we stood beside Pauline's body as I prayed again: 'Father God, I ask you through Jesus to send your Holy Spirit and do all you want to do,' and then we waited in silence. This time, I felt tingling power come all over me, and my hands became quite hot. 'In the name of Jesus,' I found myself saying, 'I break the power of death.' Immediately,

Pauline's chest area jumped like someone being defibrillated, and thus encouraged I broke the power of trauma in Jesus' name with a similar result. I couldn't be sure but after I'd done this there seemed to be a more peaceful look on Pauline's face. I said a few more prayers, and then Pete and I left.

Within 24 hours, Pauline was moved to an ordinary ward, having regained consciousness and begun to breathe unaided. Within a week, she was moved to a psychiatric hospital, no longer in need of any further physical healing. Pauline's body was completely restored in a very short while (apart from the scar around her neck), but it took considerably longer to heal her marriage, her soul and her spirit. Talking and being real with one another was a key factor, as was teaching and ministry at Ellel Pierrepont,[6] but Jesus was and is the greatest source of healing for them both. Pauline wrote to me recently: 'Nobody has ever or will ever love me as much as Jesus,' and she finished with a quotation from Habakkuk 3:2: 'Lord, I have heard of your fame; I stand in awe of your deeds.'

A New Covenant right to healing

So far in this book, I have argued that in the Gospels, Acts and Epistles, it is the Holy Spirit who heals, and nowhere in

---

[6] Ellel Pierrepont is one of four centres run by Ellel Ministries International in the UK: Ellel Grange in Lancaster; Glyndley Manor near Eastbourne; Pierrepont in Frensham, Surrey, and Ellel Scotland at Blairmore House, near Aberdeen. Info@pierrepont.ellel.org.uk

them could I find any New Covenant rights of believers to healing because of the cross. What I have now discovered in the Old Testament is that physical sickness, when it is a penalty from God for sin, can be avoided by exercising faith in the cross of Christ. This is because forgiveness is offered to us as a New Covenant right by God, through Jesus, and automatically undoes the penalty of sin when appropriated through repentance and faith.

God is still God and can punish anyone he chooses with sickness, but it is no longer a covenant arrangement with rules and regulations. On the other hand, if God were to inflict sickness upon someone due to sin, as he did with Elymas (Acts 13:11), and the transgressor was then to receive forgiveness of sins from God through the cross of Christ, it stands to reason that part of God's absolution would include healing. Unfortunately, I cannot give an example of such a healing because I have not met one. God used disease as a penalty for sin to help establish and encourage the Old Covenant, but now that we are under grace, and not under law, he uses it far less, because a new punishment system is now in place to go with the New Covenant – Christ died for our sins.

I have not met an example of someone being healed from sickness which was a punishment for sin, but there is a New Testament example of such a healing in Revelation. It comes after Jesus has returned in glory to put the final nails in Satan's coffin, and to judge (Revelation 19:11 – 20:15):

Now the dwelling of God is with men, and he will live with them. They will be his people, and God himself will be with them and be their God. He will wipe every tear from their eyes.

> There will be no more death or mourning or crying or pain, for
> the old order of things has passed away. (Revelation 21:3–4)

This is the one place in the New Testament where healing is
linked directly to the cross of Christ: 'Blessed are those who
wash their robes, that they may have the right to the tree of
life and may go through the gates into the city' (Revelation
22:14); 'They have washed their robes and made them
white in the blood of the Lamb' (Revelation 7:14). This is
obviously figurative language because red blood does not
make robes white, but its message is clear. Those who have
accepted the death of Christ on the cross for themselves are
declared righteous before God and have the right to enter
the city of heaven, where there is no more pain or crying or
death. Healing for all is presented here as a New Covenant
right. By his wounds we are healed. When Jesus returns, all
who have accepted him and his death on the cross will be
healed of all sickness for ever.

25. Raised for all eternity at 67

Edie Matthews was described by doctors as 'one in a million'. She had suffered as a child from infantile rheuma-
toid arthritis and as a result was a small person – not a
dwarf because her body was perfectly proportioned, but
even when she was seven years old she could run under
a table without ducking. At 21, she was confined to a
wheelchair, in which she spent the rest of her life. For her
last 30 years, she lived with her friend Edith, who was
also confined to a wheelchair, and together they worked,
lived and looked after each other.

I used to take communion to them once a month until the city council gave us a minibus with a tail-lift, and then we were able to bring them to church weekly. At the age of 67, Edie Matthews was admitted to hospital in some discomfort, and I visited her on the ward. Wearing my clerical collar, I was able to go in a few minutes before visiting hours, and after a brief conversation I made an offer to pray with her, which was gratefully received. At this moment, I felt rather awkward: it was a very long, old-fashioned ward, and many patients were looking at me. The visitors were due in soon so, with all eyes on me, I put a hesitant hand on her forehead and asked God to do all he wanted to do by his Spirit through Jesus, in five minutes.

I was surprised by joy when the power of the Lord came on Edie, because she was a rather formal lady who was not used to this kind of thing. She was already seated in a chair, but now her head went back, her arms went up, she started shaking and her face began to glow. I looked furtively around, but no one seemed to be worried, so I sat it out. 'Bless you, Lord; pain be gone; keep doing all you're doing,' I kept whispering, and anything else which came into my head. This went on for 15 minutes, but despite my fears we were totally uninterrupted; I think the nurses were delayed, and late in letting the hordes in.

When she came round, Edie was beaming. 'Edith believes in this sort of thing,' she said, 'but I don't. . . didn't.'

'How do you feel?' I asked.

'A million dollars,' she replied. 'The pain's all gone. You know, Peter,' she carried on, 'I reckon dying must be like this; it's glorious.'

I was thrilled, and encouraged her to let me pray for her again the next time I visited her. This kind of ministry can become addictive.

The hospital diagnosed a narrowed and restricted bowel as the problem, advised against an operation and sent Edie home with painkillers. It was not their fault they made a mistake: Edie had been used to pain all her life and no one knew how seriously ill she was. The real problem was cancer at an advanced stage.

A little while later, Edie was readmitted in pain to the hospital, where I visited her and prayed again, but by now she was much more heavily drugged and nothing visible occurred. Three weeks after my first hospital visit, I had a little nudge from the Lord. I was in my study at about lunch-time and sensed I ought to ring the ward to find out how Edie was doing, particularly as the feeling that accompanied the words was one of alarm. The sister who answered told me that Edie had enjoyed a very good morning; there was no cause for alarm, and nothing at all to worry about at present. I gave her my phone number, just in case, and told her who I was, as Edie did not have any nearby relatives.

Win some, lose some, I thought and went over to church to prepare for an afternoon meeting. I had been gone only ten minutes when Carol came running over from the vicarage to find me. 'The sister went to check Edie after you rang,' she explained. 'She's deteriorating fast.'

I left immediately, collecting Edith and her wheelchair on the way. When we reached the ward, Edie's relative had just arrived from Essex, and together we went in to see Edie behind the curtains. Edith held her hand and a little tear of recognition came on to her friend's cheek. I laid my hand on her forehead, and said: 'Come, Holy Spirit, and do all that you want to do.' As I was saying this short prayer, Edie died, feeling, I believe, like a million dollars. Edith squeezed her hand and said: 'There are no wheelchairs in heaven, Edie.'

7

The Cross

The cross of Christ stands at the centre of our Christian faith and, for those of us who love the Lord Jesus, it is very precious in our sight. Whenever I preach to Pentecostal or charismatic brothers and sisters in Christ and say it is the Holy Spirit who heals, they either nod, smile, or shout Hallelujah!, depending on their different cultures. But whenever I dare to follow it up by saying it is not the cross that heals, the heads begin to shake; the frowns appear, and all kinds of words are expressed, usually along the lines of, 'Help him, Jesus.' So the cross is worth looking at on its own, to see what part it does play in the healing ministry, if only to keep me in a job. This is what I found:

- The cross of Christ offers us the forgiveness of sins, which puts us right with God, enabling the Holy Spirit to fill our hearts with his peace. Sometimes peace with God brings health to our bodies.
- Receiving forgiveness of sins through the cross of Christ, and the assurance of 'sins forgiven' that the Holy Spirit brings, helps us to forgive others. When this happens, the

pain of unforgiveness in our hearts is taken away, and our sick bodies may recover more speedily.

- Occasionally, sickness is linked to the presence of a demon. Jesus defeated Satan at the cross, giving us the legal right to cast out demons in his name. When this is accomplished in the power of the Holy Spirit, and the Holy Spirit enters into the place where the demon has been, then our bodies, souls and spirits will often reap the benefit.

- In each case, the cross of Christ helps us to deal with the root of a sickness, which may alleviate some of the symptoms, but the authority of God and the power of the Holy Spirit coming through Jesus is usually needed to bring about complete physical healing. The cross deals with sin so that whenever sickness is directly related to sin, and not just the consequence of living in a fallen world, the cross will always be relevant.

- But there are no accounts of healing in the New Testament where sickness goes automatically as a result of sin being forgiven.

26. Saved by the cross, healed by the Spirit

Susan's father brought his children up in military fashion. They were made to go to cold, austere churches, twice on Sundays and several times during the week, where they sat on hard wooden benches, knelt on cold stone floors but were never allowed to laugh or speak in anything other than a whisper. At 18, Susan had a disagreement with her father, and was thrown out of the house. She remembers vividly standing by the bus-stop with her little bag wondering, 'Where shall I go?'

At the age of 20, Susan experienced her first symptoms of multiple sclerosis; by the time she was 40, she had chronic progressive MS which was causing her condition to deteriorate rapidly. She suffered from poor co-ordination, visual problems, bladder and bowel dysfunctions, serious mobility limitations and chronic fatigue, which were immense. Susan required the aid of a wheelchair and various other pieces of mobility equipment to assist her in day-to-day life.

Another MS sufferer, a Christian, invited Susan to her home one day and shared the gospel with her, leaving Susan feeling very angry. But words that had been spoken kept surfacing in her mind: *Could all this that I was hearing about a loving God, who gave the ultimate sacrifice of his Son for my life, be real?*

Almost subconsciously, while flicking through the TV channels, Susan began to watch a God channel. 'Before I knew what was happening,' she wrote to me, 'I found myself on my knees in my bedroom in front of the TV, giving my life to Jesus.'

Because of her childhood experiences, Susan told herself, 'I don't need church,' and made do with *Songs of Praise* on television. Then, one Sunday morning, God spoke to her, unmistakably, inside her head. 'Susan, go to church!' he said.

'So, I duly washed, dressed, and went off in search of a church,' she wrote in a note to me.

And the one she chose wasn't a bit like the churches of her childhood. 'Everyone was so loving,' Susan continued, 'so caring. There was something different about them which made me want more. It wasn't long before I was totally settled into this church, loving every bit of it, joining a Bible study group and reading God's word regularly.'

Meanwhile, Susan's health continued to deteriorate and her quality of life became very poor. She needed assistance in many daily tasks and began to feel overwhelmed by the disease. In her quiet times, while reading the Bible, Susan was struck by the number of times Jesus healed people and, consequently, she asked him to heal her and continued to do so.

Three weeks later, Jesus sent the Holy Spirit in healing power on Susan, while she was asleep in bed. This is what she wrote to me about it:

Upon waking one morning, I felt completely different physically and was able to move comfortably to sit on the edge of the bed with my feet on the floor. I stood up and my legs felt like rocks. Solid. No rubber knees. No numbness. No pins and needles. No shaking. No wobbling. Then I went to the bathroom and I didn't stagger.

Being a cautious person, I convinced myself it was probably my first ever remission, but three years later I am still fully fit and haven't felt better. Not once in this time have I suffered any of those dreadful symptoms or disabilities.

And it wasn't only Susan's body that was healed. When she became a Christian, Susan was living with Allan, so they got married. Allan became a Christian; they were baptised together, and Susan visited her father and family to restore relationships with them.

All of this came about through the cross of Christ and the healing Holy Spirit whom Jesus sent to bring total healing to Susan, body, soul and spirit, through his body the church (on satellite and in the flesh), in answer to prayer. To God be all the glory![1]

Subjects of the King

Jesus did not teach healing. Jesus did healing and taught the kingdom of God: 'Jesus went throughout Galilee, teaching in their synagogues, preaching the good news of the kingdom, and healing every disease and sickness among the people' (Matthew 4:23; see also Matthew 9:35).

I have found that three of Jesus' teachings on the kingdom of God are particularly helpful in preparing people to receive the healing of the Spirit, and each one is linked to the cross. They are:

a) Peace with God (Matthew 6:25–34).
b) Sin (Matthew 4:17).
c) Forgiving others (Matthew 6:14–15).

I cannot help thinking that if we put these three things right in our lives, then the members of the medical profession would be able to play more golf.

a) Peace with God

The path to peace with God is set out for us in Paul's letter to the Romans. First, we acknowledge our own sin: 'All have sinned and fall short of the glory of God' (Romans 3:23).

---

[1] Susan is a friend of Anne, my mother-in-law, who also lives in Spain.

Second, we believe in what Jesus has done for us on the cross: '[We] are justified freely by his grace through the redemption that came by Christ Jesus. God presented him as a sacrifice of atonement, through faith in his blood' (Romans 3:24–25).

Third, we receive peace with God: 'Therefore, since we have been justified through faith, we have peace with God through our Lord Jesus Christ' (Romans 5:1).

For the purposes of this book, it is worth noting how this peace comes to us: 'God has poured out his love into our hearts by the Holy Spirit' (Romans 5:5); 'The Spirit himself testifies with our spirit that we are God's children' (Romans 8:16); 'For the kingdom of God is not a matter of eating and drinking, but of righteousness, peace and joy in the Holy Spirit' (Romans 14:17). Jesus' death on the cross, plus our right response to that death, justifies us before God. He then sends his peace into our hearts, by his Holy Spirit – the Spirit who heals.

27. One more time

An elderly lady, we'll call her Vi, used to worship in a church I attended. She'd loved the Lord all her life and particularly enjoyed coming to holy communion, to thank Jesus for his death on the cross, to receive the assurance of forgiven sins and to be filled with his love.

Sadly, she became ill with cancer and, despite valiant efforts from the medical profession and much prayer from her brothers and sisters in Christ, she was told it was terminal. Friends and nurses visited her often, and the disease was managed well enough for her to remain at home, but eventually Vi became very weak and frail and was no longer able to get to church. At that time, those closest to her prepared themselves for her promotion to glory.

But then an idea began to grow inside Vi, bringing a twinkle to her eye and an enthusiasm to her spirit. 'One more time,' she thought to herself, and shared it with her closest friends. 'How about one more time? Do you think with the doctors' and nurses' help you could get me up and dressed, and take me to church, one more time?'

It wasn't very sensible or practical, but the idea seemed to switch a light on inside Vi, and this produced a similar response from her assistants. 'Why not?' they chorused, as they caught her enthusiasm. It wasn't a good idea, but maybe it was a God idea.

It took a lot of preparation from a number of people, and a considerable amount of hard work, but it was worth it to see Vi's grateful, beaming smile. They kept encouraging one another with the slogan: 'One more time.' Wheelchair and transport were laid on, drugs administered, plenty of time given to getting her ready, and right on schedule Vi found herself in her beloved church for the Sunday holy communion service. It was difficult and painful but Vi loved it, and her friends loved her loving it.

At the appointed time, and with a lot of help from her friends, she rose from her chair, toddled to the communion rail, and knelt at the front of church to receive the sacrament. As Vi received the elements, the song of Simeon came into her mind: 'Lord, now let your servant depart in peace. My eyes have seen your salvation' (from the Funeral Service – an adaptation of Luke 2:29–30).

Vi remained kneeling at the rail while the power of God came all over her and flooded her soul with his love, before she rose slowly with his peace in her heart. Jesus had died for her sins; she had made it 'one more time', and there was no need to fight any more. She sensed it was easier walking back, and there was no pain as she sat out the rest of the service in her wheelchair. Strangely, she felt a new person when she arrived home, and the next day, and the next, and her dream of 'one more time' turned out to be a false dawn. As Vi received the bread and the wine and God's peace entered her heart by his Spirit, complete healing came into her body. Consequently she came back to church for communion again and again, for years to come.

The bread and the wine helped Vi to focus on what God had done for her on the cross, but it was God, not the bread and wine, who healed her. Peace with God came to Vi through the cross of Christ, and the power of the Holy Spirit then healed her.

b) Sin

I managed to find three healing accounts in the New Testament where sin is mentioned:

First, in Luke 5:18–26 (also in Matthew 9:2–8 and Mark 2:3–12), some men came to Jesus carrying a paralytic on a mat, smashed a hole in the roof and lowered him down. 'When Jesus saw their faith, he said, "Friend, your sins are forgiven"' (Luke 5:20). It is fun to speculate why Jesus said this, but the New Testament does not give us an answer. These are the stages, however, about which we can be definite:

- The power of the Lord was present for Jesus to heal the sick (Luke 5:17).
- The men had faith in Jesus (Luke 5:18–20).
- Jesus forgave the man his sins (Luke 5:20).
- As a separate, later activity, Jesus healed the man (Luke 5:24–25).

For whatever reason, Jesus forgave the man his sins first, and then, as the power of the Lord was present for him to heal the sick, he healed him, five verses later. It is important to notice that the forgiveness of sins and the healing of the paralysed man's body are two separate activities; separated by Jesus' teaching about the authority he has received and prophesying that he will heal the man as evidence of that authority. The man was not healed by having his sins forgiven – he was healed *after* he had his sins forgiven.

Second, in John 5:1–15, Jesus healed another paralytic, one who had been an invalid for 38 years. This time, Jesus healed the man without receiving any positive response from him, possibly because this healing took place in Jerusalem and the man did not know who Jesus was (Luke 5:13). Afterwards, however, Jesus said two important things:

- 'See, you are well again. Stop sinning or something worse may happen to you' (John 5:14).
- 'The Son can do nothing by himself; he can do only what he sees his Father doing, because whatever the Father does the Son also does' (John 5:19).

Jesus seemed to imply that if the man kept on sinning, maybe a specific sin related to the illness, then he would become sick again, this time worse than before. However, the man was healed on this occasion without confessing any sin or faith in Jesus beforehand, because the Father was doing it and Jesus obeyed his Father.

What we can conclude from these two stories is that even if sin was the reason for them both being paralysed, and this is not definite, neither of them was healed automatically by having his sins forgiven. Both of them needed God's activity, his authority and power, to heal them. We also note a further principle that emerges from this second story. Dealing with sin may assist people in staying healthy and avoiding sickness, and the cross very definitely helps us to deal with sin. This fits well with Isaiah's vision of the Suffering Servant, whose death prevents the onlookers from becoming ill.

Third, the disciples, having heard Jesus link sin with sickness in John 5, then came across a man born blind in John 9. They asked Jesus: 'Rabbi, who sinned, this man or his parents, that he was born blind?' (John 9:2).

Jesus' reply is very important: '"Neither this man nor his parents sinned," said Jesus' (John 9:3). On one or two occasions, Jesus seemed to link sin with sickness, but on this occasion he says, 'Definitely not.' This fits well with the book of Job in the Old Testament, where, possibly before the Old Covenant (many people think the book of Job is very old), God reveals to us for over 30 chapters that Job was not sick because of sin. But it also fits well with Isaiah's vision about the Suffering Servant which came after the end of the Old Covenant. The disciples, like many Jews in

Jesus' day, were continuing to operate Old Covenant rules and regulations and seemed to still believe that all sickness was a punishment from God for sin – Jesus needed to teach them otherwise. The Pharisees certainly thought this. They said to the man born blind, who could now see: '"You were steeped in sin at birth; how dare you lecture us!" And they threw him out' (John 9:34).

Jesus' confrontation and disagreement with the Pharisees, over the relationship between sin and sickness, suggests that the Old Covenant rules and regulations for healing have now gone. The healings of the two paralytics are the only two healing stories in the Gospels where Jesus addresses sin, and interestingly, these are the two stories which most clearly demonstrate the need for the authority and power of the Holy Spirit in Jesus' healing ministry (see Chapter 2 and my comments on John 5:1–21; Luke 5:17–26).

In contrast to the Old Testament, there are no accounts of healing in the New Testament where sickness goes automatically as a result of sin being forgiven.

The cross of Christ enables us to be filled with the Holy Spirit again and again, and forgiveness through the cross of Christ clears the channels through which the Spirit of God may flow, but in the New Testament it is the Spirit who heals.

28. Choose life

A friend of mine asked me to visit her mother, I'll call her Mavis. Sciatic nerve trouble in her back was the problem – the medical profession could not help any more – Mum was now well into her eighties.

At this stage in my experience of the healing ministry, I was beginning to realise the importance of the relationship between the symptoms and the root cause of a sickness. I'd heard different doctors and psychiatrists say that illness in our country was something like 70, 80 or even 90 per cent psychosomatic, so I learnt to ask a question whenever I was requested to pray with a sick person. This is the question:

What was happening in your life when the symptoms first appeared?

Mavis was an absolute saint – a Baptist one. She loved Jesus, loved the people of God, and loved talking to unbelievers about Jesus, but when I visited her she was in pain. It had become impossible for Mavis to find any position, whether standing, sitting or lying down, that eased her pain, so our conversation was very difficult and uncomfortable for her.

'What was happening in your life when the symptoms first appeared?' I asked gently.

'My sister died,' Mavis replied, without even thinking about it.

So I probed and prodded. 'Was she a believer?' I asked.

'Of course, Peter,' replied Mavis. 'She was a Baptist.'

Of course. 'Are you sure she is with Jesus?' I dared to ask, but regretted it almost immediately. Blessed assurance poured out of Mavis's lips and put me in my place.

'How did you get on with your sister?' I enquired.

'Never a cross word,' continued Mavis. 'Saw her two or three times a week. Went shopping together. Coffee in Rackhams every Tuesday morning. We were very close, especially since both our husbands died some time ago.'

I was losing. I had this great theory but I couldn't find any facts to fit it. No worries about her sister. No guilt. No unfinished business. No regrets. I was about to offer a simple prayer before moving on to another appointment when suddenly, unsolicited, this popped out of Mavis all by itself.

'I do wish I was with her,' she announced.

Oh dear! I'd met this before and knew something of the problem, but how did I tell one of God's saints, a Baptist who had lived a much more godly life than I had, that her problem was *sin*? Satan doesn't tempt many little old ladies with wild orgies, bank-robbing or murder, so, faced with a Baptist saint, he had selected one of his more subtle ploys. Choosing death rather than life. Not choosing what God was choosing. There was no easy way of saying it, so I just said it.

'Peter,' she said, 'you're absolutely right. I must let her go. Choose life, not death. Serve God until he calls me home. Right,' she concluded, 'let's do it!'

So we did. Mavis prayed a beautiful prayer repenting of her sins, letting her sister go, choosing life not death, and agreeing to serve God for the rest of her life. Then, because of the atoning sacrifice of Jesus, I was able to speak out God's forgiveness to her. Her spirit felt much more at peace once this was done, and as I asked Father God to send his Holy Spirit in healing power on Mavis through Jesus, she was gloriously healed.

Due to her repentance, and the cross of Christ that enabled Mavis to receive God's forgiveness, there were now no barriers in the way. Mavis's face lit up, joy flooded her body, soul and spirit, and the pain left instantly. So we had a cup of tea.

I was just moving on to my second slice of cake when Mavis suddenly muttered: 'I do still miss her. I do wish I was with her.' Oh dear! Before my eyes, the theory and theology were confirmed as the pain rushed back in, all over her body, and registered on her face.

'Oh dear!' she commented. 'I've done it again.'

Believe it or not, this went on for three weeks. Mavis loved her sister, and loved Jesus, and simply wanted to be with both of them, but, until she chose what God was choosing for her, life not death, the pain kept coming back. However, each time she repented and received God's forgiveness, the Holy Spirit came powerfully upon her and the pain left. I'm pleased to record that Mavis got there in the end; the pain left permanently, and she served God faithfully for the rest of her life. She is, however, with Jesus and her sister now – sometimes sin is just a matter of timing.

c) Forgiving others

Paul wrote that God's love in Christ should motivate us to forgive one another: 'Be kind and compassionate to one another, forgiving each other, just as in Christ God forgave you' (Ephesians 4:32).

John linked this to the cross:

This is love: not that we loved God, but that he loved us and sent his Son as an atoning sacrifice for our sins. Dear friends, since God so loved us, we also ought to love one another. (1 John 4:10–11)

What if we do?

• Jesus said, 'Love your enemies and pray for those who persecute you, that you may be sons of your Father' (Matthew 5:44).
• 'For if you forgive men when they sin against you, your heavenly Father will also forgive you' (Matthew 6:14).

What if we don't?

• 'But if you do not forgive men their sins, your Father will not forgive your sins' (Matthew 6:15).

Then the master called the servant in. 'You wicked servant,' he said, 'I cancelled all that debt of yours because you begged me to. Shouldn't you have had mercy on your fellow-servant just as I had on you?' In anger his master turned him over to the jailers to be tortured, until he should pay back all he owed. This is how my heavenly Father will treat each of you unless you forgive your brother from the heart. (Matthew 18:32–35)

Some people have seen the torturers as satanic, and Paul seems to have been one of them:

If you forgive anyone, I also forgive him. And what I have for-given – if there was anything to forgive – I have forgiven in the sight of Christ for your sake, in order that Satan might not out-wit us. For we are not unaware of his schemes. (2 Corinthians 2:10 –11)

And there is one passage in the New Testament that many
scholars suggest links sickness with a wrong attitude
towards the cross and the church.

In the first place, I hear that when you come together as a
church, there are divisions among you . . . A man ought to
examine himself before he eats of the bread and drinks of the
cup. For anyone who eats and drinks without recognising the
body of the Lord eats and drinks judgment on himself. That is
why many among you are weak and sick, and a number of you
have fallen asleep. (1 Corinthians 11:18, 28–30)

William Barclay, having first made a case for the 'body of
the Lord' being the bread which represents Jesus' body on
the cross, goes on to comment most helpfully on a second
possible meaning:

The phrase *the body of Christ* again and again stands for the
church; it does so, as we shall see, in chapter 12. Paul has just
been rebuking those who with their divisions divide the
church; so this may mean that the man eats and drinks
unworthily who has never realised that the whole church is
the body of Christ and who is at variance with his brother, who
looks on his brother with contempt or who, for any reason, is
not one with his brethren. The Church of Scotland order of
service for the Sacrament invites to the Table those who are 'in
love and charity' with their neighbours. Every man in whose
heart there is hatred, bitterness, contempt against his brother
man eats and drinks unworthily if with that spirit in his heart
he comes to the Table of Our Lord. So then to eat and to drink
unworthily is to do so with no sense of reverence and no sense
of the greatness of the thing we do; and to do so while we are

at variance with the brother for whom Christ died, as He died for us.[2]

The corollary of this is that a right attitude to the cross of Christ, and to one another, is much more likely to lead to a life of health and wholeness than a wrong one. Once more, we note how the cross of Christ can help us to avoid becoming sick.

The cross motivates us to love one another and forgive one another, and the Holy Spirit gives us the power to do this. He not only convicts us of sin but enables us to see Jesus and to forgive those who sin against us (John 16:8).

> But Stephen, full of the Holy Spirit, looked up to heaven and saw the glory of God, and Jesus standing at the right hand of God. 'Look,' he said. 'I see heaven open and the Son of Man standing at the right hand of God.' . . . Then he fell on his knees and cried out, 'Lord, do not hold this sin against them.' (Acts 7:55–56, 60)

Stephen, full of the Spirit, was able to ask God to forgive his killers, just as Jesus had done before him from the cross (Luke 23:34). The cross of Christ enables us to be forgiven, and motivates us to forgive; the Holy Spirit empowers us to forgive – all of which paves the way for God to heal.

29. Drums in church

On one occasion, I was invited to speak and lead a time of ministry in an Anglican church situated in the heart of England. During the time of ministry, someone from our

---

[2] William Barclay, *The Letters to the Corinthians* (Edinburgh: Saint Andrew Press 1954) pp. 116–117.

small team gave a 'word' they thought may have come from God.

'I think there's a person here,' she began tentatively, 'who has a pain in the right ear, and I believe God wants to heal you.'

No problem. A young man claimed it was for him, so after the service I saw him, together with a lady from his own church.

'What's the condition?' I asked.

'Catarrh,' he replied. 'I've suffered with it since I was born.'

This last piece of information deflated me enormously. *From birth* was not an idea which filled me with faith, hope or charity. I had a little moan inside my head at God for landing me with this one but, instead of telling me off as I expected, he seemed to speak kindly to my inner ear.

'The word was not for catarrh, Peter,' God seemed to say. That was all, but it was enough. Of course! The word was for pain in the right ear, so I tried a new question.

'How long have you had the pain in the right ear?' I asked, hoping for something more recent than birth.

'Since we had drums in church,' he responded, without having to think about it.

When I tell this story in church, people usually laugh at this point, particularly if they are traditionalists who feel that drums in church would give anybody a pain in the ear. But on this occasion, they were wrong and the boot was on the other foot. The young man with the pain in the right ear was the drummer.

He proceeded to tell me the sad tale of how some

people on the parochial church council (PCC) had voted against drums in church, and how a number of people in the church had told him personally what they thought about it, and continued to do so. At this point, the lady from the church spoke up.

'I was one of those who voted against the drums,' she began, addressing the drummer, 'but since you've been playing them so sensitively and not bashing the living daylights out of them, I've found them a very helpful aid to worship.'

'You have?' asked the young man somewhat rhetorically, with an incredulous look on his face. 'You're the first person to say that to me.'

I then took a step back as the two of them engaged in chatting, confessing, repenting, forgiving and much holy hugging, which was a joy to behold. At the appropriate moment, I suggested we ask the Holy Spirit to come, to show the drummer what Jesus thought about drums in church.

As he stood there, eyes closed, hands held out to receive, the Spirit of God came all over him and a huge smile spread across his face from ear to ear. It was obvious that Jesus did not think the same thing about drums in church as some members of the PCC had done.

Eventually, the drummer opened his eyes, and shared with us the picture he'd seen of Jesus loving him and affirming him for offering his musical gift to God in worship. He was positively beaming as he told the story. Ultimately I asked him, 'How's the ear?'

'Terrible,' he replied. 'The pain's as bad as it's ever been.'

I have to admit I was surprised and disappointed by this, but God had named it, so I claimed it. I asked the Holy Spirit to come in healing power, and then, as my hand on his right ear became exceedingly hot, I said, 'In the name of Jesus, I command the pain in the right ear to go.' And it went. Instantly. I kept in touch with the vicar of the church, and he confirmed to me that although the drummer still struggled from time to time with catarrh, the pain in the ear never returned.

Interestingly, the 'word' from God, the guidance of God, being right with God through the cross and with one another through forgiveness, did not bring automatic healing. They all opened the way for healing, but in the end it was the Holy Spirit who healed.

Deliverance

One of my great sadnesses is that more people could be healed if only they would believe and practise what is taught in the New Testament about deliverance. Smith Wigglesworth was one of the most successful healing-evangelists in the twentieth century, and he often discerned and cast out demons as the root cause of sicknesses. Luke recorded this:

- 'When Jesus had called the Twelve together, he gave them power and authority to drive out all demons' (9:1).
- 'The seventy-two returned with joy and said, "Lord, even the demons submit to us in your name"' (10:17).
- 'He replied, "I saw Satan fall like lightning from heaven. I have given you authority to trample on snakes and

scorpions and to overcome all the power of the enemy"' (10:18–19).

This was just a foretaste of what was to come after Jesus had ascended into heaven:

- 'Crowds gathered also from the towns around Jerusalem, bringing their sick and those tormented by evil spirits, and all of them were healed' (Acts 5:16).
- 'With shrieks, evil spirits came out of many, and many paralytics and cripples were healed' (Acts 8:7).
- 'Their illnesses were cured and the evil spirits left them' (Acts 19:12).

The reason they could cast out demons was because Jesus had defeated Satan at the cross, and the authority that the accuser once possessed over the earth had now been given to Jesus. This is how it worked.

God gave the kingdom of this world to Adam and Eve, but they gave it to Satan by doing what he told them to do (Genesis 1:26; 3:6). When a king obeys someone else, then, in effect, that someone else becomes the ruler. Everyone who came after that also sinned, and obeyed Satan, until Jesus came (Romans 3:23; Hebrews 4:15). There are several theories of the atonement in Scripture, some of which are metaphors, that have stretched the minds of theologians ever since. But what actually happened in relation to Satan is that God said to Jesus: 'Go to the cross,' Satan said: 'Come down from the cross,' and Jesus obeyed God, completing a perfect life on earth (Matthew 26:43; 27:39–44; Philippians 2:8). Theoretically, until that moment Satan still had a chance, but once Jesus said, 'It is finished!' and died, Satan had lost (John 19:30). For the first time since Adam, God was now able to give authority on earth back to humanity because of the man Jesus (Philippians 2:9–11). This is why, when we repent of our sins and obey Jesus, we can cast out demons in his name. The nails on the cross were the first nails in Satan's coffin.

In the Bible, and in my experience, there are two different ways that deliverance can help with physical healing – direct and indirect.

a) Direct

'Jesus was driving out a demon that was mute. When the demon left, the man who had been mute spoke' (Luke 11:14). This is a direct relationship between the demon and the disability. The demon is causing the problem, and when it goes, the problem goes. Would that it were always that easy, but it does happen from time to time. I suspect, though I cannot prove it, that when this happens there is probably nothing wrong with the person physically that an X-ray or scan would reveal. The demon is stopping the hostage from speaking, like a bandit with his hand over his mouth, and when a greater authority and power removes the bandit, the person can speak.

I have seen blind eyes opened in similar circumstances, but you'll have to wait for that story. The common one is a headache. Headaches can have many different causes but occasionally they are caused directly by a demon. I remember on one occasion, after a meeting, ministering to a lady who had a blinding headache. We took her to a private room; she repented of the sin that had allowed the demon in; we cast it out in Jesus' name, and the headache went completely. When a demon is directly responsible for an ailment or a disability, it is a relatively straightforward procedure, but it isn't the most common scenario in my experience.

b) Indirect

Jesus met a woman 'who had been crippled by a spirit for eighteen years'. He called her 'a daughter of Abraham' and he encountered her in the synagogue, worshipping God, listening to Jesus teach. He healed her in two stages. First, there was a 'word': 'Woman, you are set free from your infirmity' (Luke 13:12). This is authority. Jesus normally cast out demons with a word of authority. Second, there was the laying-on of hands: 'Then he put his hands on her, and immediately she straightened up and praised God' (Luke 13:13). This is power. You can see the change. Jesus often healed the sick with the laying-on of hands, whenever touch seemed to be important.

I suggest that Jesus removed the demon with a 'word' and healed the back through the laying-on of hands in the power of the Spirit. In my experience, this two-stage healing is the more common one where demons are concerned. Like squatters who vandalise property, we need to throw them out first, but then we have to clean up the mess they've left behind and repair the damage.

This principle can be seen to apply to everything else in this chapter. We can lose our peace with God through sin, unforgiveness and demons, and this may lead to physical sickness. We can regain our peace with God through the cross of Christ, repentance, forgiving others and deliverance, but the physical damage that has been done remains. We then need the authority of God and the power of the Holy Spirit to heal the physical damage which is left behind, though his love and healing does seem to flow more freely whenever these barriers have been removed.

30. It's only demons

I was asked by a friend of a friend if I would visit a couple whose five-year-old son had a terminal tumour. It was located in the neck, so an operation was not possible. A Christian lady lived a few doors away, and she agreed to come with me, so we met together for prayer half an hour before our first appointment.

As we prayed, I sensed God telling us to offer three visits. With a non-churchgoing family, it is easy enough to pray for the sick in one visit, but not to share much about Jesus, and this is what we wanted to do most of all. We were delighted when the parents agreed to three sessions.

On our first visit, we shared a few of Jesus' healing stories from the Bible plus our own experience, prayed with the boy for healing, and then left. Both of us sensed a demonic reaction in the boy so, on the second visit, we read together the two stories of children who had been healed by Jesus through deliverance:

a) In Mark 7:24–30, Jesus met a Syro-Phoenician woman who exhibited great faith in Jesus. As a result, he removed a demon from her little daughter without visiting the house.

b) In Mark 9:14–29, Jesus helped a man to believe and then cast a demon out of his son.

In both cases, Jesus ministered to the parent first; only after they had responded in faith were their children healed. We shared this with the couple, who were then happy for us to pray for their son.

On our third visit, we turned to John 3 and talked about being 'born again', after which we asked if either of them would like to be 'born again'. She said yes, and he said not yet. Consequently, we led the mother of the boy in a prayer of commitment and then invited God the Father through Jesus to fill her with his Holy Spirit. The little boy remained upstairs in his bedroom while all this was taking place downstairs in the lounge.

I don't often do this but obeying what I thought was a prompting from the Holy Spirit, I asked God to give her the gift of tongues. We prayed in tongues for a short while and then stopped as a beautiful, flowing language came out of the lady's mouth in something like a Scandinavian accent. I had never experienced anything quite so impressive, and it flowed on and on.

'OK,' I said after a while, 'you can stop now.' But she didn't. 'OK,' I repeated, 'you can stop now.' But she couldn't.

The private gift of tongues is unlike any of the other gifts of the Holy Spirit, in that once received people are able to speak in tongues at any time and stop whenever they choose. But the boy's mother couldn't stop – the speaker of the tongue was controlling her.

'Demon of Satan,' I said, 'in the name of Jesus, I

command you to manifest.' (Nowadays, I seek to bind demons and loose people, but these were early days.)

Three manifestations occurred instantly with such power that we were all taken aback, and each one suggested a different identity:

i) She was thrown from side to side at lightning speed, like a rag doll – anger.
ii) Her eyes seemed to rattle around in her head like a china doll – unforgiveness.
iii) The leer of a mischievous monkey came all over her face – pretence.

I bound them all very quickly in the name of Jesus; the manifestations ceased, and I tried to explain to the startled couple that, as it was only demons, we could deal with them because of Jesus' victory over Satan. At this point, the father of the boy remembered an important appointment and left.

Prompted I believe by God's Spirit, I asked her if she had really wanted to be born again, or was she perhaps just saying it? We then had frank discussions about how she only did it because she wanted her little boy healed and hadn't really believed the stuff about demons. This was understandable, as we had gone rather quickly over the ground because of the limitations of only three meetings, and the condition of her son.

But now, after what she'd just witnessed, the stuff about demons made more sense, and she was ready to pray the prayer again, including repentance, and mean it. After this, the Spirit came on her; she could still speak in tongues, but this time under complete control.

We tackled the demons one at a time, and it was very hard work – even though the lady was able to give us their identity. The demons would not leave until her own sin had been confessed, and in particular her husband's sin against her had been forgiven. Ideally, we would have taken more time expressing the justice of God before asking her to forgive, but time was against us.

This woman was magnificent. Asked to believe in Jesus, his death for her on the cross, his supernatural healings and the existence of demons in three short visits, she made it, for her son. Asked to confess her own private sins and forgive the very serious sins of her husband against her, she got there, for her son. She was like a wounded tigress in the jungle protecting her cubs, and the courage and commitment I witnessed in her is something I will never forget. As the boy was only five, we believed that the parents' sin was the demonic root of his illness (encouraged by what we had read in the New Testament), and that helping at least one of them to be right with God would pave the way for their son's healing.

At times, she was thrown about, retching on the floor, in pain and torment as the demons would not go easily because of the rights they still had. Deliverance is, to my mind, the Rolls-Royce activity for Christians – demons will only go when there is true confession, true forgiveness, true belief and trust in Jesus. It requires 100 per cent commitment, and this remarkable lady made it in three short meetings, for the sake of her son. Those who are cynical about deliverance – *name it and blame it*, they call it – who see it as an easy option, simply have no idea.

We managed to get rid of two of the demons and their manifestations in the time we had left, and arranged to come back after the weekend to do the third one the following Monday morning, but when we returned there were no more manifestations. We asked the Holy Spirit to come; in the name of Jesus, we commanded the third demon to come to the surface, but nothing happened. We tried our best for three hours and got nowhere, so I went to the loo.

'Help, Lord,' I prayed in the little room, and one word came into my mind: 'Mother'.

'Does the word "Mother" mean anything to you?' I asked, when I returned.

'Yes,' she answered. 'I was with her all weekend.'

'And did you tell her about last Friday?' I asked.

'Yes. I always tell her everything,' she replied honestly.

'And. . .' I continued.

'She said it was a load of rubbish. Like fairies at the bottom of the garden,' she told us.

'And did you agree with her?' I asked.

'Yes,' she said.

Over lunch, as gently as we could, we reminded the sick boy's mother about the Bible stories, and what we'd experienced together that seemed to confirm them. Then, during coffee, she said this: 'OK. I believe you're right and Mum's wrong. Let's have another go.'

God came powerfully; the third demon showed itself as before, and within an hour it too had gone, with much coughing and spluttering, just like the other two. We asked God to fill her afresh with his Holy Spirit, and peace came on her face, after which she brought her son downstairs to join us. We anointed the boy with oil, asked the Holy Spirit to come upon him in healing power in the name of Jesus, waited a short while for God's Spirit to do his work, and then left.

Within 24 hours, the boy's tumour had shrunk more than 50 per cent, and by the end of the week it had gone completely. He went back for check-ups every six months, and was eventually declared completely clear and healed. I believe he's now in his twenties. Christ defeated Satan and all his forces at the cross, and the Holy Spirit enables us today to capitalise on that victory (John 12:31–33; Philippians 2:6–11; Colossians 2:13–15).[3]

The boy's mum repented of her sin, forgave those who had sinned against her and learned, as we went along, to trust in Jesus. We then took her through the process of deliverance, with the guidance and power of the Holy

---

[3] In the Church of England, the House of Bishops has produced an excellent Child Protection Policy entitled *Protecting All God's Children* (London: Church House Publishing 2004). It wisely advises that 'obtrusive healing and deliverance . . . may result in children experiencing physical, emotional or sexual abuse'. Please note that Jesus only ministered deliverance to two children at the parents' request, and ministered to a parent first in each case. Similarly, we only ministered to the young boy at the parents' request, and did not do any deliverance to the boy. Ministering to his mum, while he was elsewhere, praying gently over the boy and anointing him with oil in his mother's presence, proved to be sufficient. Most mainline denominational churches have rules and regulations about deliverance and these need to be followed carefully for the protection of all concerned.

Spirit, to a position of peace with God. Then, by the power of the Holy Spirit, as the root of the boy's illness had been dealt with, her son was wonderfully restored. None of this would have been possible without the death of Christ on the cross, for which we are eternally grateful.

8

The Kingdom of God

Jesus taught us to pray, 'Our Father in heaven, hal-
lowed be your name, your kingdom come, your will
be done on earth as it is in heaven' (Matthew 6:9–10).
In heaven, there is no more pain, no more suffering, no
more death, and no more Satan (Revelation 21:4; 20:10).
We therefore need to examine what it means, in terms of
healing, to pray, 'Your kingdom come, your will be done, on
earth.' This is what I found in the New Testament:

- Between the first and second comings of Christ, the coming of God's kingdom is the coming of the Holy Spirit.
- The purpose of the coming of the Spirit, the bringing in
  of God's kingdom, is to defeat the works of darkness here
  on earth and to usher in the kingdom of light.
- Satan's desire is to kill and destroy, but God's desire is to
  heal and restore. Whenever God's kingdom comes,
  therefore, we may expect to see some healing and deliverance.
- But, for now, this is a foretaste of what is yet to come.
  There is an already-and-not-yet tension in the New

Testament which teaches us that, until Jesus returns, we shall have problems which include disease, decay and death.

- We therefore pray and work for God's will to be done on earth as in heaven, while recognising that this will not be fully realised until Jesus returns.

Healing and healing stories are often about God's compassion, love and mercy for one person, but the coming of God's kingdom in the age of the Spirit is a much bigger truth for the whole body of Christ. It is not just about the dramatic restoration of an individual, but the reign of God over the whole of mankind and the fulfilling of his purposes, which include healing. I have therefore used stories about Heidi Baker in this chapter, as they involve the healing of large numbers of people simultaneously, which looks and feels much more like kingdom activity but which, sadly, is yet beyond my experience. The healing stories which involve Heidi in this chapter are the ones she told us on the Wednesday night in Toronto, mentioned in Chapter 1. I found them to be awe-inspiring and theologically helpful.

31. The kingdom comes for God's Makua bride

When God invited Heidi to ride in his chariot of fire, with him holding the reins, it meant, in reality, that she was expected to do everything God told her to do by his Spirit. This is what happened. God said to Heidi, 'I want you to go and get my Makua bride.'

The Bantu language of Makua is spoken by more than four million people in Mozambique, approximately 47 per cent of the population and by far the largest ethnic group in the country. They live primarily in three of the four northernmost provinces of Mozambique, some distance from where Heidi normally operates in Maputo. In the places where the wealthy tourists go, the coastal mainland is rich in elephant and lion, sable and wild dog, while the warm Indian Ocean often throws up glimpses of the marine big five (whales, whale sharks, dolphins, dugongs and manta rays). The sand on the beaches is powder white, the sea a primary blue, while the interior is deciduous woodland densely populated with birdlife. You can even fly here by Pelican Air from Kruger Park in South Africa. In the area to which God called Heidi Baker, however, there was only dirt.

'OK,' replied Heidi, 'but can I take my children with me?' God agreed to let her bring fifty of her five hundred plus orphans, aged between eight and twelve, and they became her ministry team, without badges. They began preaching on the streets near the coastal town of Pemba, and were pelted with rocks for their trouble. A big one struck Heidi in the middle of her back, and caused her considerable pain and discomfort. While the Westerners who had come to observe Heidi's work chose to lock themselves in their Land Rovers and observe this unusual form of evangelism from a safe place, the preaching and ministry continued in the open air, from the back of trucks.

On one occasion, Heidi prayed for a blind man, who was instantly healed. He accepted Jesus Christ as his Lord and Saviour and then stood on the truck, from where he evangelised the crowd. He'd only been a Christian for a minute but his preaching and testifying were as effective as Billy Graham's. When the children hugged and prayed for the sick with childlike faith, thousands were healed and saved.

Heidi was asked if she would visit a man who was crippled and blind and pray for him, as he had no way of getting to the meetings. God's healing-evangelist agreed, even though it was many miles away, and arrived during the hours of darkness. By the light of a torch, she spoke about Jesus and prayed for the man to be healed, but nothing happened. *Rats*, thought Heidi. *All this way and nothing happens.*

'Do you want to get saved?' she asked. Yes! He and his family still wanted Jesus to be their Lord and Saviour. So they did that, and then he said he had a headache. *A headache. Headaches even get healed in North America*, thought Heidi. But she prayed for him anyway, and his headache went. 'When God heals you fully,' said Heidi, just before she left, 'send a runner.'

Heidi returned to the mission near Pemba, where so many were healed and accepted Jesus that a new Christian church was planted there on the Sunday. On the Monday, Heidi sought the help of a Muslim magnate, who virtually owned the city, in order to arrange a trip to India. She was sitting in his posh car when runners arrived and began knocking on the window.

The blind and crippled man had been completely healed by Jesus, and they had run for six to seven hours to tell her the story. The magnate heard it all, begged

Heidi to pray for him immediately, received prayer in the name of Jesus and began sobbing his heart out as he accepted Christ for himself. His influence on others was then considerable. Heidi, who has a degree in theology, then did some theology with us.

'I didn't know why God did not heal the man when I prayed for him, but God did. He's God. He likes being God. We're only concerned because we're not God. He calculated that I would be talking to the influential Muslim at precisely this point in time and healed the man at the right moment for the runners to arrive six to seven hours later, as I was talking to him. God is God and likes being who he is.'

This is God's timing. This is God's activity. Neither the sick, nor the saved, nor the unsaved got what they wanted when they wanted it, but when the power of the Lord was present to heal the sick man, he was healed – not before and not after. Thanks to the obedience of Heidi, God was able to be God, and do what he wanted to do, when he wanted to do it. 'Your kingdom come, your will be done on earth', in the dirt.

To God be all the glory!

The two kingdoms

I still remember the John Wimber Signs and Wonders conferences of the mid-1980s with great affection. John had been a member of the Righteous Brothers, who'd once achieved three top ten hits at the same time, so the musical aspect of worship at the meetings was first class. God also moved powerfully amongst us by his Holy Spirit, providing us with plenty to observe and experience, and many of us witnessed things we had never seen before. But what appealed most to those of us who were in church leadership roles was his teaching on the kingdom of God.

What John taught was that signs and wonders, including healing, came with the kingdom of God package. When Jesus sent out the Twelve and the seventy-two, they proclaimed the kingdom, healed the sick and cast out demons. They were given authority and power to do this, the authority and power which comes with the Holy Spirit, and all three activities, when successful, achieved the same goal: the kingdom of God came when the Holy Spirit came, and when people responded in faith to his coming they left the kingdom of Satan, were born again by the Spirit of God into the kingdom of God, and sickness and demonisation, which characterised the dominion of darkness, were overcome when they were healed and delivered, by the same Holy Spirit. Whenever Christians proclaim the kingdom, heal the sick and cast out demons in the power of the Holy Spirit, and people respond in faith, the kingdom of God advances at the expense of the kingdom of Satan. Theologically, theoretically, this corresponded totally to what we had been taught at college, whichever shade of churchmanship we came from.

The liberal scholar Rudolf Bultmann wrote this in his *Theology of the New Testament*:

The dominant concept of Jesus' message is the *Reign of God*. Jesus proclaims its immediately impending irruption, now already making itself felt. Reign of God is an eschatological concept. It means the regime of God which will destroy the present course of the world, wipe out all the contra-divine, Satanic power under which the present world groans – and thereby, terminating all pain and sorrow, bring in salvation for the People of God which awaits the fulfilment of the prophets' promises.

He went on to write this:

Jesus is convinced that the world's present course is under the sway of Satan and his demons.[1]

The conservative evangelical scholar George Eldon Ladd, in *Jesus and the Kingdom*, used a quote from Professor T. W. Manson to make his point:

The essential thing for understanding both the ministry of Jesus and the theology of Paul is the doctrine of the two kingdoms: the Kingdom of God and the kingdom of Satan. All the evils under which men suffer, and all the evils which they commit, may be regarded as the manifestation in history of the power of the evil kingdom. All men's hopes for the future – the future of the world or of the individual – are bound up with the triumph of the Kingdom of God over the kingdom of Satan. That, when it comes, is the coming of the Kingdom of God in power.[2]

The Roman Catholic scholar Raymond Brown, in his commentary on John's Gospel, wrote this about Matthew, Mark and Luke:

---

[1] Rudolf Bultmann, *Theology of the New Testament*, Volume One (London: SCM Press Ltd 1952), p. 5.

[2] George Eldon Ladd, *Jesus and the Kingdom* (London: SPCK 1966), p. 116.

Let us begin with the Synoptic Gospels, where the miracles are primarily acts of power (*dynameis*) accompanying the breaking of the reign of God into time. The miracles worked by Jesus are not simply external proofs of his claims, but more fundamentally are acts by which he establishes God's reign and defeats the reign of Satan. Many of the miracles attack Satan directly by driving out demons. Many more heal sickness which is associated with sin and evil. The raising of men to life is an assault on death which is Satan's peculiar realm. Even the nature miracles, like the calming of the storm, are an attack on the disorders introduced into nature by Satan.[3]

And the feel of all this at the Wimber conferences was very, very positive. Normally, what happens to church leaders like me is that a request is made to go and visit an individual who is not well. I see them at home or in hospital, say some prayers and hope they get better. If they don't, I take the funeral and try to comfort the bereaved – all on an individual basis. I pray hard, asking – at times begging – that God will heal my friend, and I win some but lose a lot.

The kingdom of God coming in power felt very different from this. John Wimber invited the Holy Spirit to come on 3,000–4,000 all at once, and it seemed more like a kingdom activity. Theologically, we found ourselves moving from the isolated, negative, apologetic *say a prayer for you* mentality to the way it was always meant to be. Healing and deliverance were part of God's purposes in advancing his kingdom, on earth as in heaven, and many of us wanted to be a part of the King's army doing just that. John taught us to ask the

---

[3] Raymond E. Brown, *The Gospel According to John I-XII* (London: Geoffrey Chapman 1971), p. 525.

Holy Spirit to come, to wait for his coming and then to seek to respond to his coming, believing that by so doing God's kingdom would come among us. The results we were able to observe during the times of ministry made it look as if he was right.

Coming away from such conferences, I no longer felt that healing was just for special people to do at special times, but a bread-and-butter activity of daily Christian living that was meant to involve all of us. I've had a very exciting 20 years trying to do this stuff, in the power of the Holy Spirit, and this book is written to encourage others to have a go. Inevitably, this means we need to look at the relevant Bible verses as well as sharing the stories, to check out the solid base from which all this comes.

The kingdom comes[4]

'In those days John the Baptist came, preaching in the Desert of Judea and saying, "Repent, for the kingdom of heaven is near"' (Matthew 3:1–2). John the Baptist began his ministry by saying that the kingdom of God was near.[5]

'After John was put in prison, Jesus went into Galilee, proclaiming the good news of God. "The time has come," he said. "The kingdom of God is near. Repent and believe the

---

[4] The first part of this section appeared in *Signs and Blunders* and is reprinted here with the kind permission of Monarch Publications. Peter H. Lawrence, *Signs and Blunders* (Crowborough: Monarch Publications 1994).

[5] Matthew uses 'kingdom of heaven' when the other Gospel writers use 'kingdom of God'. They are interchangeable.

good news!"' (Mark 1:14–15). Jesus began his ministry by saying the kingdom of God was near.

'These twelve Jesus sent out with the following instructions . . . "As you go, preach this message: 'The kingdom of heaven is near'"' (Matthew 10:5–7). The twelve apostles began their ministry by saying that the kingdom of God was near.

> After this the Lord appointed seventy-two others and sent them two by two ahead of him to every town and place where he was about to go. He told them . . . 'When you enter a town and are welcomed, eat what is set before you. Heal the sick who are there and tell them, "The kingdom of God is near you."' (Luke 10:1–2, 8–9)

The seventy-two began their ministry by saying the kingdom of God was near.

John the Baptist, Jesus, the twelve apostles and the seventy-two all began by saying the kingdom of God was near. So when did it arrive? When did the kingdom of God move from being near to being here? The answer is to be found in Matthew, immediately after the Pharisees accused Jesus of casting out demons by Beelzebub. This is what Jesus replied:

> Every kingdom divided against itself will be ruined, and every city or household divided against itself will not stand. If Satan drives out Satan, he is divided against himself. How then can his kingdom stand? And if I drive out demons by Beelzebub, by whom do your people drive them out? So then, they will be your judges. But if I drive out demons by the Spirit of God, *then* the kingdom of God has come upon you. (Matthew 12:25–28; my italics)

The kingdom of God comes when the Holy Spirit comes: kicking out the kingdom of darkness; bringing in the kingdom of light. These few verses (above) in Matthew touch on all the major issues of the two kingdoms, which need a brief look.

The kingdom of Satan

Is Satan a king, and does he have a kingdom? Jesus said: 'If Satan drives out Satan, he is divided against himself. How then can *his kingdom* stand?' (Matthew 12:26; my italics). Because we know that Jesus was not casting out demons by Beelzebub, we can assume that Satan does have a kingdom and it stands. Jesus referred to it as 'his kingdom' (Matthew 12:26).

Jesus gave Satan the title 'prince of this world' three times (John 12:31; 14:30; 16:11). Paul called him 'the god of this age' (2 Corinthians 4:4), 'the ruler of the *kingdom* of the air' (Ephesians 2:2; my italics), and referred to his area of control as 'the dominion of darkness' (Colossians 1:13). In his letter to the Ephesians, he wrote this:

> Put on the full armour of God so that you can take your stand against the devil's schemes. For our struggle is not against flesh and blood, but against the rulers, against the authorities, against the powers of this dark world and against the spiritual forces of evil in the heavenly realms. (Ephesians 6:11–12)

If the devil has 'rulers', 'authorities', 'powers' and 'spiritual forces of evil' to carry out his schemes, it sounds like a kingdom to me, if not an empire, with him at the top. And he is not just one of many because John writes: 'The reason the

Son of God appeared was to destroy the devil's work' (1 John 3:8). John also writes that 'the whole world is under the control of the evil one' (1 John 5:19). The devil seems to be enemy number one. In the book of Revelation, we read this about the devil, or Satan:

> The great dragon was hurled down – that ancient serpent called the devil, or Satan, who leads the whole world astray. He was hurled to the earth, and his angels with him . . . Then the dragon was enraged at the woman and went off to make war against the rest of her offspring – those who obey God's commandments and hold to the testimony of Jesus. (Revelation 12:9, 17)

Someone who can lead the world astray and has 'his angels with him' sounds like a formidable opponent to me. In the end, he gathers the nations of the world together to wage war against God's people (Revelation 20:7–9). The good news is that he loses; the bad news is that it hasn't happened yet.

I can understand the reluctance of some to use the phrase 'two kingdoms', lest they give the impression that it is two equal kingdoms. It never has been, and it never will be. Satan is but a created being; whenever God says, 'Enough is enough,' and snaps his fingers, Satan is gone. But until then, God chooses to work with, in and through Jesus' disciples to overcome the evil that the serpent commits on the earth, and to defeat the army he uses to do it. Peter, who had the keys to the kingdom of God against which hell could not prevail (Matthew 16:18–19), certainly thought the devil was still a force to be reckoned with: 'Your enemy the devil prowls around like a roaring lion looking for someone to devour' (1 Peter 5:8).

From a brief look at the New Testament, it does seem to me that there is a case for saying that Satan does have a kingdom; he is the boss, and Christians are at war with him.

Jesus' kingdom

Jesus said, 'If I drive out demons by the Spirit of God, then the kingdom of God has come upon you' (Matthew 12:28). A key phrase here is 'by the Spirit of God'. The Spirit of God can enter into a person, which Jesus in the flesh cannot do, and kick out evil spirits from within. This is one of the reasons why Jesus said, 'The kingdom of God does not come with your careful observation, nor will people say, "Here it is," or "There it is," because the kingdom of God is within you' (Luke 17:20–21). This means that those who receive the Spirit when he comes enter the kingdom of God.

> Jesus answered, 'I tell you the truth, no-one can enter the kingdom of God unless he is born of water and the Spirit. Flesh gives birth to flesh, but the Spirit gives birth to spirit. You should not be surprised at my saying, "You must be born again."' (John 3:5–7)

The Spirit of Jesus knocks at the door of our lives, and if we let him in then the kingdom of God is within us. We become temples of the Holy Spirit (1 Corinthians 6:19). The coming of the Spirit of God, with power to all who believe in Jesus, is the coming of the kingdom of God. Whenever we pray, 'Your kingdom come, your will be done on earth' in the Lord's Prayer (Matthew 6:10), we are in effect praying, 'Come, Holy Spirit.'

From then on, when we let God do what he wants to do

in and through us by his Spirit, we are making Jesus the King of our lives. When this happens, the kingdom of God is coming on earth as it is in heaven.

In the Old Testament, the kingdom of God was Israel. It was a visible kingdom with clearly defined borders. When Jesus returns, every eye will see him and once more the kingdom of God will be a visible one with clear-cut boundaries. In between times, in the age of the Spirit, the kingdom of God is a spiritual kingdom, an invisible one not limited by time or space. For now, the kingdom of God is a reign which comes when the Holy Spirit comes to all who believe in Jesus and accept him as the King of their lives. Jesus said, 'You know him, for he lives with you and will be in you' (John 14:17).

When we become Christians, we move from the kingdom of darkness to the kingdom of light. Paul writes this to the Colossians: 'For he has rescued us from the dominion of darkness and brought us into the kingdom of the Son he loves, in whom we have redemption, the forgiveness of sins' (Colossians 1:13–14). Those who do believe in Jesus have 'passed from death to life' (1 John 3:14); they have moved 'out of darkness into his wonderful light' (1 Peter 2:9); they have gone from being under the control of the 'father of lies' (John 8:44) to being filled with the Spirit of truth (John 14:16–17).

The aims of the two kingdoms

And the purposes of the two kingdoms are very clear: 'The thief comes only to steal and kill and destroy; I [Jesus] have come that they may have life, and have it to the full' (John

10:10). The subjects in the kingdom of Satan are ruled by a king whose purpose in life is to steal, kill and destroy, whereas the subjects in the kingdom of God, ruled by King Jesus (1 Timothy 6:15), inherit eternal life and are empowered to spread God's love abroad. Darkness and light, death and life, lies and truth are all contrasts that imply there is no middle ground, with everyone belonging to one kingdom or the other. Because of the seriousness of the division and purposes of the two kingdoms, the constant battle of the two kingdoms is what born-again Christians are called to be engaged in all the time. This is why Jesus gave authority and power to his disciples and sent them out to proclaim the kingdom, heal the sick and cast out demons (Luke 9:1; 10:1–9). The result and Jesus' response were very revealing: 'The seventy-two returned with joy and said, "Lord, even the demons submit to us in your name." He replied, "I saw Satan fall like lightning from heaven"' (Luke 10:17–18).

The disciples of Jesus, given power and authority, can alleviate the darkness by building the kingdom of light. Just as Satan was defeated in heaven, so he is now being defeated on earth, and because Jesus baptises us in the Holy Spirit, all who believe in him can continue to do the same as he did when on earth (John 14:12, 16). And the power to do signs and wonders, the power of the Holy Spirit, is inextricably linked to the coming of God's kingdom. Jesus sees this coming of the Spirit of truth in power to his disciples as the coming of the kingdom of God: 'And he said to them, "I tell you the truth, some who are standing here will not taste death before they see the kingdom of God come with power"' (Mark 9:1).

On the Day of Pentecost, after one of their number had already tasted death, the kingdom of God came in power (Acts 2:1–4). Paul also mentions the power: 'For the kingdom of God is not a matter of talk but of power' (1 Corinthians 4:20).

This is the gospel of Jesus Christ. This Jesus, who proclaimed the kingdom of God, healed the sick and cast out demons, who died for our sins on the cross, and defeated death by rising again and ascending into heaven, now pours out his Holy Spirit on us – that we may continue his work here on earth. It is the work of dispelling the dominion of darkness and ushering in the kingdom of light.

32. The kingdom comes to Brazil

In Mozambique, there are no posters or media advertising that prepare people for when Heidi comes in God's chariot of fire. In the dirt, some of it caused by the horrendous floods of 2000, while ducking and weaving to avoid the stones that are being thrown, it is not difficult to give all the glory to God. But when Heidi went alone to Brazil, without her children, the church was packed and waiting for her arrival. The coming of 'The woman of power for the hour' had been advertised.

'How may you get all the glory here?' asked Heidi, who hates seeing herself on posters.

'Use the children,' replied God.

The worship was sincere and sensitive, and the people were open to God, even though they had never seen any creative miracles. Heidi got all the children – eight, nine, ten years old – to come to the front, despite the strange looks of the smartly dressed elders. 'Do you children believe God heals the sick?'

'Of course,' they replied, even though they had never seen it happen.

'OK,' said the unusual missionary. 'You're the prayer team. Those who are really sick or dying come up the front.'

There had already been some electrifying ministry sending shock waves through a number of people, but some of them were even more shocked at the thought of the children ministering to the sick and dying.

'They haven't been through class,' advised one elder. 'We haven't covered healing yet on the curriculum.'

'Just hug 'em,' responded Heidi, believing that to be the only training necessary. They hugged a guy in a wheelchair, and he got out and walked. They hugged a lady with large hearing aids, who took them out and could hear perfectly without them. They hugged a little girl of five or six, who had crippling arthritis and was blind – a girl the kids from the prayer team had teased in times past. The girl began to walk, opening and closing her hand, and full sight came to one eye. She did not have the other eye, and it was not healed, but when the Holy Spirit came and the kingdom of God came, she saw with the other one. Many others were also healed. Heidi confessed that she could not do miracles, and God got all the glory because he used the children, who had not done healing in their classes.

Our God reigns

The kingdom of God comes today when the Holy Spirit comes, and the kingdom comes in us whenever we allow him to do whatever he wants to do. This means that healing for us, body, soul and spirit, is a by-product of his coming, not the main agenda.

The main agenda of the Spirit who comes is to bring glory to Jesus, the King, and healing tends to come to us when we seek to do the same. This is why Heidi works so hard in her missions to point people to Jesus and not to herself, and understanding this can help us to grasp the significance of healing in relation to the kingdom in the New Testament.

The problem with healing and 'healing services' is that we who are sick want God to do for us what we want. Sometimes people call for me, the vicar, like they call for the gas man or the television mechanic. They don't want anything to change. They just want their heating, their television and their bad foot fixing – as it was before. But the coming of the kingdom of God, the coming of the healing Holy Spirit, is not like that. The coming of a new kingdom is intended to be the coming of a new reign – when the king can do whatever he wants, and his subjects say yes to him in all things.

The perfect Son of God lived amongst the people of Nazareth for something like 25 years. During that time, Jesus did whatever they told him to do. He was obedient to his parents, the religious and political laws of his day, and his schoolteachers. As a carpenter/builder, the client would give him orders; Jesus would obey them, and for 30 years everyone was very happy with this.

But when Jesus was anointed with the Spirit and began teaching and demonstrating the coming of the kingdom of God, even though healing came with it, they were not happy bunnies. When he claimed to be the Messiah and to have authority over them, they tried to overthrow him, over a cliff (Luke 4:28–30).

Korazin, Bethsaida and Capernaum were just as bad (Matthew 11:20–24): they wanted healing but they didn't want the healer. They wanted the King to heal them, to fix them, like the gas man, but they didn't want a new kingdom which made demands on their lives and changes to their lifestyles.

This is one of the major drawbacks of the covenant-right teaching. It is all about our rights to healing, health and wholeness for our sake, or our church's sake, or our community's sake. Sometimes, because God loves us, he graciously grants our requests, but this is not what Jesus taught nor demonstrated about the kingdom. Rather, we are exhorted to seek first the kingdom of God (Matthew 6:33) and his lordship over our lives, and then other things such as healing will be added unto us, as he directs, after that. Ironically, many of us are sick with stress and worry because we are not totally surrendered to the King.

When the Spirit comes, then the kingdom of God comes, and then the power of God begins pulling down the dominion of darkness and replacing it with the lordship of Christ. Because Satan's aim is to destroy, and God's desire is to heal, and because there is no sickness in heaven, degrees of healing and deliverance will always take place when the Spirit comes in power and is welcomed. But this is why it often doesn't look very pretty. It is what John Wimber called a 'clash of two kingdoms'. When the Spirit comes, that which is hidden in darkness comes to light and needs dealing with; strongholds need to be broken; wrong thinking needs to be changed, and yes needs to be said to Jesus in total surrender, if his will is to be done on earth as in heaven.

The person most surrendered to Jesus I have ever seen is Heidi Baker, and she has experienced the greatest number of healings in 2005 that I've heard about. Of course, Heidi lives and works and has her being amongst the powerless people of the world. When power comes to them, they don't care what it looks like and many healings take place, whereas the powerful, with everything to lose, locked in their Land Rovers, who raise their eyebrows when strange things take place, don't regularly see the healings that Heidi sees.

And the thinking and the theology play an important part in this. I believe that if individuals, groups and churches regularly asked the Holy Spirit to come, to do whatever he wants to do, rather than trying to tell him what he ought to do, then God's kingdom would come more powerfully, more often, and begin to change the world. I am sure we would then see more healings, as a kind of by-product, as well.

33. The kingdom comes to Chicago

'Chicago? I don't want to go to Chicago,' said the American, Heidi Baker. 'Nothing happens in Chicago.'

'I'm going to Chicago,' responded God. 'Will you come with me?'

'Sure,' replied Heidi. 'If you're going, I'm going.'

So the chariot moved into Illinois, beside Lake Michigan,

to the city more noted for its ungodly activities than its godly ones. It was difficult here to find ways of giving all the glory to God because all the kids had been moved out to do colouring. There were two or three who had sneaked in and the rest of the ministry team had to be made up of radical-looking teenagers who had 'everything everywhere'.

'Do you believe God does things?' asked Heidi.

'Yeah,' they said, so they became the ministry team.

'Who's dying in the house?' enquired the all-American lady missionary. And the dying came up in their little cars, or were carried to the front by friends.

There was a man with a brain tumour, and a lady with tumours throughout her whole body with less than three weeks to live. Another lady looked as pale as a ghost, as if she was about to expire there and then, and there were two really big guys who were crippled. The radical-looking teenagers, despite having 'everything everywhere', and despite the non-too-affirming looks of the smart elders, just hugged them.

Heidi hugged the whiter-shade-of-pale lady, and then shrieked at her. 'Spirit of death, I rebuke you in the name of Jesus. Get out,' she commanded. And then she added, by way of clarification, 'No. Not you, lady. The thing on you.' Apparently it left, at which point Heidi invited the corpse to dance.

'I'm paralysed,' she explained quietly. But get up and dance she did, while her husband fell apart at the realisation that his wife had been fully healed, despite being so close to death.

Encouraged by this, Heidi grabbed the big guys and said, 'Let's dance.'

'Actually,' one of them replied, 'we can't walk.' But dance they did, not elegantly, but successfully. Despite their size, they blubbered across the platform, tripping over their trousers which had never been fitted properly, as previously they couldn't walk.

Heidi hugged the lady full of tumours for 20 minutes until, in the power of the Holy Spirit, she began vibrating visibly all over her body. She was totally healed and joined in the dance, spinning round and round. Some people think dancing is of the devil, but God was doing it that night – the night the kingdom of God came to Chicago.

Already and not yet

When the Holy Spirit comes and people welcome him, then the kingdom of God comes, but how much of heaven can we expect here on earth before Jesus returns? Will Heidi Baker keep doing what she is doing until the whole world is evangelised, healed and delivered, and the Christian church emerges triumphant, or can we only expect the full benefits of the kingdom of God to be realised when Jesus returns?

Bible-believing scholars often write about the 'already' and 'not yet' tension of the New Testament – what they classify as 'realised eschatology' and 'future eschatology', what is offered when the Spirit comes now, compared to what is yet to come. This now needs our attention.

Some people teach that as Satan was defeated at the cross of Christ, and Satan is responsible for all sickness, we can all be healed of everything today because of Jesus' victory. This will indeed be true in the New Jerusalem, but we need to ask, 'What is prophesied and promised in the Bible for today?'

The second coming of Jesus. . .

The tension between the 'already' and the 'not yet' can be seen clearly in the doctrine of the second coming, particularly as prophesied in Isaiah.

Already Jesus has been conceived (Isaiah 7:14), born (Isaiah 9:6), anointed (Isaiah 11:1–2), healed the sick (Isaiah 35:5–6), died (Isaiah 53:8), risen (Isaiah 53:10–11), brought in the New Covenant and sent the Holy Spirit to us (Isaiah 59:20–21). But *not yet* has the Prince of Peace caused the world to 'beat their swords into ploughshares and their spears into pruning hooks' (Isaiah 2:4), the leopard to lie down with the goat (Isaiah 11:6), the nations to be judged (Isaiah 2:4), or the new heavens and new earth to bring an end to premature death, with healing for all (Isaiah 65:20).

On the other side of the same coin, we note that although Satan has *already* been defeated twice, both by the Archangel Michael (Revelation 12:7–9) and also by Jesus (John 12:31), the accuser is *not yet* dead, chained, or removed from the earth. In Revelation 12:17, after Satan, the dragon, has been thrown out of heaven by Michael and the holy angels, he goes off to 'make war against the rest of her offspring – those who obey God's commandments and hold to the testimony of Jesus'.

Timing is often confused in the book of Revelation but 'war against' those who 'hold to the testimony of Jesus' looks to me very much like a post-Easter war, in which Satan is still alive and active. In 1 Peter 5:8, after Jesus has died, risen and ascended, we read of the devil prowling around 'like a roaring lion looking for someone to devour'. Peter seems to think the devil is not only still alive but dangerous.

In 1 John 5:19, more than half a century after Jesus has ascended into heaven, John writes about 'the whole world' being 'under the control of the evil one'. To say that Jesus has already completed his defeat of Satan is, therefore, a little premature. When Jesus told a parable about wheat and weeds, good and evil, he said this: 'Let both grow together until the harvest' (Matthew 13:30). And the angel in Revelation said: 'Let him who does wrong continue to do wrong . . . let him who does right continue to do right; and let him who is holy continue to be holy' (Revelation 22:11).

George Eldon Ladd, in his book *Jesus and the Kingdom,* discusses the 'tension between the Kingdom of God and a sinful world, between the age to come and the present evil age'. His conclusion regarding the second coming of Christ is particularly relevant:

> The consummation as Jesus viewed it would not be a 'historical' event like other events but would be the inbreaking of God into history. This means we can expect no relief from the tension of the already and the not yet until the final consummation. History is not moving towards it: when it happens God will break in sovereignly and until then faith rather than sight will be our pathway.[6]

---

[6] George Eldon Ladd, *Jesus and the Kingdom*, pp. 334, 331.

Disease. . .

According to Revelation, Jesus' final victory over Satan is yet to come (Revelation 20:10), and Jesus, the Prince of Peace, says that until then there will be all kinds of trouble, including diseases: 'Nation will rise against nation, and kingdom against kingdom. There will be great earthquakes, famines and pestilences' (Luke 21:10–11).

The world we live in does not look like one in which Satan has *already* been finally defeated – that is *not yet*. For now, before the *not yet* becomes the *already*, it looks much more like the one that Jesus prophesied we'd experience before he returns. According to Jesus, there will be 'pestilences', diseases, until that time and, according to Paul, as we noted in Chapter 4 on the Epistles, the whole world will continue to decay as we wait for the new creation.

Decay. . .

Paul writes in Romans that the Spirit gives us the 'firstfruits' but not the full glory, especially in our bodies, which is yet to be revealed, and until then our bodies will continue to suffer from decay (Romans 8:22–23). The 'firstfruits', or foretaste, of what is to come happens when the Spirit releases the gifts of healing, miracles and faith among us and we taste something of the joys that we await eagerly. Can we claim healing from decay as well as disease because of the cross of Christ? I suspect not, or else we'd all be living longer than Methuselah (Genesis 5:27), which brings me naturally to death.

Death. . .

Death is probably the easiest example in the Bible to understand in terms of the 'already/not yet' tension of the age of the Spirit, between the first and second comings of Jesus. Paul writes, 'For as in Adam all die, so in Christ all will be made alive' (1 Corinthians 15:22). When Adam sinned (Eve too), human beings became mortal, and those who were not killed by the sword eventually became ill (like Isaac, Jacob and Elisha), and died. Jesus has indeed defeated Satan at the cross; all authority in heaven and earth has been given to Jesus, and he offers eternal life to all who believe and trust in him; 'in Christ all will be made alive' – but physically, not yet. Jesus said this: 'I am the resurrection and the life. He who believes in me will live, even though he dies; and whoever lives and believes in me will never die' (John 11:26).

Jesus' promise of eternal life does not end physical death, even though the Spirit of Jesus enables believers to experience abundant life now. Jesus said 'even though he dies', implying the inevitability of death. Jesus said this just before he raised Lazarus from the dead, but even Lazarus had to die again. All of Jesus' first disciples are now dead and, even in Paul's time, some believers in Thessalonica had fallen asleep. When Jesus was on earth, it was the age of Jesus; when he returns, it looks from Scripture that it will be the age of Jesus again, but for now, between the first and second comings of Jesus, we live in the age of the Spirit, who chooses his timing and opts to work with, in and through fallen, sinful people, who are still subject to disease, decay and death (1 John 1:8).

Already, we can receive the gift of eternal life and have a foretaste of heaven, the 'firstfruits', as we experience the presence and power of the Holy Spirit, and sometimes this includes temporary healing, but not yet have we been saved and healed from the ultimate pain of physical death and mourning. Satan has already been defeated but he is not yet dead. Jesus has already been victorious, but his true reign has not yet been fully realised, and the demonic has not yet been chained or removed from the earth. The healing ministry of the Spirit, in Jesus' name, reflects this tension – some are healed, some are not, but all die.

Joni Eareckson Tada is a good example of this tension.[7] From a wheelchair, her writing, preaching, singing, painting and films have helped more people to know Christ than most fit and able-bodied Christians have ever managed. While she groans as Paul did, waiting for a new body, God has used her and her suffering mightily to spread his kingdom on earth.

Not easily, and not without many problems, Joni has tried to yield herself and her life to the will of God, bringing positive results to God's kingdom. Following a different path, Heidi Baker has sought to do the same, also in very difficult and painful situations, and by the grace of God has brought positive results too. Our prayer continues to be: 'Your kingdom come,' but it is also: 'Your will be done,' for: 'Yours is the kingdom, the power and the glory.'

---

[7] Joni Eareckson and Joe Musser, *Joni* (Glasgow: Pickering & Inglis 1978).

34. The kingdom comes to Sierra Leone

When the chariot of fire took Heidi Baker to Sierra Leone, she saw the kingdom of God come with power and glory in a way she'd only dreamed about before.

There was a big problem for Heidi in terms of publicity and posters, which meant she couldn't go out of the house without being mobbed. The room she was in had no light, no electricity, no water, and was very hot, so despite the success of the meetings she felt pretty miserable for most of the time she was there.

On the first night, she removed all the elders who were sitting on the stage behind her dressed in smart suits, and danced with the kids in the dirt. The hierarchy were not greatly impressed, but even so, thousands were saved and healed.

On the second night, people got out of wheelchairs, blind eyes were healed and this time thousands and thousands were saved and healed. But on the third night, Heidi was really struggling to help people take their eyes off her and to focus on Jesus.

'Let me see your glory, Lord,' she prayed. In the Bible, the glory is often seen as the manifest presence of God, and this is what Heidi desired so that the people would give all the glory to Jesus.

'If you'll get low,' Jesus seemed to say to the missionary, 'I'll walk across the field pouring out oil and everyone will be healed.' So right in the middle of the meeting, Heidi stopped speaking, knelt down on the ground and put her face in the dirt. The interpreter began to freak out and kept trying to say something, but the speaker said, 'Shhh,' and eventually he did.

Gradually, everyone else did the same. The whole football field was packed with people who got down on their knees and put their faces in the dirt. Heidi didn't comment on this when she told the story, but as the majority of people were Muslims who were used to doing this in their mosques, it seemed to me to have special significance as they were now bowing down to Jesus.

Not a baby cried; not a mother moved; not a teenager wriggled. Heidi then saw Jesus walking over the field pouring oil on everyone who was sick.

'Now,' said Jesus by his Spirit, 'tell them what I've just done.'

Heidi told them, and the once blind, deaf and paralysed Muslims came forward to testify to being healed, giving all the glory to Jesus. That night, tens of thousands of people were saved.

The sick were healed as Jesus anointed them with oil – the outward symbol of being anointed with the Holy Spirit. Heidi finished by saying, 'The glory of God filled the house.' When we get low with abandoned love and yield ourselves to his glory, then the kingdom of God comes among us by his Spirit, and healing often comes with the glory.

9

Name It and Claim It

The Pentecostal church is the fastest growing church in the world. Throughout the twentieth century, they have taught the rest of us that Jesus heals today and have demonstrated it in their meetings. Some of their best-known preachers encourage everyone to name their sicknesses before God and to claim their healing from him in Jesus' name, and regularly – especially in their larger gatherings – some are healed. The Pentecostal church probably sees more healings per square metre than any other church.

So I searched the New Testament to find out if 'name it and claim it' is a biblical notion, and this is what I discovered:

- The New Testament exhorts us to claim it, if God names it.
- We do not have a written word from God in the Bible to claim healing for all diseases, at all times, and in all places.
- We do sometimes receive a spoken word from God, through his Spirit, for healing in Jesus' name.

• When God names it by his Spirit, we are encouraged to exercise faith in him by claiming it, in the name of Jesus.

35. Healing in the car park

In the autumn of 1988, after 24 hours of travelling, I arrived in the warm heart of Africa one Saturday night.[1] I was extremely tired, but as I lay down to sleep a 'God thought' began to swirl around in my head. 'In the Blantyre congregation tomorrow there will be a teenage boy who can't see very well.' As I prayed into it, God seemed to say, 'He wants to go to university but is hampered in his studies. I want to heal him.'

I arrived at the church at 7.30 am, feeling lonely as well as tired. 'I'm all on my own,' I moaned to God, 'and nobody will be up praying for me as it is only 5.30 in the morning back home.'

'I am with you,' God seemed to say, 'and Sister Mary is already on her knees praying for you in chapel.'[2] I checked it out when I returned home, and Sister Mary, from the community of St John, was in fact on her knees in chapel at 5.30 am, praying for me. How wonderful!

I met the Anglican vicar, Father Zimbe, who helped me into all kinds of colourful, heavy robes in preparation for the 8 o'clock mass, and as he did so I mentioned my conversation with God.

---

[1] I visited Malawi on behalf of SOMA, at the invitation of Tom Walker.

[2] Sister Mary was from the community of St John, Alum Rock, in the parish where I used to be the vicar.

'Last night,' I began, 'I thought I heard God say he wanted to do some healing this morning.'

'No, no, no,' responded Father Zimbe instantaneously, 'we don't do healing. It's the mass. We do the mass.'

I finished robing, complimented those present on the beautiful vestments they had provided for me, and tried again. 'I really did believe God was telling me he wanted to do healing,' I said, as kindly as I could.

'No, no,' he replied, 'you can speak for ten minutes, with an interpreter, and then we'll get on with the mass.'

'So I can't do healing?' I asked for the last time.

'No, we'll do the mass,' Father Zimbe concluded, 'but you can speak on healing.'

So much for Sister Mary's prayers, I thought – wrongly. At ten to eight, the phone in the vestry rang and Father Zimbe carried on a conversation in Chichewa for a few minutes, during which he occasionally mentioned my name. 'That was the bishop,' he announced as he put the receiver down. 'He said Peter Lawrence is to be allowed to do whatever he wants to do.'

'Healing,' I proclaimed.

'No more than ten minutes,' concluded Father Zimbe. We then processed with a group of people dressed as angels into the large, impressive, packed church.

When I stood up to speak, there were approximately 200 women in blue-and-white Mother's Union uniforms facing me on my right-hand side, and about 200 men in normal apparel on my left. Behind me, in an ornate chancel as long as the nave, Father Zimbe sat behind the high altar surrounded by a host of angels.

At the end of my talk, I gave the 'word' I thought God had given me: 'I believe God may be saying there is a teenage boy here who wants to go to university, but he is hampered in his studies because he can't see very well. I think God wants to heal him.'

Without waiting for the translation, an elderly man in his seventies leapt to his feet at the very back of the church, with his hand in the air, and declared loudly in English, 'That's me. That's me.'

Before I could respond, Father Zimbe rose up at the other end of the church and shouted back in perfect English, 'No it's not, you silly old fool. Sit down.'

The old man, however, was not going to be distracted that easily, and kept walking towards me as he responded: 'But I can't see very well and I want to be healed.'

At this, the vicar came out from behind the candles and marched menacingly towards the man who couldn't see very well, like the sheriff facing a gunslinger at high noon. 'That may be so,' he said in a firm voice, 'but you're not going to university I do know.'

Undeterred, the elderly man kept coming towards me and, without deviation, Father Zimbe made his way towards the portable lectern where I was standing, and there they met eyeball to eyeball in front of my nose. At this point, I believe God gave me a word of wisdom. 'It's all right, Father Zimbe,' I said, 'we'll have a quick prayer with him and then we'll get on with the mass.'

'Ah yes!' he drooled. 'The mass.'

Nothing happened to the elderly man when I prayed for him, and as I moved to join the angelic host my mind was full of non-angelic thoughts. *All this way – tried to be obedient – Sister Mary praying – taking a risk for Jesus but nothing happens – and now I have to sit here in all this hot, heavy clobber, as the temperature rises beyond sweating-point, in a capacity crowd.* At least the incense kept the mosquitoes at bay.

Afterwards, having divested but still wishing the ground would swallow me up, I was making my way across the car park to the hall for a coffee, when I found myself surrounded by a group of excited teenage boys. 'This is the boy,' they said virtually in unison. 'This is MacDonald.'

Well you're too late, was my first thought, and *Push off!* was the second, but fortunately neither of them crossed my lips. I certainly wasn't feeling very holy or full of faith at the time.

'Why didn't he claim the word in church?' I asked, as politely as I could.

'In this country, we respect our elders,' their spokesman began, 'and after the old man had jumped up so speedily it was not possible for MacDonald to claim it.' This was blatantly true, as the old man had been very quick off the mark, so somewhat pacified I turned my attention to the patient.

MacDonald, aged 16, was virtually blind and had to be led everywhere. In truth, he could see less than a metre, but he seemed a very nice lad who believed in Jesus. I put my hand on his head, asked God the Father through Jesus to send his Holy Spirit, and then waited, but not for long.

MacDonald's face became agitated and distorted almost at once, while tension rose up from his stomach and went through his chest to his face where a foul-sounding language came flooding out of his mouth. 'Is this Chichewa?' I asked the bystanders, but they assured me they didn't recognise the language, and had never heard anything like it before. Consequently, I knew what to do.

'Demon of Satan,' I said firmly, 'in the name of Jesus, I command you to leave.' At the name of Jesus, there was an immediate response from MacDonald, who doubled up in discomfort, while a visible tension rose once more from his stomach, but this time it went out through his mouth as he coughed and spluttered for a few moments. MacDonald then opened his eyes and, to the amazement of everyone around, especially his friends, described detail he could see on the furthest horizon. He was completely healed, as God said he would be, in the car park, and it only took about two and a half minutes.

I shall never forget this moment as long as I live. Once he was blind; now he could see – and I was there to witness it. I meet many doubters, including clergy, who do not think God performs signs and wonders today, and certainly do not believe in the existence of demons. Sometimes they express their doubts, unbelief and cynicism to me and try to unload their own non-biblical theories on me – but all I can say to them is, 'I was there. Once he was blind – now he could see.'

I spent a week with Father Zimbe and 30 other clergy from Malawi immediately after this. When I told this story as part of a talk, he laughed and laughed until tears streamed down his face, and then he stood up to give his testimony. 'It's true,' he said, 'every word – just as Peter has told you.' Father Zimbe gave me full permission to use this story whenever I chose to do so.[3]

Three weeks later, MacDonald wrote a long and beautiful letter to me in perfect English, claiming to be the fittest boy at school, and saying he was now looking forward to attending university. God is very good!

Name it

Mark 11:22–24 is one of the Bible references frequently used to justify what some people describe as 'name it and claim it' theology:

> 'Have faith in God,' Jesus answered. 'I tell you the truth, if anyone says to this mountain, "Go, throw yourself into the sea," and does not doubt in his heart but believes that what he says will happen, it will be done for him. Therefore I tell you, whatever you ask for in prayer, believe that you have received it, and it will be yours.' (Mark 11:22–24)

On its own, this looks very much like: choose anything you want – from owning a Rolls Royce car to peace in the Sudan – name it and claim it, without doubting before God, and you'll get it. When we put it with all the other 'name it and claim it' verses from the New Testament, however, we get a slightly different picture. That is why I always like to

---

[3] Father Zimbe died a year or two later, and a colleague and I paid for his tombstone.

gather the relevant verses together on a particular topic and allow Scripture to ask the questions and provide the answers. This helps me to understand what God is saying, and it also gives me scriptural authority for my conclusions. I have been able to identify the following 15 references which seem to be relevant, and assembled them in the order they appear in the New Testament. May they increase your faith as you meditate upon them:

- 'Ask and it will be given to you; seek and you will find; knock and the door will be opened to you. For everyone who asks receives; he who seeks finds; and to him who knocks, the door will be opened.'(Matthew 7:7–8)
- 'And I tell you that you are Peter, and on this rock I will build my church, and the gates of Hades will not overcome it. I will give you the keys of the kingdom of heaven; whatever you bind on earth will be bound in heaven, and whatever you loose on earth will be loosed in heaven.' (Matthew 16:18–19)
- 'I tell you the truth, if you have faith as small as a mustard seed, you can say to this mountain, "Move from here to there" and it will move. Nothing will be impossible for you.' (Matthew 17:20–21)
- 'I tell you the truth, whatever you bind on earth will be bound in heaven, and whatever you loose on earth will be loosed in heaven.'

    'Again, I tell you that if two of you on earth agree about anything you ask for, it will be done for you by my Father in heaven. For where two or three come together in my name, there am I with them.' (Matthew 18:18–20)
- Jesus replied, 'I tell you the truth, if you have faith and

do not doubt, not only can you do what was done to the fig-tree, but also you can say to this mountain, "Go throw yourself into the sea," and it will be done. If you believe you will receive whatever you ask for in prayer.' (Matthew 21:21–22)

- 'Have faith in God,' Jesus answered. 'I tell you the truth, if anyone says to this mountain, "Go, throw yourself into the sea," and does not doubt in his heart but believes that what he says will happen, it will be done for him. There- fore I tell you, whatever you ask for in prayer, believe that you have received it, and it will be yours.' (Mark 11:22–24)

- 'So I say to you: Ask and it will be given to you; seek and you will find; knock and the door will be opened to you. For everyone who asks receives; he who seeks finds; and to him who knocks, the door will be opened . . . how much more will your Father in heaven give the Holy Spirit to those who ask him!' (Luke 11:9–10, 13)

- The apostles said to the Lord, 'Increase our faith!' He replied, 'If you have faith as small as a mustard seed, you can say to this mulberry tree, "Be uprooted and planted in the sea," and it will obey you.' (Luke 17:5–6)

- 'Believe me when I say that I am in the Father and the Father is in me; or at least believe on the evidence of the miracles themselves. I tell you the truth, anyone who has faith in me will do what I have been doing. He will do even greater things than these, because I am going to the Father. And I will do whatever you ask in my name, so that the Son may bring glory to the Father. You may ask me for anything in my name, and I will do it.' (John 14:11–14)

- 'If you remain in me and my words remain in you, ask whatever you wish, and it will be given you.'(John 15:7)
- 'You are my friends if you do what I command. I no longer call you servants, because a servant does not know his master's business. Instead, I have called you friends, for everything that I learned from my Father I have made known to you. You did not choose me, but I chose you and appointed you to go and bear fruit – fruit that will last. Then the Father will give you whatever you ask in my name.' (John 15:14–16)
- 'I will see you again and you will rejoice, and no-one will take away your joy. In that day you will no longer ask me anything. I tell you the truth, my Father will give you whatever you ask in my name. Until now you have not asked for anything in my name. Ask and you will receive, and your joy will be complete.

  'Though I have been speaking figuratively, a time is coming when I will no longer use this kind of language but will tell you plainly about my Father. In that day you will ask in my name.' (John 16:22–26)
- If any of you lacks wisdom, he should ask God, who gives generously to all without finding fault, and it will be given to him. But when he asks, he must believe and not doubt, because he who doubts is like a wave of the sea, blown and tossed by the wind. That man should not think he will receive anything from the Lord; he is a double-minded man, unstable in all he does. (James 1:5–8)
- Dear friends, if our hearts do not condemn us, we have confidence before God and receive from him anything we ask, because we obey his commands and do what pleases him. (1 John 3:21–22)

• I write these things to you who believe in the name of the Son of God so that you may know that you have eternal life. This is the confidence we have in approaching God: that if we ask anything according to his will, he hears us. And if we know that he hears us – whatever we ask – we know that we have what we asked of him. (1 John 5:13–15)

I found it very faith-building to read through these verses and to realise how much Jesus and the New Testament writers encourage us to ask God in faith for things. Physical healing is definitely one of those things implied in John 14:11–14 but phrases like 'whatever you ask for' or 'ask whatever you wish' can obviously be seen to include healing as well.

Mark 11:22 begins, 'Have faith in God', and most of the 15 passages suggest it is faith in God we need rather than faith in our faith. As I read these particular verses through, it became obvious to me that specific asking in prayer flows out of the relationship with Jesus rather than a legalistic formula that will work for all people in all situations at all times. The New Covenant is all about how we can have a right relationship with Father God, and this is where the Johannine verses are so vital, because they explain much more clearly how this relationship enables us to ask God for things.

When, through the cross, we are in the Father and the Father is in us (John 14:10, 20; 1 John 2:24–25), we love him, obey him and follow him (John 14:15, 21; 12:26), as friends of God (John 15:14; 1 John 3:21). Then, when we ask in his name (John 15:16), according to his will (1 John

5:14), he will grant whatever we ask, as long as we really believe and have 'faith in God' (Matthew 17:20; 21:21; Mark 11:22–23; Luke 17:5–6; John 14:12–13). In a sense, this is really quite obvious. Can we ask God to help us jump from the pinnacle of the Temple, turn stone into bread, or become the ruling princes of this world if God is not doing it (Matthew 4:4–11)? Jesus only taught what the Father taught, said what the Father said, and did what the Father was doing (John 8:26, 28–29). The simple truth is that if we have faith the size of a mountain and God is not in it, we shan't move a mustard seed. But the glorious positive truth on offer here is that if we come to God through the cross of Christ, and get to know Jesus through his indwelling Holy Spirit, and ask properly in Jesus' name, then he will grant our requests.

'In Jesus' name' is certainly a key phrase. What this means is spelt out in John 15:7, 14–16: 'If you remain in me and my words remain in you . . . If you obey my commands . . . Then the Father will give you whatever you ask in my name.' I think when the 15 New Testament passages are looked at together, and Scripture is allowed to interpret Scripture, then the overwhelming evidence is that we will receive what we ask for when our faith is 'in Christ', 'in his name', and 'according to his will'. This is why we need to recognise God's word to us, and obey his commands, before we can begin to pray in faith. There is a distinct difference between faith in Christ and faith in our own minds, between the power of the Holy Spirit and the power of positive thinking.

In today's busy world, we have a good example of what it means to do something in someone else's name; it is called the secretary. If someone rings my secretary Liz while I am away, and asks, 'Would Peter like to go horse-riding next Wednesday?' my secretary would reply: 'Peter thinks horses bite at one end and kick at the other. I can say with absolute authority in his name, on his behalf, no, he would not like to go horse-riding next Wednesday.' And she would be right. And she would be right because she knows me well and has done so for many years (she's over 75). But if someone rang and asked, 'Would Peter be available for a free round of golf at Wentworth next Wednesday?' (normally £260 a round) my secretary would say, 'I haven't got his diary here, but I can say with absolute authority that no matter what is in his diary, he will definitely be available to play golf at Wentworth next Wednesday, and he would like me to say yes in his name.' And she would be right. A newcomer to the office, however, who did not know me so well, would not be able to speak so definitely on my behalf; they might, in hesitancy, lose me my heart's desire – or land me on a bucking bronco.

If a friend says to me, 'I'll pick you up by the postbox at 6 pm and give you a lift to church,' I exercise faith in my friend by going to stand beside the postbox at 6 pm. If no one says they'll pick me up, and I go and stand by the postbox at 6 pm in the hope of a lift, then I'm stupid. The difference between faith in God and stupidity is sometimes very small, like building an ark on dry land (Genesis 6:11–22), and it all depends on hearing the voice of God, knowing the mind of Christ, or interpreting the Scriptures correctly.

Most people would agree with this interpretation of the relevant 'name it and claim it' verses. We obviously cannot ask God to help us to be successful in robbing a bank, or mugging an old lady, and this means that 'naming' in accordance with God's will is important. The negative side of this argument is even more compelling. Can we ask God to grant something contrary to his will? Of course not! Knowing his will is therefore vital, and here is the story of the first time I realised God was willing, from time to time, to reveal his will to us by his Spirit. I was very young at the time.[4]

36. The sticking gate

One morning, I read this in the Bible passage that my daily notes had chosen for the day:

> Beloved, do not be surprised at the fiery ordeal which comes upon you to prove you, as though something strange were happening to you. But rejoice in so far as you share Christ's sufferings, that you may also rejoice and be glad when his glory is revealed. (1 Peter 4:12–13, RSV)

The passage didn't seem particularly appropriate for me, so I did some praying, and then went out into the parish to do some visiting. I'd been asked to visit two people I didn't know and been given a piece of paper with their names and addresses on it.

I visited the first name on the list and found myself listening to an old lady who would have sent a chronic insomniac to sleep, and who never seemed to pause for

---

[4] In 1974, I was training for ordination at St John's College, Nottingham, during which time I was attached to St Margaret's Aspley, where John Finney was the vicar.

breath. I played the nodding donkey for a while and then tried to make my escape by suggesting politely, while she was still talking, that maybe I should visit somebody else. 'You should visit my next-door neighbours,' she said, with a real firmness in her voice. 'One of them is blind, the other is deaf, and they used to be keen church people until they became too frail to get out of the house. Nobody from the church has visited them for years.'

This was just the opening I was looking for, and I grasped it with both feet. 'Right,' I said, as she tried to change the subject, 'I'll go next door then.' As I stood up and made my way to the exit, she kept on talking while I kept on walking, but eventually I made it to territory beyond earshot.

I went next door, tried to open the gate, but failed. Normally I can manage gates, but on this occasion I couldn't budge it; it was completely stuck. While I was standing there nonplussed, a strange thought came into my head: 'Don't go here. Visit the other address.' Inwardly, I protested. 'This chap is blind, his wife is deaf, and no one's visited them for years,' but the thought remained. 'Not here, not now; visit the other address.' In rebellion, I attacked the gate with new gusto, but to no avail, so in failed desperation I went to the other address (I went back the next day and had no trouble opening the same gate).

At the second address, a big, middle-aged man came to the door. Bill Fox was the sort of person from whom I would normally run a mile, particularly if I met him in a dark alley at night, but he was crying, and when I said I'd come from the church, he invited me in. As soon as I entered his lounge, I became aware of his mother sitting in the corner of the room, and she was crying too.

Bill's wife, Lucy, had been ill with cancer for two years, and more than one organ of her body had been removed in an attempt to save her life; she was upstairs in bed when I called. Bill asked me if we would pray for Lucy in our services but under no circumstances did he want me or anyone else to see her or to pray with her. That was basically it – end of conversation. As a parting gesture, I scribbled down our phone number for him, and was just about to leave when a second strange thought entered my head: 'Stay where you are.'

This was crazy, but for some reason I froze to the spot. I looked at him and he looked at me. I couldn't think of anything else to say to him, and he couldn't think of anything else to say to me: like a pair of lemons, we just stood there. Suddenly, he grabbed my arm. 'She's heavily drugged,' he said, 'and probably won't wake for several hours. If you come up quietly, you can say a quick prayer.'

When we entered the bedroom, Bill was dismayed to see Lucy sitting up in bed, wide awake. Oh dear! He apologised most profusely to her, explaining that I was from the church and in a mad moment he'd given me permission to pray for her.

At this point, the Spirit seemed to move within me as I found myself taking over and asking Lucy if she'd like me to pray for her. She gave me a lovely warm smile and said yes. I asked her if she believed Christ could heal her. At first, knowing how ill she had become, Lucy was hesitant, but after a quick, loving glance at her husband, she said, 'Yes, I do.' I laid one hand on her forehead, one on her hand, and prayed a simple prayer. After I'd finished, she said, 'I'll be all right now,' and I left – fast.

I drove to church, knelt at the communion rail and, trembling inside, burst into tears. The words of my morning Bible reading came into my mind:

> Beloved, do not be surprised at the fiery ordeal which comes upon you to prove you, as though something strange were happening to you. But rejoice in so far as you share Christ's sufferings, that you may also rejoice and be glad when his glory is revealed. (1 Peter 4:12–13, RSV).

Maybe they were Christ's tears I was shedding.

Two days later, we were asked to do the funeral. I was apprehensive at visiting big Bill Fox again, afraid he might blame me for his wife's death, but when I arrived with John, the vicar, I found a completely changed man. He told me how his wife had dramatically recovered following my prayer and been able to get up and do the housework for the first time in months. Both of them believed she had been healed. Two and a half hours later, she went to bed and in the morning, after a good night's sleep, woke up, hugged her husband, told him she loved him, gave him a kiss, and died.

For several weeks, Bill had asked the doctors to end Lucy's life because of the pain she was suffering and, in his anger at their refusal, had sworn at God repeatedly, pleading with Christ to come and take her. Christ had now come, and he was at peace. Every night since she died he'd slept soundly, which was something he'd not done at all in the previous six months. At the gate of the house, our vicar, John, who came with me, said, 'What a lovely man,' and we went quietly home.

People from the church continued to visit Bill, who, twelve years later, accepted Christ for himself, was confirmed in the church, became the church warden and attended church regularly with his second wife, Janet. He has now gone to glory. God's willingness to speak to me, guide me and use me gave me the great privilege of being a part of what he was doing. Sometimes God heals the sick for further work on earth, and sometimes he heals them for rest in his presence.

Claim it

Most Christians would agree that the 15 'name it and claim it' passages encourage us to believe that if God names it, we should claim it. Most Christians would agree that if God gives us a 'spoken' word for healing then we should believe for it without doubting and claim it in Jesus' name. The difference of opinion comes as to whether the Bible gives us a 'written' word for healing, authorising us to claim healing in Jesus' name for every sickness. I need to ask, therefore, in the light of this study, whether the Bible gives us the authority to do this.

A promise and a command

In the Gospels, in relation to healing, there is a promise and a command from God which encourages us to try and heal the sick.

a) The promise. Jesus healed the sick and gave his disciples this promise: 'Anyone who has faith in me will do what I have been doing. He will do even greater things than these, because I am going to the Father' (John 14:12). This is an important promise because it is made to 'anyone' who believes in Jesus – that's us. Four verses later, Jesus links this promise to the coming of the Holy Spirit (John 14:16). We have already seen that Jesus could only do what he saw the Father doing – so this promise is a great encouragement to all of us to have a go, but it is not a promise that enables us to 'name it and claim it' for all people, at all times, in all circumstances. When the Spirit of God gives us the authority and the power of God, then we can heal the sick as Jesus did, in Jesus' name.

b) The command. The disciples were sent out by Jesus, first the Twelve and then the seventy-two, to heal the sick (Luke 9:1; 10:1). He gave this command to them: 'Go and make disciples of all nations . . . teaching them to obey everything I have commanded you' (Matthew 28:19–20). Again, this is for us, and again we note that Jesus and the disciples healed the sick in the power of the Holy Spirit, whenever the power of the Lord was present to heal the sick. As Jesus taught and commanded the disciples to heal the sick, so these verses inspire us to get out there and have a go – but without the guarantee of 100 per cent success. When the Spirit of God gives us the authority of God and the power of God, then we can heal the sick as Jesus' disciples did, in Jesus' name.

We also note that Jesus and the disciples raised the dead; this is included in the promise and the command, but history suggests not all of them, all of the time. We have a biblical word that encourages us to minister to the sick, indeed commands us to minister to the sick, but not a covenant word that enables us to claim healing for all people, in all places, at all times.

As we move on to consider other relevant scriptures, and especially the interpretation of other verses, we begin by noting the importance of context.

The importance of context

Whether we believe that God bypassed human free will and dictated the Bible infallibly to the world, or whether we believe God breathed his Spirit into and through fallible human beings and provided his authoritative word as treasure in earthen vessels, or whether we believe the Holy Scriptures are simply mankind's written account of the glorious works and revelations of God in history, the Bible still comes to us as a written document, or a written 'word' from God. This means the context is vital in understanding it and interpreting it correctly. Let me give a stupid example to illustrate the point: the Bible declares: 'There is no God.' Look it up. Psalm 14, verse one, second line. Clear, unmistakable, authoritative. 'There is no God.' Putting it into context, however, gives us a better understanding and interpretation: 'The fool says in his heart, "There is no God"' (Psalm 14:1).

Now the problem with context is that it is hard work and takes a lot of time – time which most people do not have. In my stupid example, the verse itself gives us the answer. However, sometimes it takes the whole chapter, the whole book, the whole of the New Testament, or even the whole Bible to give us the correct understanding and interpretation of God's written word to us.

Sadly, many of the 'name it and claim it' preachers that I have heard do not seem to have the time and don't bother much with context at all. I have heard preachers say, 'As the whole Bible is the word of God, all its verses, whether Old or New Testament, are equally valid.' This is the crunch exegetical problem. This is why many preachers say we have a covenant right to healing, or that God has promised it, because healing in the Old Testament is seen at times to be an Old Covenant right, providing, of course, that we don't sin. But if we take that line, then pork chops come off the menu, sacrificing animals has to take place in church services, and all males have to be circumcised. The Bible, however, in both Old and New Testaments, declares that the Old Covenant is over, broken, obsolete, and healing in the New Testament, under the New Covenant, is no longer a covenant right.

The gift of the healing Holy Spirit is our New Covenant right through Jesus, and that is why we need a 'spoken' word to give us God's authority and power to heal the sick. There is no 'written' word, under the New Covenant, that enables us to name and claim healing for all people, in all places, at all times.

There is, however, a 'written' word that encourages all Christians to pray for the sick, and to minister to them in the power of the Holy Spirit.

37. While the vicar's away. . .

Julia used to suffer from a bad back. On one occasion, her family prayed for her; she went over in the Spirit at home, and afterwards felt better, but, some time later, the back trouble returned and no amount of praying or ministering from others would shift it. Each time people prayed, Julia felt blessed, loved and a little better for a short while, but not healed.

During my visit to South Africa in 1988, Christine, our lay reader, led the monthly Sunday healing service.[5] As it progressed, Julia, just like the woman in the Bible (Matthew 9:21), kept saying to herself, 'If only I go forward, I'm sure I will be healed.' Faith grew inside her to the point where she testified afterwards, 'I just knew I was going to be healed.'

This is the work of God. This is a 'spoken' word from God. This is the gift of faith from on high. It is not a person deciding for herself what to do and believing it – the initiative comes from God. Julia had several times received appropriate 'words' for others, and this seemed to be one for herself. At the healing service, Christine invited people to come forward to the communion rail for prayer, but nobody moved. It is amazing how hard British people find it to get out of their chairs or pews once they are in them, especially when compared to people in Malawi, and this lack of activity greatly challenged Julia's faith in God. The battle raged for a while inside, but eventually Julia rose slowly, eased her way forward, and, as she did so, others followed her example. She found it very painful kneeling and, even though she

---

[5] I was part of a British team under the leadership of John Mumford, a former curate of Canford Magna, supporting John Wimber's Signs and Wonders conference in Johannesburg.

felt God's anointing as Mary and Alicia prayed, her back became no better, so they stopped.

Still sensing that God wanted to heal, Julia found her faith in him sorely tested at this moment. She was kneeling in agony at a communion rail; two ladies on the other side were praying, God was still saying he wanted to heal, but Julia was experiencing no improvement. This was particularly difficult for Julia, as so many had tried before. But even so, she stayed with it.

'You need to lay hands on my back,' said Julia. So Mary leaned over the rail and put her hand in the right place and, as they commanded the pain to go in Jesus' name, Alicia felt something move, and Julia's back was healed.

Next morning, the pain was back just as before, and the test of Julia's faith increased in difficulty. 'Did God really say. . .?' (Genesis 3:1). Because Julia was convinced God had spoken and was speaking, she continued to resist Satan and the pain in her back, and fought in prayer for a whole week. After that, the pain left and did not return.

When God speaks, when power comes on people as we pray for them, then I believe we need to 'name it and claim it'. We believe God has said he wants to heal; we believe the Holy Spirit is giving us the power; so in Jesus' name we command the sickness and pain to be gone, and we hang in there for as long as we can, providing it is not causing distress to the sick person. On one occasion, Jesus needed two attempts to heal a blind man (Mark 8:22–26), and this should encourage us not to give up easily the first time we try. Sometimes when God says he wants to heal, and he names it by his Spirit, then claiming it in Jesus' name and going on claiming it will bring healing. When Jesus said, 'Ask and it will be given to you,' the aorist tense is used by the New Testament writers, which suggests, 'keep asking' (Matthew 7:7). And that is just what Julia did.

Faith in God

Rather than having faith in faith, or a legalistic formula, our 15 passages encourage us to have faith in God. But, as with his apostles, the cry of our hearts is often: 'Increase our faith,' or, like the father of the demonised boy: 'Lord, help me overcome my unbelief' (see Mark 9:24). Understanding how faith, signs and wonders from the New Testament work may help us to increase our faith. We should also be aware of three vital ingredients – obedience, experience and the gift of faith.

a) Obedience

When we have no experience of God's healing power, then obedience will often do instead of faith. In fact, obedience is frequently the starting-place that leads to faith. John Wimber prayed for 200 sick people before he experienced his first healing, and he always said he kept going out of obedience to what he believed God commanded him to do in the Bible (Matthew 28:19–20).

In 2 Kings 5, Naaman the Syrian had not seen God heal anyone, so when God's prophet Elisha told him to dip seven times in the River Jordan, the problem he faced was not faith but obedience. When he was eventually persuaded to do as he was told, he was completely healed. When God names it and we claim it, obedience alone will sometimes do.

John's Gospel informs us that Jesus' first sign was to turn water into wine at Cana. This meant that nobody had seen Jesus do any miracles before, so obedience, not faith, was the key: 'His mother said to the servants, "Do whatever he tells you"' (John 2:5). As servants, obedience was all that was necessary.

b) Experience

There is no doubt, however, that it is easier to have faith the second time than the first. Experts say that faith is often caught rather than taught, and it must have been immensely helpful to be around Jesus when his healing ministry took off in Capernaum.

Having been anointed by the Holy Spirit, Jesus moved from Nazareth to Capernaum. On the Saturday, he went to the synagogue, where a demonised man shrieked out, and Jesus healed him. The people were amazed. Jesus went for Saturday lunch at the house of Simon and Andrew, only to find Peter's mother-in-law, who was supposed to be cooking the lunch, in bed with a fever. So Jesus healed her too.

It was the sabbath until 6 pm, so they spent a quiet afternoon at home beside the lake until the sun went down. Then, as the town clock struck six, there was a tap at the door. Whoever answered it found the whole town in the front garden, wanting Jesus to come out and heal their sick friends and relatives – scores of them. So Jesus did (Mark 1:32–34).

Very early the next morning, Jesus escaped from Capernaum and visited the nearby villages, where he did some more healing, and 'people still came to him from everywhere' (Mark 1:45). A few days later, Jesus came home to Capernaum and was mobbed by the crowds, so much so that four vandals had to smash a hole in the roof in order to bring their paralysed friend into the presence of Jesus, who, rather than ringing up his insurance company or calling the police, noted their faith (Mark 2:1–5). This is quite extraordinary faith, and we are bound to ask: 'Where did it come from?'

Forgive me for speculating, but in those days the seriously ill used to live together in colonies, and friends and relatives would take food etc. to them. Theologically, they were judged by many to be sinners whom God was punishing, and therefore they would be outcasts until they were healed. I suggest that all the able-bodied, ambient inmates of Capernaum hospital got healed on Saturday night. The ones that didn't were those who couldn't walk, but if you yourself had been healed, I think you'd have gone back for your friend who hadn't been able to get there, and told him all about it. And when you've seen Jesus heal and maybe been healed yourself by him, it is as much natural as supernatural to have faith. Mark wrote, 'Jesus saw their faith' (Mark 2:5), a faith which undoubtedly arrived with the many healings experienced or witnessed a few days ago. And it continued.

An official came from Capernaum to Cana to ask Jesus to heal his son (John 4:46–47); Jairus, a ruler of the synagogue in Capernaum, asked Jesus to heal his daughter (Luke 8:41–42); a Roman centurion, who had built the synagogue in Capernaum, asked Jesus to heal his servant (Luke 7:1–10), and Jesus said, 'I tell you, I have not found such great faith even in Israel' – faith which had undoubtedly been fuelled by all that had gone on before in Capernaum.

For 30 years, Jesus did not heal anybody that we know about. However, once the Holy Spirit anointed him to heal and a wave of healing began, then belief in Jesus as the Anointed One was all that was necessary. When the power of the Lord is present to heal the sick, then asking and believing is all that is required (Luke 5:17–26). This is the context in which the 15 asking passages will lead to God's healing through faith in Jesus. Obedience can be taught, but such faith as this comes more easily when it is caught, and I would encourage everyone who wants to have a go at ministering to the sick to get alongside someone who has been used by God before, and is full of faith.

c) The gift of faith

Paul writes: 'Faith comes from hearing the message, and the message is heard through the word of Christ' (Romans 10:17). It was a teaching that Paul had found to be true in his own experience:

> In Lystra there sat a man crippled in his feet, who was lame from birth and had never walked. He listened to Paul as he was speaking. Paul looked directly at him, saw that he had faith to be healed and called out, 'Stand up on your feet!' At that, the man jumped up and began to walk. (Acts 14:8–10)

Paul preached the message, the crippled man believed, and the faith to be healed rose up within him. Paul later recognised the value of faith as a gift from the Spirit when he wrote to the Corinthians, especially when Christians come together: 'Now to each one the manifestation of the Spirit is given for the common good. To one there is given through the Spirit . . . faith' (1 Corinthians 12:7–9).

In church, prayer for healing usually follows the worship of God, through Jesus, in the Spirit, and the preaching of 'the word of Christ', the word of truth. This can sometimes release the gift of faith in the gathered assembly, particularly where spiritual gifts are given by God to build up the congregation. On four occasions, I've had the privilege of visiting the Toronto Christian Fellowship and, knowing John and Carol Arnott personally, I have been able to mingle with the leadership backstage, as it were.[6] What struck me as a Church of England clergyman was the spirit of unity among the leaders going for the same goals, believing the same things and despite huge criticism from all over the world, encouraging and building one another up. In my experience, I believe God has begun to move powerfully among us on four or five occasions, only to see the Spirit quenched by the cynicism and criticism that is so much a part of British culture. Creating atmospheres of love, encouragement and acceptance, and building faith in worshipping communities in Britain, is so difficult but so essential, I believe, to seeing God's gift of healing released among us.

---

[6] In 1991, John Arnott invited me to speak at the Stratford Vineyard, two years before the 'Toronto Blessing' came to our attention. In 1995, I hosted the Waves of the Spirit conference in Bournemouth, where John and Carol Arnott were our main speakers.

God's power and authority to heal needs to find a home in welcoming hearts and bodies but sometimes, by his grace, he helps us in our weakness.

38. A dumb telephonist

Quite recently, my phone rang at 8 o'clock in the morning, and even though I am not at my best so early, I answered it. On the other end of the line was a lady who had lost her voice and couldn't speak. When I cannot hear a sick person speaking, then I find it quite helpful if I can discern God's voice instead.

'Hello,' I said. 'Who's there?'

'Mmmmm!' came the reply, but it sounded quite an urgent and important 'Mmmmm'! As my body and mind were half asleep, I prayed in tongues under my breath, to activate my spirit, and then spoke whatever came into my head in English. It came out like this.

'Is that someone who has lost her voice?' I asked.

'Mmmmm!' was the answer.

'Is that someone from our church whom I know quite well?' I continued.

'Mmmmm!' was the sound that came leaping back down the line, but in a louder and more affirmative sort of way.

'Do you want me to pray for you?' I enquired.

'Mmmmm!' she said positively.

'Is it Sue?' I guessed.

At this, the phone decidedly bounced with 'Mmms'.

'Shall I come round now?' I asked and, as the humming sounds seemed to reach the highest and most positive decibels so far, I grabbed my coat and went round.

Sue was due at work shortly, and as she spent most of her mornings on the telephone, she was hoping I might be able to help her regain the use of her vocal cords. It was one of those rare moments when words and faith rose up inside me at the same time, so I went for it. I spoke and she replied by writing everything down on a piece of paper – it was rather fun.

'You won't get your voice back until you forgive your father,' I found myself saying.

'Is there no other way?' she asked, looking resignedly unhopeful as she passed me her scrap of paper.

'No,' I replied.

'So if I want to go to work, I've got to forgive him now?' she wrote, not really asking a question as she scribbled away.

'Yes,' I agreed.

'Huh!' she seemed to say. Pause. More writing. 'OK then,' she wrote.

'Write your prayer down,' I suggested. 'Then pray it.'

So Sue wrote it down, then she prayed it silently with her eyes closed – then I declared God's forgiveness through Jesus and invoked the Holy Spirit. He came quickly and powerfully, and once Sue was engaged by the Spirit I claimed her healing in Jesus' name. After this, Sue began to speak to me, croakily at first, but more easily as time went by. Eventually, she went off to work, arrived on time and answered the phone all morning, even though we needed another session before her voice returned to complete normality.

Hearing from God, being obedient to his instructions

and claiming his healing are all in the story somewhere. No, it wasn't quite a penalty for sin, more the consequence of unforgiveness, but God certainly allowed it and used it to bring about his will and his healing. Life is rarely boring when we seek to do whatever he tells us to do and to claim in Jesus' name whatever he tells us to claim by his Spirit. The blind see; the lame walk; the deaf hear; the dumb speak.

False belief and its problems

When the Holy Spirit guides us and empowers us to heal, and we exercise faith by naming it and claiming it persistently in Jesus' name, then, I believe, we can expect to see healing take place. The New Testament says again and again that in the power of the Holy Spirit, under the authority of God the Father, Jesus and the disciples and his other followers healed the sick. But, to believe that healing is mine as a covenant right because of the atonement is to deny *everything* the Gospels, Acts and Epistles say about physical healing, and to claim something as true that they *never* say. It is a belief that has many problems.

a) There are theological problems

John Stott writes:

> Bearing the penalty of sin is readily intelligible, since sin's penalty is death and Christ dies our death in our place, but what is the penalty of sickness? It has none. Sickness may itself be a penalty for sin, but it is not itself a misdemeanour which

attracts a penalty. So to speak of Christ 'atoning for' our sick-nesses is to mix categories. It is not an intelligible notion.[7]

b) There are biblical problems

If people were healed by claiming their covenant rights, we would not need the Holy Spirit to heal us, and we would not need spiritual gifts. Who needs the spiritual gift of heal-ing if healing is already mine by right? Who needs to hear from God, and who needs to discern when he comes in power? In fact, who needs God at all? If God put my heal-ing in the bank at Calvary, I can simply go and draw it out without bothering him. The Bible suggests otherwise. The New Testament links healing to the coming of the Holy Spirit in power, and describes spiritual gifts as the keys to tapping into that power.

c) There are assurance problems

It is a doctrine which can lead me to doubt my own salva-tion. I am saved by believing in what Jesus did for me on the cross. If I am also healed by believing in what Jesus did for me on the cross, where does that leave my salvation if I am not healed? If I have not enough faith for healing, what makes me think I have enough for salvation? The logical conclusion is that every so-called Christian who wears spec-tacles, needs a hearing-aid, has a cold, or dies of a disease is not saved.

---

[7] John Stott, *The Cross of Christ* (Leicester: Inter-Varsity Press 1989), p. 245.

d) There are compassion problems

I have heard people shouting at those in wheelchairs to have more faith. That is not healing; that is abuse. And who should have the faith, anyway? In the New Testament, it is often the one ministering, or the friend or relative who has the faith. Even those who are naturally full of faith tend to lose some of it when they become ill. Such people often need love, mercy, compassion and the power of God to help them, not a lecture.

e) There are historical problems

It is a belief which totally denies the history of revivals. At times, during revival, such as Indonesia in the 1960s, many people were healed. However, the same people who laid hands on people either before or after the revival found that far fewer people were healed then than *during* the revival. Why? Because supernatural healing comes from God and a movement of his Holy Spirit. That's what the New Testament says, and that's what the history of revivals demonstrates.

f) There are practical problems

It doesn't work, and in particular it doesn't work in the West. Those who preach it see some healed, occasionally many, but never all of everything. They don't empty hospitals. The belief that healing from all sicknesses can be claimed as a covenant right for all Christians, for all times, has never been demonstrated, even by Heidi Baker.

g) There are decaying problems

The world record for a man under 40 running the 100 metres is less than 10 seconds. The world record for a man aged between 95 and 99 is 22 seconds. Paul does not seem to expect us to be healed of decay and old age before Jesus returns (Romans 8:22–25).

h) There are post-mortem problems

Raising people from the dead was something Jesus, Peter and maybe Paul did, and it is on the list of healings in Matthew 10:8 that the Twelve are given authority and power to do. It is, however, one kind of healing where it is very difficult to ask the patient to claim his or her covenant rights – and indeed, contacting the dead is forbidden in Scripture. I suggest, therefore, that raising the dead requires the same kind of authority and power that raised Jesus from the dead (Romans 8:11).

i) There are healing and lifestyle problems

It is a doctrine that inhibits us from looking at the roots of a sickness with the intention of changing wrong beliefs or lifestyle. Ironically, the one area where the cross of Christ is most powerful in helping with healing is when sin is connected to sickness, but if we think that all we need is faith in what has already been done, then we may miss out on the benefits of the cross. In my experience, it is a belief that often stops people receiving the healing God wants to give them. Several times, I have spent time counselling those who have been told to claim their healing without success when in fact a change of lifestyle was all that was needed to remove the sickness. It is, of course, a belief that has no room for the medical profession, or undertakers.

j) There are evangelism problems

In the Gospels and Acts, non-believers are often healed first, before they come to faith in Jesus – and the same is true today (John 4:53; 9:35–38; Acts 3:8–9; 8:12; 9:18; 28:8–10). Rather than being healed by believing in the cross and claiming their covenant rights, some are healed first by Christ, then believe in the cross and then enter the New Covenant relationship with him. Sometimes, people are healed and do not go on to become disciples of Christ. If physical healing is *only* available as a covenant right to all who have entered the New Covenant through faith in Christ, then we are bound to ask, 'What about those who are sick and do not yet believe?' The very good news is that, because it is the Spirit who heals, non-Christians can be healed too.

39. A pain in the neck

One Saturday morning, I was doing some work in my study when I began to feel strangely warmed. I immediately stopped what I was doing, went over to an armchair, sat down, closed my eyes and waited for God to speak to me. As I sensed his Holy Spirit upon me, my thoughts turned to Roger Jones, a friend and professional Christian musician, who I knew was ministering at a church weekend away.[8] This thought then came to my mind: 'Tell Roger to give out this "word" at the Sunday evening service. "There will be a teenage girl present with a pain in the neck where it meets the shoulder."' And then a further instruction: 'Tell the person who sees her that the pain in the neck is not the main reason I want her to come forward.' I phoned my message through to Mary Jones, who relayed it to her husband late on Saturday night.

Two teenage girls attended all the meetings. One of them was a committed Christian who worshipped regularly in the church, and she had persuaded her non-Christian friend to come with her. At the very first session, Roger's talk seemed to give the friend a pain in the neck. It was a genuine physical pain which stayed with her all weekend, until after Roger's final sermon. She told her friend all about it.

When Roger gave the 'word' about a teenage girl with a pain in the neck, on Sunday evening, the Christian girl nudged her friend. 'That's for you,' she said. The friend nodded and agreed to go with her to the front. As soon as she left her chair, the pain in the neck also left, never to return, but they still came forward.

Gill was waiting for them. Roger had told her the further instruction, so when the girls shared their story and why they had come forward, Gill asked a few sensitive

---

[8] Roger Jones works for Christian Music Ministries, writing and producing Christian musicals, speaking at parish weekends and conferences. Details of all his activities and publications can be found on: www.cmm.org.uk

questions. Yes, one was definitely a committed Christian but no, her friend was not. Encouraged by the 'word', and the physical healing of her neck, she accepted Jesus Christ as her Lord and Saviour, and her friend promised to look after her and nurture her in the Christian faith. It is wonderful when God speaks to a non-Christian and heals them even before they accept him as Lord. It is much easier to do evangelism that way round.

Summary

The New Covenant is indirectly linked to all Christian healing because through it we can all know God, from the least to the greatest (see Hebrews 8:7–13). It is this 'knowing' which enables us to discern when God wants to use us to heal the sick. The alternative approach, of trying to claim healing for every condition as a covenant right for today, seems to me to be fraught with difficulties. I dare to suggest it is untenable, flying in the face of Scripture and experience, and I certainly want to retain the option of praying for non-Christians, who have not, as yet, any covenant rights, as well as for Christians.

The Old Covenant is over, but the glorious New Covenant is here, enabling us to receive the forgiveness of sins, a right relationship with God and the gift of the healing Holy Spirit. One day, the New Covenant will allow all believers to enter into a world of total, permanent healing, harmony, justice and peace, but, for now, the Holy Spirit still enables us to glimpse and receive a foretaste of heaven. Sometimes we pray for people and they are healed. Sometimes we lay hands on people and they are healed. Sometimes when we gather in Jesus' name he releases spiritual gifts among us and people are healed. Sometimes when people's lifestyles are changed to be more like Christ, they are healed. And sometimes healing is delayed a season until we meet Jesus face to face, when all who believe in him will be totally healed, as a New Covenant right, because of the cross.

10

The Wind of the Spirit

A fter Jesus rose from the dead and ascended into
heaven, he poured out his Spirit on all believers,
and has continued to do so ever since. Until Jesus
returns, we live in the age of the Holy Spirit and during that
time, the Bible informs us, it is the Spirit who heals. This
chapter is my understanding of the implications of that
biblical truth for all who would seek to heal the sick in the
power of the Holy Spirit.

- The wind of the Spirit blows wherever he chooses.
- As children of God, born again of the Spirit of God, we are
  encouraged to:

  a) ask God to come;
  b) wait for him to come;
  c) seek to respond to his coming.

- When we do this, and by his grace and mercy respond
  appropriately, God's will is done on earth as it is in
  heaven.

Good timing

The timing of God is important in all of the above three areas, and the writer of Ecclesiastes spells it out for us:

> To everything there is a season, and a time to every purpose under the heaven:
>
> > a time to dance . . .
> > a time to build up . . .
> > a time to speak . . .
> > a time to weep . . .
> > a time to keep silence . . .
> > a time to heal . . .
> > and a time to die. (Ecclesiastes 3:1–9 KJV)

The Bible was written by a nation of farmers who knew more about the seasons than our permanently-well-stocked-instant-supermarket society. They knew all about the time to burn the stubble, plough the land, sow the seed and wait for the harvest. They also knew about the good times and the bad, just as my friend Juliette does.

40. A time to dance

Juliette is one of the young people at our Lantern church, and she wrote this for me about her physical problems.

> Before 2001 I can't remember a time when I was not in pain. Taking painkillers, time off school, not involved in school sports, time out during exams (sitting in one position for a length of time was very painful), unable to sit or stand for long. I always went forward for healing at church but the only thing that happened was the pain went away for a short time.

An orthopaedic consultant who examined her explained that the positioning of her thigh was such that both knees faced inwards while her feet were positioned outwards at 10 to 2, which was how she was born. During the summer of 2001, Juliette attended the New Wine and Soul Survivor conferences at Shepton Mallett.[1] On the penultimate night, a guy in a wheelchair was healed, and on the last night Mike Pilavachi, the leader, gave the session over to healing, and called people forward.[2]

Juliette went forward, and a lady (without knowing what was wrong) asked God through Jesus to send the power and love of the Holy Spirit upon her. Juliette takes up the story:

> Suddenly I felt a wave of heat hit me like I was burning up. I started to shake and the woman, guided by God, moved her hand over my legs. Where her hand moved, my leg rippled. I then felt slammed to the ground by God, with extreme pressure running down my body, and began to shake violently, feeling God was pushing me around all over as if I was experiencing a supernatural, surgical operation.
>
> Eventually it stopped as suddenly as it started, leaving me feeling exhausted and sweaty. I went to get up, pulled my knees in to get up and couldn't believe they were in alignment with my feet. I pulled my legs back down and pulled my jeans up. I couldn't believe they were straight. I just kept

---

[1] Details of the Soul Survivor summer camps and conferences for young people can be found at: www.soulsurvivor.com – Details of the New Wine summer camps and conferences for families can be found at: www.new-wine.org

[2] Mike Pilavachi is the leader of the Soul Survivor church, in Watford.

pulling them up and down to see the difference. I then carried on dancing.

I went to tell my friends but they weren't listening to me as all they noticed was the gold dust which was covering my neck, face, hands, legs and arms. [A few people in our church have privately experienced this wonderful gift of being lightly covered in gold flakes, including my youngest daughter, Hazel. It seems as if the Holy Spirit occasionally brings some pavement with him when he comes to give us a taste of heaven (Revelation 21:21).]

Juliette's mother adds a postscript:

When I brought her home the next day and we examined her, there was the colouring of new bruises all along her legs, which intensified during the next few days.

And yes, at the start of 2005, when this was written, the legs are still straight, normal and regularly used for dancing. To God be all the glory, and bless him for New Wine and Soul Survivor.

Discerning the wind of the Spirit

Once we have acknowledged the important role of the Holy Spirit in healing the sick, then there is a problem to face. While talking to Nicodemus about the necessity of being 'born again by the Spirit', Jesus says this to him about the Spirit: 'The wind blows wherever it pleases. You hear its sound, but you cannot tell where it comes from or where it is going' (John 3:8). What a pity! If only I could tell God what to do, where and how to do it! If only I could control God! In reality, the only New Testament method for healing is to try and catch the wind, as with a yacht or a hang-glider. But what do I do if the wind doesn't blow, or doesn't blow in the direction I would choose? This, I suspect, is the root problem that causes many Christians to come up with all kinds of interesting and varied theologies to avoid facing the pain of this biblical truth – the pain of following a God who heals some and not others.

The *non-interventionists* say: 'We cannot believe in a God who heals some and not others, so we don't believe that God ever intervenes or heals anyone.' This is not biblical. God intervened in the history of mankind from the beginning of Genesis to the end of Revelation – it's just that Peter was released from prison by an angel while James was beheaded (Acts 12:1–10) and others were sawn in two (Hebrews 11:37); 'And there were many in Israel with leprosy in the time of Elisha the prophet, yet not one of them was cleansed – only Naaman the Syrian' (Luke 4:27).

The *cessationists* say: 'For a short while, Jesus and his disciples healed everybody, to reveal his Lordship to the world, but now he doesn't heal anybody.' This is not biblical. The Gospels do not teach this, and neither the Acts of the Apostles nor the Epistles come to this conclusion.

Some of the *'healing-evangelists'* that I have heard seem to believe that we have a right to complete healing for everyone from everything, here and now. As I have argued already, this is not biblical either.

Trying to put God in a box is what Charles Davis described as 'the lust for certitude'.[3] A God who heals no

---

[3] Charles Davis, *The Temptations of Religion* (London: Hodder & Stoughton 1973). 'The Lust for Certitude' is the title of the first chapter.

one is fine; we all know where we stand. A God who once healed everybody but now heals nobody is also fine; we can handle that. A God who heals everybody of everything is a nice idea and a realistic future hope and even though it sacrifices intellect and biblical principles for the sake of a black-and-white theology, it gives us a certain certitude. A God who heals some and not others, however, is unacceptable to all three groups because it means I am not in control. I do not know what God is going to do next. And yet, when one becomes like a little child who doesn't understand everything but still trusts, then the way forward is incredibly simple: God holds all the reins and I come along for the ride.

We cannot know all the reasons why God does not choose to heal all believers of everything right now, but here are a few which may be helpful, and which I have observed over the years.

The priorities of God

a) The priority of salvation. . .

God wants everyone to be born again, to believe in his Son Jesus, to become Christians (1 Timothy 2:4). This is more important to him and to us than healing bodies that are still going to die. On many occasions, people who have been told they have a terminal illness ask to see the vicar, even though they don't normally attend church. Frequently, it has been my privilege and pleasure to lead them to Christ before they die and then conduct a Christian funeral. Strangely, in the purposes of God, the illness has helped the

THE WIND OF THE SPIRIT

person to come to know him and to be healed permanently for all eternity.

Sometimes Christians who are told they have a terminal illness then help others to know Christ before they die, by witnessing to them. People often listen to a dying Christian friend or relative far more readily than to a fit and healthy one. Sometimes they witness successfully in hospital to other patients or members of the medical staff.

Sometimes people like Joni,[4] who have a chronic illness rather than a terminal one, can be used by God to lead others to Christ more easily than when able-bodied. A Christian's wheelchair can be a key that opens the door to God's kingdom for others. In short, salvation is a higher priority to God than physical healing, and sickness is sometimes used by him to bring others to himself. Healing the spirit is always more important than healing the body.

b) The priority of healing the soul. . .

Christian counsellors often define the soul as 'emotions, mind and will'.[5] If I feel badly about myself or others, if I think and believe wrong things about myself or others, if I keep making wrong choices because of bad feelings, bad thoughts or unforgiveness, then God may want to heal my soul before my body.

---

[4] Joni tells her own story in the book *Joni.*

[5] Tom Marshall is one of the respected teachers and counsellors who define the soul as 'emotions, mind and will'. He does this in his book *Free Indeed* (Chichester: Sovereign World 1983), p. 42.

c) The priority of righteousness. . .

Perennial sins or addictions can affect our churches and destroy our witness to the world. Forgiveness, cleansing, deliverance or teaching about right conduct may be higher on God's list than physical healing.

d) The priority of holiness. . .

Why do I want to be healed? For what purpose? Holiness means being set apart – set apart to serve God. If I want to be healed for my sake rather than his sake, it may be that holiness becomes a higher priority for God than healing.

e) The priority of right relationships. . .

Sometimes a person comes forward for prayer with a bad foot and God says, 'I would rather heal his marriage than his foot today.' Our priorities are not always God's priorities.

f) The priority of healing roots rather than healing symptoms. . .

If between 70 per cent and 90 per cent of all physical illnesses in this country are due to psychosomatic reasons, as some doctors say they are, then God may want to heal the root cause of our sickness more than the symptoms. This may look like short-term non-healing, but it may be better for us in the long term.

There may be many, many reasons why God does not want to heal us now, instantly, of a physical illness, even though in the long term it is always his desire to heal every Christian of everything. Some of God's priorities I have listed take a long time to accomplish, even a lifetime, and in such cases God's healing may be delayed until the New Jerusalem. What is important is believing in a God who knows best, and because he views life from an eternal perspective and he is God, trusting him is always better than knowing all the answers.

In the next story, dealing with righteousness issues first led to healing, which led to trust and eventually God's blessing for a whole congregation.

41. A time to build up

A few years ago, I was asked to speak at a seven-day retreat for clergy. During the course of the week, everyone became more and more open to the gentle waves of God's Spirit, bringing to the surface a few problems, allowing some grief to be expressed, and encouraging many with feelings of warmth, love, forgiveness and acceptance.

Following these general sessions, a number of individuals asked for private ministry. Several came to me determined to change sinful aspects of their lives, and I particularly remember one who came seeking healing.

He was a clergyman with poor mobility in his legs, who was in constant discomfort, which meant that on some days he could hardly stagger more than a few yards. But he was also a man who was bowed down with guilt and shame and needed to be forgiven, built up and affirmed. He shared some personal sins, repented of them and then accepted the forgiveness of God that I was able to pronounce over him because of the cross of Christ. After we'd taken some time to do all that, I asked God the Father through Jesus to send his Holy Spirit upon him.

At first God came with the assurance of sins forgiven, and a few tears surfaced, but after a while his face became hot, his hands began to shake, and then he slid to the floor, where he remained for about 15 minutes with signs of power all over him.

'I felt power,' he said, 'slowly working its way down my body, removing the pain, taking it down my legs and out through my toes.' The forgiveness of sins he was able to receive through the cross of Christ cleared the channels through which the healing power of the Holy Spirit was then able to flow. When I saw him later in the church where he was the vicar, his legs seemed to be absolutely fine, and his spirit had come alive.

'I asked God to come,' he said excitedly, 'just like you taught us at the retreat, and he came. Our folks had never experienced anything like it.'

God's priority was righteousness first, then healing, and then the trust in God which grew inside him and in turn motivated the vicar to ask God to come on the congregation; this brought great blessings for all. Those whose lives have been mended, spiritually and physically, by the cross and the Spirit, are usually the best at giving away what God has given to them.

Come, Holy Spirit

Once we have accepted that it is the Spirit who heals, and have worked through the pain of letting him blow wherever he pleases, then our method for proceeding is very straightforward:

- We ask God to come.
- We wait for him to come.
- We seek to respond to his coming.

a) We ask God to come

In Luke 11:1–13, Jesus teaches his followers to pray. He tells them to ask and go on asking, to seek and go on seeking, to knock and go on knocking, just as a hungry friend asks for bread, or as a child asks his father for food. It follows the Lord's Prayer, when we are encouraged to ask for daily bread. Jesus promises that the Father will send the Holy Spirit to God's children, not satanic forces, whenever they do this (see Luke 10:17–20; 11:11–13).

I take this to mean that God's children, those who are born again, can and should ask God the Father through Jesus to send his Holy Spirit again and again, and that God will respond positively to this request. Hopefully, by now, you will have noticed some of the things that have happened when we have prayed this prayer: blind eyes have been opened, the lame have walked, the deaf have heard, the dumb have spoken, cancer has gone, and the dead have been raised to life. I always recommend this biblically based method to everyone, and not as an optional extra. Even though the Spirit blows where he chooses, we are still exhorted to ask, seek and knock. When it comes to healing in Jesus' name, then the initiative is in our hands as the body of Christ here on earth who are commanded to 'be filled with the Spirit' (Ephesians 5:18).

But some will say – they always do – why ask the Holy Spirit to come when he is already here? I gave a complicated answer to this question in my second book,[6] but here is a simpler answer. Most theological questions and problems about asking God the Father through Jesus to send his Holy Spirit can be solved by putting the work of the Holy Spirit into two categories.

i) The *presence* of the Holy Spirit.

ii) The *activity* of the Holy Spirit.

God was obviously with Jesus, even from birth, and by the time he was twelve (at least), he knew God as Father in an unprecedented way (Luke 2:49). This means that God, who is Spirit, was *present* with Jesus for the 30 years before his baptism. When the Holy Spirit came upon him at his baptism, it was an anointing for *activity* – the specific activity of defeating Satan by proclaiming the kingdom, healing the sick and casting out demons (Matthew 4:23–24). We can see these two categories, the presence and activity of the Holy Spirit, in what happened to, with, in and through Jesus' followers in the early church.

i) The presence of the Holy Spirit

These are the last words of Matthew's Gospel, Jesus' own words: 'And surely I am with you always, to the very end of

---

[6] Peter H. Lawrence, *Doing What Comes Supernaturally* (Bristol: Terra Nova Publications Ltd 1997).

the age' (Matthew 28:20). This is the permanent presence of Jesus, by his Spirit, promised by him to his disciples and those who will become his disciples (see Matthew 28:19–20).

In Romans 8:9, Paul writes: 'If anyone does not have the Spirit of Christ, he does not belong to Christ.' In John 3:6–7, Jesus says this to Nicodemus: 'Flesh gives birth to flesh, but the Spirit gives birth to spirit. You should not be surprised at my saying, "You must be born again."' The permanent presence of Christ, by his Spirit, comes then to all who are born again – who become Christians.

Religious language about the unseen is naturally imprecise, but the biblical word used most commonly for obtaining the permanent presence of the Holy Spirit in our lives is '*receive*' the Holy Spirit. After the resurrection of Jesus, before his ascension, Jesus breathed on his disciples and said: '*Receive* the Holy Spirit' (John 20:22; my italics). Coming as it does towards the end of John's Gospel, it corresponds well to Jesus' statement at the end of Matthew: 'And surely I am with you always' (Matthew 28:20). One is visual, one is verbal, but the message is the same.

On the Day of Pentecost, Peter said to the crowd:

Repent and be baptised, every one of you, in the name of Jesus Christ for the forgiveness of your sins. And you will *receive* the gift of the Holy Spirit. The promise is for you and your children and for all who are far off – for all whom the Lord our God will call.(Acts 2:38–39; my italics)

This whole package is about becoming Christians, and the word used is '*receive*' the gift of the Holy Spirit. Peter assures us that it is a promise for us as well as them (Acts 2:39).

Philip went to Samaria and preached the gospel, and when they responded positively, for the first time, he sent for Peter and John:

> When they arrived, they prayed for them that they might *receive* the Holy Spirit, because the Holy Spirit had not yet come upon any of them . . . Then Peter and John placed their hands on them, and they *received* the Holy Spirit. (Acts 8:15–18; my italics)

When Peter was used by God to bring the gospel of Jesus Christ to the Gentiles at Caesarea, he commented: 'They have *received* the Holy Spirit just as we have' (Acts 10:47; my italics).

In Ephesus, Paul found some 'disciples' who had not really become Christians, and asked them, 'Did you *receive* the Holy Spirit when you believed?' (Acts 19:2; my italics). As they had not received the Holy Spirit, Paul then preached Jesus to them; they believed, were baptised in water and received the Holy Spirit (Acts 19:4–6).

At Samaria and Ephesus, the believers received the Holy Spirit after water baptism (Acts 8:14–17; 19:5–6), but Paul, Cornelius and friends received the Holy Spirit before they were baptised (Acts 9:17–18; 10:44–48). So we must be careful about turning description into prescription, and stories into doctrines, but we can say that all four groups received the Holy Spirit as part of their Christian births.[7]

---

[7] I am well aware that when Ananias went to pray for Paul, he said, 'The Lord . . . has sent me so that you may see again and be filled with the Holy Spirit' (Acts 9:17). This was obviously part of Paul's conversion package. It may be the one verse that stops people like me from trying to put everything into neat parcels, or it may be that the

Paul continued to use the word 'receive' in his epistles for the moment when Christians received the permanent presence of the Holy Spirit into their lives.

> For you did not *receive* a spirit that makes you a slave again to fear, but you *received* the Spirit of sonship. And by him we cry, '*Abba*, Father.' The Spirit himself testifies with our spirit that we are God's children. (Romans 8:15–16; my italics)

> I would like to learn just one thing from you: Did you *receive* the Spirit by observing the law, or by believing what you heard? Are you so foolish? After beginning with the Spirit, are you now trying to attain your goal by human effort? (Galatians 3:2–3; my italics. See also 2 Corinthians 11:4)

We all receive the permanent presence of the Holy Spirit when we become Christians, and it is not a passive presence. The presence of the Holy Spirit corresponds well with Paul's teaching on the fruit of the Spirit, when his presence in our lives begins to change us from the inside, helping us to become more like Jesus as we give him more and more room (Galatians 5:22–25). It is a process that takes time.

In 1984, I was a counsellor at the Billy Graham crusade in Aston Villa, and followed up a number of people who had made decisions for Christ.[8] After about three months, they nearly all said the same thing to me: 'It's not working. I feel worse now than I did before I became a Christian.'

---

activities of being healed and anointed for special service (see Acts 22:14; 26:16–18) required the word 'filled' rather than just 'received'.

[8] I first trained as a counsellor for Billy Graham crusades when I was a schoolboy in the sixties. We held a number of Billy Graham satellite outreach campaigns in our church in the eighties. I am a fan.

When they said this, I knew, in a strange kind of way, that they had been truly converted, and had the permanent presence of the Holy Spirit in their lives. Before they became Christians, they often felt OK when they sinned – everyone was doing it – but now they felt distinctly uncomfortable when they sinned because of the presence of the Holy Spirit in their lives. This is the beginning of holiness and righteousness – they felt worse, but their friends and relatives said they were now much easier to live with. The presence of the Holy Spirit in our lives produces the fruit of the Spirit, in time, even though the process sometimes feels uncomfortable.

In my limited experience, ministering mostly in the Western nations, I have noticed how healing comes more easily to Christians who regularly practise the presence of Christ than those who see the Holy Spirit as an absentee landlord, or frantically seek much frenzied activity from him. Heidi Baker spends hours every day in the presence of God; seeking his face rather than his hand. The activity that flows through her, which everybody wants to know about and write about, comes out of practising God's intimate presence. Smith Wigglesworth lived his life in much the same way.

42. A time to speak

When I moved to Dorset, I was overjoyed to meet Smith Wigglesworth's granddaughter, Amelia, who lived nearby and invited me round for tea. When I arrived, Amelia introduced her sister Alice to me, another granddaughter, and Alice's husband, Harold, who had known

Smith quite well. Her own husband, who had not met their grandfather, was also present.[9]

Amelia was soon sharing with us how she'd received three healings through the prayers of Smith, who, on one occasion, led an assembly of several thousand people in prayer for her when, as a child, she was critically ill. For years afterwards, people who'd been at this meeting were always pleased to meet the 'miracle child'.

The Reverend Harold Berry then went on to tell me two very remarkable stories – this is the first one:

> When I was in my twenties, and Grandfather would have been in his eighties, I went to stay with him for a week in Yorkshire. While I was there, he walked over the road to the local park and sat down on a bench beside a man he'd never seen before, who seemed to be suffering badly. As always, Grandfather opened his Bible and began reading and praying, hardly seeming to notice his near neighbour. Then, virtually without looking up, he asked the man why he was so downcast.
>
> The man explained he had cancer, was not expected to live long, and would be leaving a wife and several young children behind to fend for themselves. He was in deep distress about it all.
>
> 'Sorry to hear it,' muttered Smith, and then returned to his Bible and prayers. Eventually, the man got up to leave, whereupon Grandfather remarked: 'As your key goes into the lock of your front door, the Lord will heal you.'

---

[9] Harold and Alice Berry were missionaries in Africa for 45 years. Harold has written a book entitled *The Call of God* (published by Harold Berry, printed by Emmanuel Press 1986).

The man continued on his way, not quite knowing what to think of this strange pensioner, but as his key entered the lock of his front door, power like an electric current and light like a car headlamp flooded his whole being, and he was completely healed. For several days, he returned to the park looking for Smith, to thank him, until finally he found him and narrated the full story to him.

A 'word' from the Spirit of God to Smith, while he was enjoying his presence, enabled the man to receive God's healing and give all the glory to God. Smith was simply the messenger who discerned a time to speak.

ii) The activity of the Holy Spirit

Jesus said:

> I tell you that if two of you on earth agree about anything you ask for, it will be done for you by my Father in heaven. For where two or three come together in my name, there am I with them. (Matthew 18:19–20)

If Jesus is with us always, why does he single out the prayer meeting as a place where he will be? The answer seems to be in the *activity* of prayer. He gets involved; he reveals his will, enabling us to ask in his name. Jesus is always with us, but he promises to take an active part when we meet together in his name to pray.

The biblical word most commonly associated with the *activity* of the Spirit is being 'filled' with the Spirit. Between the resurrection and the ascension, the disciples *received* the Holy Spirit, but on the Day of Pentecost 'all of them were *filled* with the Holy Spirit and began to speak in other tongues as the Spirit enabled them' (Acts 2:4; my italics).

The disciples who had already *received* the Holy Spirit are now *filled* with the Holy Spirit and begin to speak in tongues. This is like the daily bread filling of the Holy Spirit that Jesus promised in Luke 11. We are filled with the Holy Spirit just as we are filled with food and drink but, as with food and drink, once it has been used, we need to be filled again, and again – daily bread. *Receiving* is like being born – we receive life permanently and it stays with us until we die. It is just the same when we are born again, except we 'never die'(John 11:26). *Filling*, on the other hand, is like feeding – food comes and goes while the new life we received at birth remains.

Just as Jesus makes an analogy with food, Paul links drinking with being filled with the Spirit. In his letter to the Ephesians, Paul writes this to Christians who have already received the Holy Spirit (Ephesians 1:13): 'Do not get drunk on wine, which leads to debauchery. Instead, be *filled* with the Spirit' (Ephesians 5:18; my italics).

In the original Greek, 'be filled' means 'go on being filled'. Being filled with the Spirit is like having a drink, and this time it leads to the activity of psalms, hymns and spiritual songs (Ephesians 5:19).

In the Acts of the Apostles, being filled with the Spirit continued to be an activity of the Spirit for the believers, again and again. 'Then Peter, *filled* with the Holy Spirit,' spoke words beyond his natural schooling and amazed the Sanhedrin (Acts 4:8–13; my italics). Peter was filled again when praying with others: 'After they prayed, the place where they were meeting was shaken. And they were all *filled* with the Holy Spirit and spoke the word of God boldly' (Acts 4:31; my italics). Once more, those who have already received the Holy Spirit are filled with the Holy Spirit, and further spiritual activity follows. In Cyprus, 'Paul *filled* with the Holy Spirit' prophesies blindness for Elymas the Sorcerer (Acts 13:9–12).

Just as the permanent presence of the Holy Spirit fits well with the fruit of the Spirit, so the activity of the Spirit corresponds well with the gifts of the Holy Spirit (1 Corinthians 12:1–11). The gifts enable Christians, who have already received the permanent presence of the Holy Spirit, to do something which God wants them to do, and which they wouldn't have been able to do otherwise. Gifts of the Spirit are not status badges or signs of maturity, like the fruits of the Spirit can be seen to be, but they do enable Christians to do what God is doing.

It is a shame that people muddle up the presence of the Spirit with the gifts of the Spirit, and sometimes say that people are not Christians, or cannot be in a position of leadership, if they do not speak in tongues. Fruit of the Spirit, the evidence of the permanent presence of the Holy Spirit – not gifts of the Spirit, which come and go – are the signs of maturity, and should be our yardstick for choosing leaders (Matthew 7:16). Christians have the permanent presence of the Holy Spirit in their lives but being filled daily with the Holy Spirit gives them the anointing and equipping they need for each day's tasks.

The baptism in the Holy Spirit: The common use of the phrase 'the baptism in the Holy Spirit' amongst charismatic Christians has often stopped people from asking the Holy Spirit to come again and again, and needs to be looked at briefly. In the 1960s, when the charismatic movement came to many of the mainline churches, this became a hotly debated phrase.

'Have you got it, or haven't you got it?' keenie charismatics were always asking. Some thought you got it when you became a Christian; some thought it was a subsequent second blessing, and some thought you only knew you'd got it when you could speak in tongues. The problem really was the phrase itself – a fourfold problem:

a) The phrase 'the baptism in the Holy Spirit' is not a biblical one. Jesus is the baptiser in the Spirit. It is never a noun in the Bible but always a verb[10] – always active, never passive, denoting activity rather than just presence.

b) More recently, 'baptism' has come to mean a 'once only' occasion. In my denomination, being baptised twice, or re-baptised, is forbidden.

c) The phrase leads to division and the setting up of first- and second-class Christians – i.e. those who can speak in tongues and those who can't.

d) The problem with a second-blessing theology is that many people stop there and never get to number

---

[10] Acts 19:1–7 is one place in Scripture which is often quoted to justify the noun 'baptism'. But a careful look at the text soon reveals that this was a discussion about the baptism of John in contrast to the baptism in water into the name of Jesus. After they were baptised in water, in the name of Jesus, then they received the Holy Spirit. The passage is not about 'the baptism in the Holy Spirit'. The phrase is not used here, or anywhere else in the Bible.

three. In the 1970s, 'charismatic' came to mean those who can speak in tongues, have a music group and use an overhead projector. In truth, the second blessing should merely come between the first and the third.

The problem can be solved quite simply by asking one question of the New Testament. Peter experienced the coming of the Holy Spirit on him at least five times, according to the New Testament. Which one was the baptism in the Holy Spirit? These are the five:

i) In Luke 9, Jesus gave him authority and power to heal the sick, and it worked.

ii) In John 20, Jesus breathed on him and said, 'Receive the Holy Spirit.'

iii) In Acts 2, Peter spoke in tongues on the Day of Pentecost.

iv) In Acts 4, Peter spoke bold words to the Sanhedrin in the power of the Spirit.

v) Also in Acts 4, the place where Peter was shook, and again he spoke boldly.

Which one of these five was the baptism in the Holy Spirit? The favourite has got to be number iii), the Day of Pentecost, because in Acts 1 Jesus told the disciples to stay in Jerusalem and wait to be baptised with the Holy Spirit. But what did Luke say happened on the Day of Pentecost? 'All of them were *filled* with the Holy Spirit and began to speak in other tongues . . .' (Acts 2:4; my italics). And what did Luke say happened before the Sanhedrin? 'Then Peter, *filled* with the Holy Spirit, said to them . . .' (Acts 4:8; my italics). And what did Luke say happened after the prayer meeting?

'They were all *filled* with the Holy Spirit and spoke the word of God boldly' (Acts 4:31).

So, if number iii) is the baptism in the Holy Spirit then so are numbers iv) and v). The biblical truth is that on all three occasions Peter was baptised in the Holy Spirit – i.e. immersed, soaked, or filled. Paul, writing to Christians, says, 'Be filled with the Holy Spirit,' and the tense means go on being filled. In other words, being baptised in the Holy Spirit is not a once-only occasion, but fits the *activity* of the Spirit better than the *presence*.

And it is the *activity* of the Spirit which includes healing. When the Spirit fills us, immerses us or baptises us with healing power, then we can heal the sick. We don't get the gift of healing to keep – we are filled with the gift in order to give it away, and if the next time we pray for a sick person we are not filled, then the healing activity will probably not take place until the anointing and equipping comes again.

But here we may need to add a note of caution about the gifts and the fruit of the Spirit. Without the fruit of the Spirit growing in our lives, activity – even spiritual activity – can easily become a 'resounding gong or a clanging cymbal' (see 1 Corinthians 13:1). Here is the second story the Revd Harold Berry told me.

43. A time to weep

Shortly after Smith Wigglesworth met the man in the park, he announced he was going to York by train and would like Harold to accompany him. A lady who had been greatly used by God in the healing ministry was in the 'lunatic asylum' there, and a group of people from her church had asked Smith to visit her. 'You are the only one who can get her out of there,' they said.

It was a silent journey. In reality, it had been quite a silent week as Grandfather did not bother with 'small talk' and rarely had much to say, but this was particularly silent. The well-known preacher bent over his Bible all the way from Bradford to York in some distress and anguish of soul. At times, his lips moved as if he was in communication with an unseen presence, but no sound ever came out. The deep turmoil which was expressed on his moist brow mirrored the internal pain of his inner wrestling, so Harold spent the time looking out of the window, not wishing to intrude on personal grief.

They eventually completed their silent journey to the mental hospital, where they were welcomed and given seats while the white coats went to find the lady. 'I heard her coming long before I saw her,' said Harold to me. '"Take your hands off me," she was demanding. "I'm a princess. I'll tell the king to put you away if you touch me."' She kept up the charade until this well-heeled, well-dressed, painted lady stood before the throne of the plumber from Bradford, who was representing Jesus. At once, her demeanour changed, the staff let go of her arms, and as her eyes met those of Smith Wigglesworth it seemed as if each one was looking through the windows of the other's soul. There was no longer any pretence. After a significant pause, the princess spoke.

'You're the only one who can get me out of here,' she said, with a touch of pathos in her voice.

'No,' replied Grandfather. 'You'll never leave here.' Her elegance swirled round immediately, somewhat defiantly, but seemed to accept the definitive judgement as she returned loudly and arrogantly to princess-mode.

They were nearly back in Bradford before Harold dared ask for clarification and, as he spoke, he felt like a small boy intruding on adult matters. 'Why could you not help her, Grandfather?' he asked, timidly. 'Pride,' said Smith. 'She was too full of herself to ever be set free.'

God's ways are not our ways, and his thoughts are not our thoughts, but sometimes, if we can accept this truth, he shares his thoughts with us. And always, as Christians, we seek only to do what the Father is doing. Smith Wigglesworth, so often used by God to bring healing in the name of Jesus and in the power of the Holy Spirit, was not able to help this particular sick soul, even with sweat and tears.

b) We wait for God to come

Waiting on God, or waiting for God expectantly, is a very biblical concept but very difficult to accomplish in our busy, rushed and instant world. Even as Christians who supposedly put aside Sunday as a day of rest for God, we are now most comfortable with one church service, no more than an hour long, with a ten-minute sermonette, after which we rush home for Sunday lunch and a film or sports programme on the telly. People are amazed when I tell them I do not have a television – the TV licensing people harass me regularly – but I have to say I have heard God more often and more clearly since we gave our television set away.[11] Here are some biblical verses to meditate on during the adverts:

- Psalm 27:14 'Wait for the Lord; be strong and take heart and wait for the Lord.'
- Psalm 33:20–21 'We wait in hope for the Lord; he is our help and our shield. In him our hearts rejoice, for we trust in his holy name.'
- Psalm 37:7 'Be still before the Lord and wait patiently for him.'
- Psalm 40:1 'I waited patiently for the Lord; he turned to me and heard my cry.'
- Psalm 130:5–6 'I wait for the Lord, my soul waits, and in his word I put my hope. My soul waits for the Lord more than watchmen wait for the morning.'
- Proverbs 20:22 'Wait for the Lord, and he will deliver you.'
- Isaiah 8:17 'I will wait for the Lord . . . I will put my trust in him.'
- Isaiah 26:8 'Yes, Lord, walking in the way of your laws, we wait for you; your name and renown are the desires of our hearts.'
- Isaiah 40:31 'They who wait for the Lord shall renew their strength. They shall mount up with wings like

---

[11] I have written two publications on listening to God speak, since giving away our television. *The Hot Line* was first published by Kingsway in 1990, and is now published by Terra Nova Publications Ltd, Bristol. *Explaining Hearing from God* is a shorter work (Tonbridge: Sovereign World Ltd 1992). Both publications are still available from our parish office – office@canfordparish.org

eagles; they shall run and not be weary, they shall walk and not faint.' RSV

- Lamentations 3:25–26 'The Lord is good to those whose hope is in him, to the one who seeks him; it is good to wait quietly for the salvation of the Lord.'
- Micah 7:7 'But as for me, I watch in hope for the Lord, I wait for God my Saviour; my God will hear me.'
- Acts 1:4 '[Jesus] gave them this command: "Do not leave Jerusalem, but wait for the gift my Father promised, which you have heard me speak about."'

Consider Jesus. . .

- He waited until he was 30 to begin his ministry (Luke 3:23).
- He waited to be filled with the Holy Spirit (Luke 3:22).
- He waited in the wilderness another 40 days (Luke 4:2).
- When Lazarus was sick, Jesus waited until his friend died (John 11:6–11).
- Jesus only did what he saw the Father doing (John 5:19).

Consider Peter. . .

- He was naturally quick and impetuous (Matthew 14:28; 26:35).
- Jesus told him to go into Jerusalem and wait (Acts 1:4).
- He was told to wait for the Holy Spirit (Acts 1:4).
- At the dead body of Dorcas, he put everyone out and waited on God in prayer. Only after that did he act (Acts 9:40).

Consider Paul. . .

- He was an activist (Acts 9:1–2).

- God struck him down, and he became blind (Acts 9:8).
- God waited three days before healing him and filling him with the Holy Spirit (Acts 9:17).
- After an initial burst of preaching, Paul waited for ten years in Tarsus before being called to begin his missionary activity (Acts 11:25–26).
- Paul waited on God in prayer before he laid hands on Publius's father and healed him (Acts 28:8).

We ask God to come. THEN we wait in the stillness – giving way, not being restive – for his coming (Psalm 46:10). Scripture and experience tell me that after we have asked God to come, we need to wait patiently, quietly and expectantly for him to come.

A time to be silent

In his excellent book, *Crafted Prayer*, the oft-anointed and gifted Graham Cooke writes this:

> Being still opens a channel of communication between us and Heaven. All of us have a background conversation going on in our minds. Head noise . . . is an internal voice, a sound track for our lives . . . Stillness is not about getting somewhere quiet, although that often helps, but about stilling that voice in your head.[12]

---

[12] Graham Cooke, *Crafted Prayer* (Tonbridge: Sovereign World 2003), pp. 17–18. I am very grateful to Sovereign World for allowing me to use this teaching and two further stories from *Crafted Prayer*, pages 49 and 47.

Graham often teaches others about stilling the voice, helping them to hear God and act upon his word, encouraging everyone to learn about the time to be silent – and healing sometimes flows out of this silence.

44. A time to heal

John was diagnosed with a brain tumour, which grew from the size of a pea to the size of a tennis ball. Graham Cooke led a prayer meeting of about 200 people and eventually, after much waiting on God in silence, God gave a number of people the same prayer to pray. They met regularly and prayed this same prayer together on 73 occasions. On the day John was scheduled for surgery, Graham told him to insist on a CAT scan, even though he had been scanned twelve times before.

The medics were not keen on this, but eventually they concurred – and found nothing there. Thinking the scanner had broken, they took John to another hospital – where the same nothing was revealed to them. 'There's absolutely nothing,' the doctor said. 'Not only is there nothing there, but there doesn't seem to be any trace that anything ever was there.'

Sometimes when we ask the Spirit to come, and we wait long enough for his coming, God reveals to us when it is a time to heal.

c) We seek to respond to God's coming

When God comes amongst us by his Spirit to say something or do something, it is then our responsibility to respond to his coming. This is a lifetime's study that, even in eternity, will never be exhausted because it involves the God who loves to do a new thing.

Years ago, I wrote this in *The Hot Line*, about the various ways God heals:

> Jesus touched one leper, but not the ten; he touched others while healing some from a distance; he made mud paste, spat and stuck fingers in ears; he asked one person to stand up publicly and took another away from the crowd. The disciples even saw effective healing with shadows and handkerchiefs.[13]

And they are just a few examples of the diverse methods God used to heal people in the New Testament. In virtually every healing, either Jesus or his disciples discerned God doing something different with each person. Perhaps Jesus taught about the kingdom and not about healing because he was leaving it to the Holy Spirit to give the necessary guidance each time: 'But when he, the Spirit of truth, comes, he will guide you into all truth' (John 16:13).

You may have noticed that in some of the testimonies I have shared, we asked God to come, we waited for him to come, we sought to respond to his coming, and as it was frequently different each time in the New Testament, so it was with us. The whole point of waiting on God is to hear his voice or discern his activity so that we may respond by doing what he is doing – which is not always healing.

---

[13] Peter H. Lawrence, *The Hot Line*.

45. A time to die

When a person has been diagnosed with terminal cancer in the fellowships I have served, we have usually come together to pray; frequently, someone has a word from God that the person is going to be healed, but often I end up taking the funeral service. Inevitably, the so-called 'word from God' comes out of our 'head noise', but it is difficult to hear God clearly when someone we love is dying.

Graham Cooke has more experience at stilling the voice in his head than most of us, and one day he asked the Lord about his friend George, who was deathly ill.[14] 'He's going to die,' said God. In front of his loved ones, George asked Graham, 'Am I going to live or die?'

'Have a great death,' replied Graham, gently and lovingly. After a few moments, George changed the atmosphere around his hospital bed when he announced, 'Grae, I'm going to have the greatest death you've ever seen.'

George then made a list of 24 people he knew who were not yet Christians and asked them to visit him. He led the first 23 to Christ while he was alive and the 24th, who saw the peaceful smile on George's face as he died, knelt to accept Jesus immediately afterwards. That's a great death. Stilling the voice in the head, waiting upon God, and then responding to him enabled this to happen.

Sometimes when we wait upon God in silence and then act upon his word, people are healed, and sometimes it is a time to die.

---

[14] Cooke, *Crafted Prayer*, p. 47.

Ministry for all

We ask God to come; we wait for him to come, and then we seek to respond to his coming, and I like to do this with the whole congregation present at the end of a service. I realise there are practical problems in doing this at a Sunday morning service before Sunday lunch (especially if we have left it cooking in the oven), but theologically I always wonder about the place of private ministry in public worship. Inviting people to come forward for ministry usually ends up with the same few keenies every week, but inviting God to come to them all helps the shy, reluctant and sometimes hurting souls to be touched by God as well.

I am writing this early in 2005, the day after I spoke at an evening service in the lovely village church of Iver. After I'd spoken, everyone stood with their heads held high as sons and daughters of the King, eyes closed and hands held out expectantly. As they did so, I prayed: 'Father God, I ask you through Jesus to send your Holy Spirit on us, and do whatever you want to do.'

Clergy, musicians, ministry team members and congregation then waited in silence for God to come. There were no huge manifestations or exciting instant signs and wonders, but God came. There were faces beaming, eyelids fluttering, hands shaking and eventually a number of tears. Ministry team members who'd come with me, and some from the local church, eventually wandered around and blessed what the Father was doing with a gentle hand on the shoulder. And I just stayed at the front and watched. No one left, and gradually everyone was either praying for someone or being prayed for. Problems and tears were shared; the musicians worshipped God, and it looked to me like Jesus was wandering amongst his disciples, his bride, by his Spirit, with compassion, love, reality and peace. Even the shy and reticent ones seemed to be touched by God in one way or another.

Tony, the vicar, wrote this to me afterwards:

> A large proportion of those at the service were touched deeply and significantly by the Holy Spirit and we felt, at our staff meeting afterwards, that the evening was a significant moment in our church life.[15]

I do so enjoy the moments at the end of a time of ministry when there is total participation, as there was at Iver, even if no one is healed; it seems to me it is how the body of Christ was meant to function, and God's Spirit moving gently among us facilitated it all.

Try and catch the wind

If we look carefully at the healings in the Bible and the examples I have given in this book, we find people from Jesus to Graham Cooke who have discerned the wind of the Spirit, hoisted the sails and arrived at the place chosen by God. In none of these examples did people work out a repetitive formula from Scripture that could be applied to all sicknesses, in all places, at all times, to produce the results the people wanted. God is God, and the way to God's healing is to get in touch with God by his Spirit and do

---

[15] The Revd Tony Holmes is the associate vicar of St Peter's and St Leonard's, Iver.

whatever he directs us to do. This, I believe, is a biblical way to proceed, which works in the good times and the bad.

For nearly a hundred years since the outpouring of the Spirit at Azusa Street in 1906, the Pentecostal Church has helped the people of God to know, believe and experience the power of the Holy Spirit.[16] As with the ministry of Jesus and the ministry of the early church, the first Pentecostals experienced the power of the Holy Spirit unleashed on the world, with healing in his wings. When God is healing virtually everybody, then 'name it and claim it' theology works beautifully. If God wants to heal everyone, whatever and whoever we name will be in accordance with his will, and claiming it with unswerving faith will bring about healing. When God's Spirit moves among us in healing power, I am sure we need to pray for more boldness in claiming what God is naming, and go for it, as many Pentecostals and healing-evangelists have encouraged us to do. I often long for more of their confidence and boldness.

Since Azusa Street, there have been a number of revivals, renewals and times of refreshing: in the Hebrides, Indonesia, Latin America, Africa, and even in the woolly West, there has been the charismatic movement, the Third Wave, Toronto and Pensacola. At such times, teaching that Jesus died for sickness, and claiming our healing, actually works, and sometimes may work well. But when the wind stops blowing, or changes direction, such teaching and practice

---

[16] The story of the Azusa Street Revival is well told in two books: Frank Bartleman, *Azusa Street* (New Kensington, USA: Whitaker House 1982); *Azusa Street and Beyond,* edited by L. Grant McClung, Jr (South Plainfield, NJ, USA: Bridge Publishing, Inc. 1986).

leaves a mass of broken bodies, hurting souls and discouraged, guilt-ridden spirits strewn across the pews of our churches. Such teaching and practice does not work in the hard and barren times because it is not the word of God for all times and seasons, as revealed in the Holy Scriptures.

The Bible teaches us that through the cross of Christ we who are born again can ask God the Father through Jesus to send his Holy Spirit to us again and again, and he will always come. What he does or wants to do when he comes, however, is like the blowing of the wind. One day, the 'not yet' will become the 'already', and those who accept the death of Christ in place of their own will receive complete, permanent healing. But until then, in the age of the Spirit, the New Testament teaches us to seek God, his will, his timing and his purposes. It is my belief that if we learn to practise and enjoy the presence of the Spirit in the hard times, we will be better prepared to catch the wind in the good times – but even in the hard times, the worst we get is blessed, which is still glorious. I would like to encourage everyone who wants to see Jesus heal the sick to ask God to come, wait for him to come, and then seek to respond to his coming.

11

Born Again

On a warm, idyllic summer's day, beneath a cloudless sky, my daughter Amanda punted me on the River Cherwell in the morning, and my daughter Heather punted me on the River Cam in the afternoon. What a day! Slapstick films often portray incompetent punters stranded up the pole, but my daughters had both rowed for their colleges, and I was in safe hands. Lying back on the soft cushions without a mobile phone, I was able to enjoy the delights of trailing my hand in the cool water while the dazzling dragonflies darted all around us.

A few days before, I'd taken the funeral of Sharon, who'd served God faithfully as a nurse on a mercy ship bringing healing to many, before cancer took her life. We'd prayed much for her, and there was peace at the end, but it still left a husband and two daughters feeling bereft. Sharon asked me to speak about dragonflies at her funeral because they, like Sharon, had been born again. Once they had been ugly grubs, living in darkness beneath the colourless waters, before they'd risen, taken on new bodies and begun to fly in the sunlight. All who have been born again by the Spirit of Jesus have been born again from a world of black and white into the technicolor kingdom where one day they will rise, receive new bodies and fly in the light of the Son. Sharon wanted me to tell everyone who came to her funeral that this had now happened to her, and invite them to follow her there one day, by accepting Jesus now.

I did, and it helped, a little. But after the relaxing rivers, I was now on my way to Wales – alone because no one was free to come with me – to speak at a church in Bargoed on healing. I'd just been told that my friend Clive from the golf club had inoperable cancer and, to be honest, after Sharon's death and Clive's news, I'd much rather have been with my family and the dragonflies than going anywhere on my own to speak about healing.

As I drove along the M4, nearly 40 years since I first saw the T. L. Osborn films, I continued to think of the pain I always feel when people are not healed, and I found my thoughts going to the book of Isaiah. Full of the Spirit of God, this guy prophesied that Messiah, the one anointed by the Spirit of God, would heal the sick (Isaiah 35:5–6), and one day, in the new heavens and the new earth, there would be healing for all believers from everything (Isaiah 65:17–25). This spoke to me immediately in spirit, mind and emotions. This is the heartbeat of God – the desire of his heart. Whatever gets in the way, and for however long it does so, this is God's intention, and this is where he desires to take all his children who choose to follow him; to the land of technicolor and dragonflies where the Son always shines and there is no more pain.

This, I realised, is what I shared with T. L. Osborn and all the healing-evangelists who claim and command healing whenever they encounter sickness. I share with them the heartbeat of God, because the same Holy Spirit who is in them is in me. The desire of God's heart is healing and wholeness for his children for ever, and when life falls short of that, his pain is our pain, and his frustration is our frustration. I always feel encouraged when I understand that my pain is God's pain – that we are on the same side and want the same things – but it still hurts when those I know and love are suffering.

I moved on in my thinking from God's frustration and pain at non-healing, to the frustration and pain I sometimes feel when I hear some healing-evangelists teach and promise what God in his word does not teach and promise. Already, through the cross of Christ, he promises the gift of the Holy Spirit, the Spirit who heals and longs to heal, but not yet does he promise healing for all, not until we rise out of the darkness of death and inherit new dragonfly-type bodies.

Several times, I have picked up the pieces after a healing-evangelist has been to town, and, on each occasion, I found there were two major problems:

a) Those who were not healed.
b) Those who were healed on Saturday but were ill again on Wednesday.

a) Those who were not healed

When you teach that all you need is faith to be healed, because Jesus has died for all sicknesses, then those who have been prayed for many times and are not healed become the most wretched and pitied of people. When someone dies prematurely from sickness in a Christian fellowship that teaches this, the pain of the family and friends becomes almost intolerable. I have known families in this situation who felt they had to leave the church because of the added pain of guilt and shame or, in some cases, anger, at a time when they needed the body of Christ most. For those suffering from the disability of a chronic illness, the feelings of failure and inadequacy are also heaped upon them as they become an embarrassment to the preacher whose message doesn't fit – and people know it doesn't fit. And the sad thing is that it isn't what the New Testament teaches.

In my experience, ordinary people are less concerned about everyone being healed and more concerned to ask whether anyone is ever really healed. Two or three miracles in a meeting of several thousand are enough to lift people's faith and help them to believe in Jesus, and knowing the Healer is far more important than receiving the healing. That is why in the Alpha course,[1] Nicky Gumbel has a week with the title, 'Does God heal today?' In many churches, one healing would do to answer the question and make the point. Perhaps that is why healings in the Gospels, Acts and Epistles are referred to as 'signs'.

As I crossed the new Severn Bridge, I remembered the day Cynthia came to our church and shared how Jesus had appeared to her and healed her when in a wheelchair

---

[1] The Alpha course is an opportunity to explore the meaning of life: www.alphacourse.org

(Chapter 4, story no. 12). You could have heard a pin
drop, and everyone was thrilled. There were some there
who were very ill, and they knew it was most unlikely
that Jesus would ever appear to them in a vision and heal
them, but they still rejoiced. There was a feeling of, 'It is
true! The Lord has risen' (Luke 24:34). If Jesus appeared
to everyone like he did to Cynthia, and healed every
Christian, then Christianity would no longer be faith but
sight. It was enough for us that he had appeared to one of
us and healed her, and this added great assurance to our
faith.

b) Those who were healed on Saturday but were ill again on Wednesday

For those who are healed on Saturday and become ill
again on Wednesday, the problem is not normally lack of
faith. The problem is that the simplistic message of the
healing-evangelist does not address the root cause of
the sickness. It is very easy, but not always accurate, to say
that people in the Third World see more healings because
they have more faith. One of the main reasons why there
are more healings in Third-World countries is because
more of their sicknesses are due to physical reasons than
in the West (poor sanitation, poor nutrition etc.), and God,
in his compassion, often does more for the needy who live
out of the glare of the media than he does for us. In the
West, if 70, 80, or 90 per cent of all sicknesses have
psychosomatic roots, as many doctors and psychiatrists
say they do, then faith for healing on Saturday will not
be sufficient to keep the healing beyond Wednesday, if

the roots are not addressed. Marie was healed when she forgave her mother, but knowing the root of her sickness helped her to keep her healing by continuing to forgive her mother out loud every day for six months, and so far she has stayed well for 15 years (Chapter 5, story no. 16).

I continued to reflect as my car headed north of Cardiff and into the hills and valleys of South Wales. What saddened me most about the healing-evangelists who believe in the New Covenant right to healing was that I don't believe they would see fewer healings if they preached and taught what the Bible reveals to us about the Holy Spirit. In practice, when the Spirit moves in power, then naming healing and claiming healing with confidence and faith in Jesus still brings healing to the sick. In fact, if they would listen to God by his Spirit and learn to discern the root causes of a sickness, especially in the West, then I believe they would actually experience more healings, not fewer, and more people would stay healed for longer.

Frequently, when I consider the healing ministry of Jesus today, my thoughts go back to the stories I have read about the Bradford plumber. Even if only one-tenth of the tales told about Smith Wigglesworth were true, then he must have been one of the most successful healing-evangelists ever to minister in Western civilisation. Apparently, there were: 14 raised from the dead; cancers dropping on the floor with tentacles attached to them; piles of discarded crutches left behind after every meeting; scores of people healed by his anointed handkerchiefs, or by his shadow, or by touching his clothes, as he walked by. He 'named it and claimed it' with greater power than anyone, as his great rallying cry, 'Honly Believe', rang around every auditorium he visited. (Smith often added an 'h' when it was not required and dropped one when it was.) But according to Julian Wilson's recent biography, 'His method of praying for people always depended . . . on "what the Father had to say".'[2] He only claimed it if God was naming it, and many coming after him have failed to grasp this truth. Having read most of the books on Smith Wigglesworth, and spoken to his relatives, one thing seems very clear to me: Smith Wigglesworth healed the sick because God anointed him with the Holy Spirit, and Smith only did what he saw the Father doing, as revealed to him by the Spirit.

Towards the end of his life, he said to his friend Albert Hibbert: 'People have their eyes on me. Poor Wigglesworth. What a failure to think that people have their eyes on me.'[3] He was, in fact, one of the greatest 'successes' of all time, but others coming after him might have been able to do more if he had been able to model what he did, with them in mind. There were times, for example, when the security forces asked Smith Wigglesworth not to have long queues of people waiting for him to pray for them, when he asked God to heal everyone in their places, and notable healings were still recorded. I've always preferred this method because everyone receives prayer for a considerable time (in queues, people sometimes only get ten

---

[2] Julian Wilson, *Wigglesworth: The Complete Story* (Milton Keynes: Authentic Media 2002), p. 121.

[3] Julian Wilson, *Wigglesworth*, p. 212.

seconds each); it teaches others to have a go and, most importantly, it teaches that it is God who heals, not a super-hero, which is what Smith Wigglesworth always desired.

When critical people like me, who find trusting others difficult, can experience the number of healings that I have, how many more healings would take place if more people believed in the work of the Holy Spirit, as described in the Bible? I began to see people being healed, not after I had read books on Smith Wigglesworth, but after John Wimber taught me how to do it – or, rather, how to make room for God to do it by simply asking him to come, and waiting in silence for his coming.[4]

As I drove past the town of Caerphilly, I tried to answer in my mind the questions I'd asked in Chapter 1 of this book. Having studied the Scriptures and tried to heal the sick for 40 years, I was now totally convinced that Francis MacNutt and John Wimber were right in their books when they linked healing to the work of the Holy Spirit. In revival times, when the Spirit indicates that God is doing a lot of healing, then I am sure the healing-evangelists are right to encourage us to name it, claim it and believe for healing. I am even more convinced after 40 years of seeing God heal that the lecturer at St John's College was totally wrong when he said God heals no one today, as are the non-interventionists, who either have not read the same book as I have (the Bible), or not had the same experience. Even

---

[4] I learned a lot from attending John Wimber's conferences in the eighties, and also from his book, *Power Healing* (London: Hodder & Stoughton 1986).

so, as the history of revivals suggests, the lecturer was right to note that at different times and in different places, God does more healing than at others. I still ponder on how, years after God was healing many with shadows and hankies, Paul advised Timothy to take wine for his poorly tummy. Was this the beginning of the Christian medical profession?

'Dying for sicknesses' no longer made any sense to me, and I was now sure it is not a biblical idea, whereas dying for sin, in the light of the Jewish sacrificial system and scapegoats, made total sense, and is argued clearly in the New Testament. The end of the Old Covenant, where sickness was seen as a punishment for sin, and the bringing in of the New, sealed by the blood of Christ, where it is not, was very helpful to me in understanding Isaiah 53 and the Suffering Servant. Where sickness is the consequence of sin, then applying the cross to the root of the problem is helpful, but otherwise, whenever the medical profession is unable to help, I am sure we need the Holy Spirit to bring healing. The wonderful news of the New Covenant is God's promise to give his children the healing Holy Spirit, again and again, if they ask in Jesus' name.

We also need the Holy Spirit to help us in finding the root causes of a sickness, especially if the person who is sick is unaware of any problems themselves. Once we have discerned the root cause of a sickness, the Bible comes into its own as it shows us how to put it right. Thinking about the Bible, and the church's experience down the ages, I was still totally convinced that the biblical way to approach healing in all circumstances is to:

i) Ask God to come.

ii) Wait for him to come.

iii) Seek to respond to his coming.

So, even with the pain in my heart for the loss of loved ones and the recent news about Clive, I knew what I would do and teach as I drove into the friendly town of Bargoed. I got lost trying to find the church (as I always do when my wife, Carol, is not with me), but once I found it – despite how I felt – I practised what I preached to a most welcoming and open group of people. After worshipping God and listening to his word, I prayed: 'Father God, I ask you through Jesus to send your Holy Spirit upon us and do whatever you want to do.'

And despite how I felt, and the funerals I'd just taken, and the news about my friend Clive, God came. This is what Andrew, the vicar, wrote to me afterwards.[5]

> There were about 60 people who attended the day, about 25 of whom were from our parish. It has made a very positive impact on those who went from our parish, some of whom were relatively new to that kind of prayer and ministry through the Holy Spirit. There have been two clear instances of healing:
>
> Ann had suffered a lot with arthritic pain in her legs, which badly affected her walking (she needed a stick). When you invited the Holy Spirit to come during the second session, her legs went from under her (and she sat down heavily on the pew!). Swelling on one of her ankles went right down, and

---

[5] Andrew Bookless is the vicar of Bargoed and Deri with Brithdir. The church where we held the meetings was St Gwladys.

when she went over to the hall for lunch she found her walking was vastly improved and the pain in her legs had gone. She is now walking around without her stick, and freely telling lots of people about what God has done. She has said that she never expected this sort of thing to happen to her.

Later, Ann wrote this in their parish magazine:

> After the worship and teaching, with prayer and the power of God's Holy Spirit, I can say I was healed. Many of you know the pain I had and also that I could not mobilise myself without a walking stick. This healing experience was a wonderful feeling.

Dorita also gave her own version of how she was healed, in the parish magazine:

> During one of the prayer times, when we stood and asked the Holy Spirit to come, I felt something like a wind blowing on me and I couldn't stay on my feet. As I sat on the pew I had a very powerful experience of God's Holy Spirit coming upon me, which affected me physically (e.g. feelings of heat, shaking and tears). It is hard to describe how I felt but I sensed that God was doing something deep in me and it was really wonderful. I felt so good afterwards. On the next day, Sunday evening/night I had popping/cracking sounds in my right ear. I'd had ear problems for years with deafness on that side. My hearing has since been fine. I kept a pre-arranged appointment with the nurse nine days after this happened, and she confirmed that my ear is completely clear.[6]

A year later, I met her husband, who confirmed to me that his wife is still healed.

---

[6] The quotes are from: *Parish Messenger,* July 2004.

Paul, in his letter to the Corinthians, was worried that if unbelievers wandered in off the street they might think the believers were out of their mind, but perhaps it is not so likely in Wales. Andrew continued by writing this in his letter:

> Another young man, whom we didn't know, came into the church during the afternoon session, attracted by the sound of the worship as he walked past the church. He has been into Buddhism and other religions and said what a powerful experience he'd had in being there. He came to church this morning for our weekday service, having said to me that he now wanted to have Jesus as his guru.

I returned to Bargoed the following year and met the young man for myself. He'd been attending church regularly, and as I laid my hands on him, Guru Jesus blessed him. I could tell he was really blessed because he bought two of my books.

It was a full day, but despite feeling very tired I managed to drive myself home safely without getting lost. It wasn't a great day for feelings but God showed up anyway, as he usually does.

I visited Clive a few days later, and he was very pleased to see me. I only knew him through golf, as he didn't attend church, but he was very happy for me to pray with him before I left. I asked God to come and, as I sensed his presence through warmth in my hands, I asked God to heal him.

After this, I spent some time on my own at home, praying for Clive and waiting on God, but each time I sensed God saying he was not going to heal him. I found this very hard. There were all sorts of very good reasons why I thought God should change his mind and do what I wanted:

- Clive was a really nice bloke.
- His family and friends would miss him.
- I would miss him.
- He was a good golfer.
- Non-Christian friends might believe in Jesus if Jesus healed him.

I tried to catch God out by sticking in quick prayers at odd moments, when I thought he might not be concentrating, but he never changed his mind. He did, however, assure me that Clive would be OK and God's name would be glorified.

So I wrote to Clive and sent him a copy of Nicky Gumbel's booklet, *Why Jesus?*, and kept on praying.[7] The next time I visited, Clive said he'd read it through four times and wanted to ask me about the cross. 'I'm not too comfortable,' he began, 'with a God of love who nailed his only Son to a cross.'

Quite. Put like that, it didn't sound too loving or helpful. I prayed madly for help, and this verse came into my mind: 'God was reconciling the world to himself in Christ' (2 Corinthians 5:19). I did my best to explain that Jesus is God, who freely chose to die for us, so that we might take our sin and his love seriously. Clive seemed to accept this, so I laid hands on him once more in Jesus' name before I went home.

When I saw him again, Clive said he'd prayed the prayer

---

[7] Nicky Gumbel, *Why Jesus?* (London: Alpha International 1997).

and great peace came over him from that moment. Shortly before he died, Clive's wife Pauline commented on it again: 'He's been at peace ever since you prayed for him,' she said gratefully, but with a look of resignation and sadness in her misty eyes.

About 140 people attended the funeral, mostly from the golf club. After Clive accepted Jesus as his Lord and Saviour, he won the seniors' club championship and painted the outside of the house for Pauline, a month before he died, so I was able to give thanks for his life, a lovely man, and glory to God for revealing himself to Clive.

Then, a strange thing happened. Two people at the door told me how they'd left the area ten years ago; they used to discuss Christianity with Clive often, and had been praying for him daily. Liz, who'd been the ladies' club captain just before Clive had been the men's captain, shared how she'd been praying for Clive. Two couples from our church also shared meetings they'd had with Clive; another spoke of an outreach meeting he'd attended, and suddenly I realised I was simply one member of a large team that I knew nothing about. I thought it had been easy. We are all still devastated at losing Clive but I can now look forward to chatting with him again among the dragonflies, rivers and golf courses in the New Jerusalem. Which brings me to me.

46. The naked rector

When I write books on healing and God turns up at meetings to make me look as if I know what I'm talking about, people always want to know how I am. Am I fit and well? Do I always stay robustly healthy? The truth is that like many doctors and nurses I am a terrible patient. Tom Walker once invited me to Africa to speak about healing and, having shared a room with me, said he'd never seen anyone who travelled with so many tablets and medicines in his life.[8]

In 1985, John Wimber gave a 'word' from God in a meeting of several thousand, for someone present who had a problem with a testicle that had never dropped at puberty.[9] I ask you. What a word. It was me – and it was pertinent because at that time I was booked into hospital to have it removed, just in case it turned cancerous. I saw David Pytches for prayer, wasn't healed and had the operation, but I was greatly blessed. It was a life-changing kind of moment when I realised God had used John Wimber to give a 'word' for me, which seemed to have my name on it.

More recently, I noticed, while having a bath, that my one remaining testicle had developed a lump, which brought fear and dread to my soul. Only those who've been this way themselves can begin to understand how it felt as the pretend mask came on to get me through the day, but was taken off when I went to bed at night. I knew how Christian leaders were supposed to behave, and did my best to fit into the mould, but it only seemed to work some of the time. While using a few of the laments in the Psalms, I poured it all out to God, after which I felt freer to tell my wife, Carol, who then made the necessary appointment at the surgery.

---

[8] This was on a trip sponsored by SOMA in 1988.
[9] Signs and Wonders conference, Sheffield, 1985.

'It might just be a cyst,' said the doctor, fortunately a male, 'but we'll have to have a scan to check it out; I'll arrange for an appointment.' Waiting on God is one thing, but waiting on the NHS is quite another. More nights of doubts and fear followed while, during the day, I helped the people of the parish to celebrate Advent. The coming of God. I was still hopeful.

The appointment came through just before Christmas. 'No, it's definitely not a cyst,' said the photographer. 'Look on this screen.' I tried to look without knowing what on earth I was looking for but I couldn't really get past the words which were ringing in my ears. 'No, it's definitely not a cyst.'

'It may not be cancer, of course,' continued the photographer, 'but it's definitely not a cyst.'

I had to make another appointment at our local medical centre to hear the results and she (only one available) confirmed what he'd said. She promised to get me an appointment as soon as she could with the urologist, but in the meantime it was a case of: 'Have a happy Christmas'.

I didn't. I went into deep, bottom-of-the-garden-eating-worms mode and relied on experience rather than inspiration to get me through the services. I prepared myself to die, thanked God for all he'd let me do in my life, wished the family well and started planning the funeral. Having had to sing 'The Lord's My Shepherd', and 'Abide with Me' hundreds of times, I thought I'd make others sing it at my farewell.

Carol read the signs and contacted my friends David,

Tony, Phil and their wives. How we need loving Christian friends at such times, and yet how difficult we men find it to ask for help. I was so grateful for their love, counsel and prayers. David and his wife Irene had both suffered from cancer, and beaten it, and being a more senior clergyman than me, David gave me a helpful lecture. He told me off. He told me to choose life instead of death and, knowing it to be biblical, I did as I was told. I repented of my wormwood attitude, asked for forgiveness, chose life and waited patiently while they asked God the Father through Jesus to send his Holy Spirit on me, and do whatever he wanted to do.

He came. His love overwhelmed me. I sensed his presence, and then some words came into my mind in the form of a question: 'Would you like me to let you have cancer, be really ill, and then be dramatically healed at the last moment, giving great glory to my name, or would you rather be told by the urologist that it is not cancer and you are fine?'

Sadly, I didn't even need time to think it through. 'The second one please,' I asked, rather timidly.

'It shall be so,' said God kindly, as the vision and power faded.

When is a 'word' a 'word'? When it comes true. I wasn't at all sure it really was God, but following this ministry from my friends I felt a much greater sense of peace, and the nights became more bearable.

In the New Year, I drove on my own to see the urologist at the hospital where I'd visited many other patients before. I was the first appointment of the day, and I hadn't managed to do much of the crossword when my name was called. I went in and a rather matter-of-fact, tell-it-the-way-it-is, robust-looking nurse told me to go into the examination room, take all my clothes off and lie on the bed.

'Can I keep my socks on?' I asked, innocently.

There then followed what can only be described as a quizzical, old-fashioned look before she agreed to my request. I went in, closed the door and despite feeling extremely vulnerable did as I was told. I had only been lying there a few moments when in walked the cleaning lady, as bold as brass, mop and bucket in hand.

'Morning ducks,' she said, and began cleaning. As team rector of Canford Magna, I'm not used to being called 'ducks' – certainly not dressed only in my socks – but at least I didn't have my dog-collar on, so she wouldn't have known I was holy. Praise the Lord I had the crossword with me.

I had to laugh. Here I am about to be told whether I'm going to live or die, dressed only in my socks, when in walks Mrs Mop. It may have been a ministering angel for all I know, but it certainly didn't look like one at the time. Little did I know that worse was to come. As Flossie finished and departed through the door, so the elderly male urologist turned up, bringing with him a most gorgeous-looking 18-year-old, fresh-from-school, female medical student, who'd come with him to examine my crown jewels. In those circumstances, give me Mrs Mop any day. I took a deep breath and concentrated on twelve across.

'Look at this,' he said to her. 'Put your hand there and feel that,' he continued.

'Satan departs leaving born-again creatures,' eleven letters. I'd no idea. Couldn't concentrate, but at last the verdict arrived.

'Do you know what I think that lump is?' asked the expert.

'No,' I replied.

'I think it's scar tissue from your previous operation,' he explained. 'It's certainly not a cancerous lump. I'm 99 per cent sure that's what it is.' He went on, 'You'll be fine. It'll clear up by itself. If it doesn't, come and see us again.'

'Fine,' I said. 'Can I get dressed now?'

'Yes,' she said. 'We've seen all we want to see, thank you.'

God moves in mysterious ways, which are not necessarily our ways, but are always the best. I was spared by God while Sharon, who in my opinion was serving God more faithfully than I was, and Clive, a much kinder and gentler person than I was, were not. I cannot begin to answer the question 'Why?' but then, not being God myself, maybe I don't need to do so. Maybe God thinks being a dragonfly is more fun than being a grub. But for those who want to do whatever God is doing, even if they don't always understand why, then I recommend asking him to come, waiting for him to come and seeking to respond to his coming. I believe God has said to me that if individuals, groups and churches regularly ask him through Jesus to send his Holy Spirit, and wait patiently for his coming, then the global Christian church would be more greatly blessed and the world would be changed. Through Jesus, God loves to send his Spirit to us again and again to do his works; always he comes to bless, and often he comes to heal. I believe this fits the biblical teaching on healing far better than most I have encountered, because the New Testament reveals to us that in the age of the Spirit, it is the Spirit who heals.

Final Note

At a church near you

I am very happy to come with a team from Canford Magna to other churches and conferences, to speak and lead times of ministry. The parish office (email: office@canfordparish.org) can handle enquiries about inviting us, and can also give you details about my other books that are still available.

Unfortunately, due to my parish and preaching commitments, I am not able to see individuals for personal ministry. I have personally received ministry from the following groups of people, and recommend them most highly to you:

The Christian Healing Mission –
www.healingmission.org
Ellel Ministries – www.ellel.org
The Harnhill Centre of Christian Healing –
www.harnhillcentre.freeserve.co.uk
Trelowarren Christian Fellowship –
trelowarren@fellowshipt.co.uk
Wholeness through Christ –
www.wholenessthroughchrist.org